QUICK WIN MEDIA LAW IRELAND

Answers to your top 100 Irish media law questions

Andrea Martin

Published by
OAK TREE PRESS
19 Rutland Street, Cork, Ireland
www.oaktreepress.com

A catalogue record of this book is
available from the British Library.

ISBN 978 1 904887 46 1 (Paperback)
ISBN 978 1 904887 62 1 (PDF)
ISBN 978 1 904887 63 8 (ePub)
ISBN 978 1 904887 64 5 (Kindle)

DISCLAIMER

This book provides information that has been carefully researched and
presented. Neither Oak Tree Press Ltd, nor any director or shareholder of
Oak Tree Press Ltd, nor the author can accept responsibility for the
consequences of reliance placed by the reader on any information in this
book. It is important that any reader takes case-specific legal advice from
their legal advisor when such advice is required.

INTRODUCTION

QUICK WIN MEDIA LAW IRELAND is aimed at those who work in the media industry seeking quick and practical answers to legal questions they encounter day-to-day. It will provide students on media-related courses with a plain English explanation of the legal principles they will learn about in media law modules. It will be useful to public relations, advertising, publishing and digital media professionals faced with legal queries arising in their work, as it will be to non-specialist lawyers and their clients when faced with a media-related problem. The book is practical and written for non-lawyers. It is descriptive rather than analytical of the law. It is intended to provide 'signposts' to understanding the relevant law to anyone grappling with a media law issue.

Case law examples, illustrating the principles being discussed, are provided where they may be useful. Lawyers and law students will find further useful precedent law in the full case reports referred to. Neutral citations for cases have been given, where available, and these judgments can be located online on the website of the British and Irish Legal Information Institute website – **www.bailii.org**. Where neutral citations are not available, access to a legal library or a subscription service such as LexisNexis (**www.lexisnexis.com**) may be required to access the full case reports in question.

QUICK WIN MEDIA LAW IRELAND is divided into six sections:

- The Irish legal system: This section provides an explanation of the sources of Irish law, how it has developed and continues to develop, the personal rights guaranteed by the *Constitution* that are relevant to the media, as well as an explanation of how the Irish courts system functions.

- Defamation law: Perhaps the most important area of law for anyone involved in the media, Irish defamation law was overhauled and updated by the *Defamation Act, 2009*. This book outlines the underlying principles of defamation law and provides an explanation of Irish defamation law subsequent to the 2009 Act, which took effect on 1 January 2010. The application of defamation law to the Internet and various forms of e-publishing also is discussed.

- Defamation court procedures: For anyone involved in defamation litigation, whether as plaintiff or defendant, this section provides an explanation of the defences and court procedures they are likely to encounter in the course of a defamation action. New defences and procedures introduced by the *Defamation Act, 2009* also are explained.

- Media content regulation: This section looks at the regulatory bodies for the print and broadcast media, how they operate and the codes and standards they are charged with preparing and policing. It discusses non-judicial remedies available to members of the public who feel that those codes have been breached. It also considers how hate-speech legislation and censorship affect Irish media content.

- Privacy and data protection: What is often seen as 'intrusive' media reporting and the proliferation of personal information about individuals on the Internet raise major questions concerning the extent of privacy protection available under Irish law. Irish privacy law has developed rapidly in recent years, to the point where potential liability for breach of privacy is an increasing concern for broadcasters and publishers. Furthermore, the importance of understanding data protection law in an age where anyone with a broadband connection and a personal computer is potentially a data controller with legal obligations under that law cannot be underestimated.

- Copyright: Journalists, publishers, advertisers, television and radio producers, website proprietors and those working in new media encounter copyright issues on a daily basis. Despite this, many media professionals are not always clear on their position when faced with a copyright query. This section considers copyright law generally, as well as how it affects TV and film producers, newspaper publishers, Internet users, authors, book publishers and music industry personnel in particular.

QUICK WIN MEDIA LAW IRELAND is designed so that you can dip in and out seeking answers to your top Irish media law questions as they arise. Answers to your queries can be located not only from the contents list but also by using the subject grid at the start of the book and by following the thread of cross-references provided at the end of each Q&A.

The questions asked and answered in this book include questions I have encountered time and again from journalists, producers, presenters, publishers, editors and musicians over many years through my legal practice and training work in the media industry. I hope you find it helpful.

Andrea Martin
Co. Clare
April 2011

ACKNOWLEDGEMENTS

The author acknowledges the help and support of many colleagues and friends in the preparation of this book, especially Brian Flynn and Sarah Kieran, also Marie McGonagle, Bernadette O'Sullivan and Sharon McLaughlin, all of NUIG, Teresa Hanratty of Learning Waves, Eamonn Kennedy of RTÉ, Rosemary Day of Mary Immaculate College UL, Ailish Farragher of Eugene F. Collins Legal Resource Centre, Brian O'Kane of Oak Tree Press, Lisa Devanny, Hilarie Owen, Keara Robins, Bernardine Maloney and others happily too numerous to name individually, including my colleagues at Eugene F. Collins, Solicitors, and Judy Goldman for her legal proofreading. Your assistance and encouragement are very much appreciated.

This book is dedicated to

Brian Flynn

CONTENTS

Search by theme:

Or search by topic:
Broadcast media
Civil law
Criminal law
Defences
Online media
Print media
Remedies
Rights
using the grid overleaf.

THE IRISH LEGAL SYSTEM	Broadcast media	Civil law	Criminal law	Defences	Online media	Print media	Remedies	Rights	Page
Q1 What are the sources of Irish law?								☑	2
Q2 What is the difference between civil law and criminal law?		☑	☑						6
Q3 How is the Irish Courts system structured?		☑	☑						9
Q4 What is the role of the District Court?		☑	☑						11
Q5 What is the role of the Circuit Court?		☑	☑						13
Q6 What is the role of the High Court?		☑	☑						15
Q7 What is the role of the Supreme Court?		☑	☑						17
Q8 What cases are heard by a jury?		☑	☑						19
Q9 What are damages and how are they assessed?		☑					☑		21
Q10 How is the right to freedom of expression protected under Irish law?								☑	23

DEFAMATION LAW	Broadcast media	Civil law	Criminal law	Defences	Online media	Print media	Remedies	Rights	Page
Q34 What is the fair and reasonable publication defence?	☑	☑		☑	☑	☑			90
Q35 Does offering a right of reply avoid liability for defamation?	☑	☑		☑	☑	☑			93
Q36 Can texts be defamatory?	☑	☑		☑	☑		☑	☑	95
Q37 Can emails be defamatory?		☑		☑	☑		☑	☑	97
Q38 Can a defamation action be brought in respect of someone who is dead?	☑	☑			☑	☑	☑	☑	100
Q39 Can employers be held liable for defamatory publications made by their employees?	☑	☑		☑	☑	☑			102
Q40 Can repeating a story sourced from another media outlet be defamatory?	☑	☑		☑	☑	☑			105
Q41 Does using the word 'alleged' avoid liability for defamation?	☑	☑		☑	☑	☑			107
Q42 Does defamation law apply to social networking sites?		☑		☑	☑				109
Q43 What can a business do to protect its social networking site from a defamation claim?	☑	☑		☑	☑	☑			112

DEFAMATION LAW	Broadcast media	Civil law	Criminal law	Defences	Online media	Print media	Remedies	Rights	Page
Q44 Can an apology be construed as an acknowledgment of liability in a defamation action?	☑	☑		☑	☑	☑	☑		115
Q45 What is malicious falsehood?		☑					☑		117
Q46 Can someone with a criminal conviction sue for damages for defamation?		☑	☑	☑			☑	☑	120
Q47 What approach will the courts take if a plaintiff does not deserve the reputation she / he seeks to vindicate?		☑		☑	☑	☑	☑	☑	122
Q48 Can satire be defamatory?	☑	☑		☑	☑	☑		☑	124

DEFAMATION COURT PROCEDURES	Broadcast media	Civil law	Criminal law	Defences	Online media	Print media	Remedies	Rights	Page
Q49 What does a plaintiff need to prove in a defamation claim?		☑			☑	☑	☑		128
Q50 How is it decided whether a statement has a defamatory meaning?	☑	☑			☑	☑	☑	☑	130

DEFAMATION COURT PROCEDURES	Broadcast media	Civil law	Criminal law	Defences	Online media	Print media	Remedies	Rights	Page
Q51 How are damages assessed in a defamation case?		☑		☑			☑		132
Q52 Can an award of damages for defamation be overturned by an appeal court?		☑					☑		136
Q53 How long after a publication is made does a plaintiff have to bring a defamation claim?	☑	☑			☑	☑	☑	☑	137
Q54 Can a plaintiff from abroad sue for defamation in the Irish courts?	☑	☑			☑	☑	☑	☑	139
Q55 Can a plaintiff from Ireland sue for defamation in foreign courts?		☑					☑	☑	142
Q56 What is a correction order?	☑	☑			☑	☑	☑		144
Q57 What is a declaratory order?		☑					☑		146
Q58 What is a verifying affidavit?		☑					☑		148
Q59 Can an injunction be obtained to prohibit publication of a defamatory statement?		☑					☑		150
Q60 Can a lodgement in satisfaction of a claim be made in a defamation action?		☑					☑		153

DEFAMATION COURT PROCEDURES	Broadcast media	Civil law	Criminal law	Defences	Online media	Print media	Remedies	Rights	Page
Q61 What is an agreement for indemnity?	☑	☑		☑	☑	☑			155
Q62 What is an offer of amends?		☑		☑			☑		156

MEDIA CONTENT REGULATION	Broadcast media	Civil law	Criminal law	Defences	Online media	Print media	Remedies	Rights	Page
Q63 What is the Press Council and what does it do?						☑			160
Q64 What is the Broadcasting Authority of Ireland and what does it do?	☑								162
Q65 What regulatory requirements apply to broadcast programme content and advertisements?	☑								165
Q66 How does the Broadcasting Authority of Ireland secure compliance by broadcasters with regulatory obligations and codes?	☑						☑	☑	169
Q67 Is 'hate speech' unlawful?	☑		☑		☑	☑			174

MEDIA CONTENT REGULATION	Broadcast media	Civil law	Criminal law	Defences	Online media	Print media	Remedies	Rights	Page
Q68 Does equality legislation apply to media content?	☑					☑		☑	177
Q69 How do censorship laws affect the media?	☑	☑	☑		☑	☑		☑	179

PRIVACY AND DATA PROTECTION	Broadcast media	Civil law	Criminal law	Defences	Online media	Print media	Remedies	Rights	Page
Q70 How is privacy protected under Irish law?	☑	☑			☑	☑	☑	☑	186
Q71 What legislation provides for the protection of privacy under Irish law?	☑	☑	☑		☑	☑			193
Q72 Are image rights protected under Irish law?	☑	☑			☑	☑		☑	198
Q73 Can it be an invasion of privacy to 'doorstep' someone?	☑	☑	☑			☑	☑		206
Q74 Is consent required to broadcast or otherwise publish a person's voice or image?	☑	☑			☑	☑	☑		211
Q75 Is it illegal to record a conversation without consent?	☑	☑	☑		☑	☑	☑		215

PRIVACY AND DATA PROTECTION	Broadcast media	Civil law	Criminal law	Defences	Online media	Print media	Remedies	Rights	Page
Q76 What remedies are available to a person whose privacy has been breached?	☑	☑	☑		☑	☑	☑		219
Q77 What are the fundamental requirements of data protection legislation?	☑	☑	☑		☑	☑		☑	223
Q78 How is data protection law enforced?		☑	☑				☑		228
Q79 What is the purpose of online privacy statements?		☑	☑		☑				232
Q80 What is the difference between the law of privacy and the law of confidentiality?	☑	☑			☑	☑	☑		234
Q81 Do celebrities and politicians have the same rights of privacy as private citizens?	☑	☑			☑	☑		☑	238

COPYRIGHT	Broadcast media	Civil law	Criminal law	Defences	Online media	Print media	Remedies	Rights	Page
Q82 What is intellectual property?	☑	☑			☑	☑	☑	☑	244
Q83 How are intellectual property rights protected by legislation?		☑	☑						245
Q84 What is copyright?	☑				☑	☑		☑	249
Q85 Who owns the copyright in a copyright work?	☑	☑			☑	☑			251
Q86 What rights does copyright confer on a copyright-owner?	☑	☑			☑	☑			254
Q87 How can a copyright-owner protect their copyright?	☑	☑			☑	☑	☑	☑	257
Q88 What is the duration of copyright?	☑	☑			☑	☑		☑	261
Q89 What is the difference between an assignment and a licence of copyright?	☑	☑			☑	☑			263
Q90 What remedies are available where a breach of copyright has occurred?	☑	☑	☑		☑	☑	☑		266
Q91 What steps can a copyright-owner take to protect their copyright online?	☑	☑			☑	☑	☑	☑	269
Q92 What is 'fair dealing'?	☑	☑		☑	☑	☑			275

COPYRIGHT	Broadcast media	Civil law	Criminal law	Defences	Online media	Print media	Remedies	Rights	Page
Q93 What does 'public domain' mean?	☑	☑		☑	☑	☑			281
Q94 What are moral rights?	☑	☑			☑	☑		☑	284
Q95 What is meant by 'underlying rights' in a copyright work?	☑	☑			☑	☑		☑	288
Q96 What are performers' rights?	☑	☑			☑	☑		☑	291
Q97 How do music collection societies work?	☑				☑	☑	☑	☑	296
Q98 What music collection societies operate in Ireland and what do they do?	☑				☑	☑	☑	☑	298
Q99 What is the role of the Irish Copyright Licensing Agency?		☑				☑	☑	☑	303
Q100 What is the Public Lending Remuneration scheme?		☑				☑	☑	☑	304

THE IRISH LEGAL SYSTEM

Q1   What are the sources of Irish law?

There are five principal sources of Irish law:

- The *Constitution*.
- Common law.
- Legislation.
- European Union law.
- Other international treaties.

The *Constitution*

The *Constitution* sets out the fundamental principles that inform all law-making in Ireland. It sets out in detail how officers of the State are to be appointed, how the parliamentary system is to function, how legislation is to be passed and how the courts are to be established. It also sets out certain personal rights of the citizen, including the right to freely express convictions and opinions, as well as the right to protection and vindication of one's good name. All laws enacted and all actions of State bodies and individuals in the State must comply with the *Constitution*. It is, in effect, the touchstone for all law in the State. The Irish *Constitution* was adopted by the Irish people in a referendum in 1937, replacing an earlier *Constitution* of 1922. Since 1937, the Irish *Constitution* has been amended by referendum over 20 times, most recently in 2009 to allow the ratification by the State of the *Lisbon Treaty*.

The common law

The common law is a body of judge-made law that has evolved over centuries in the courts, originally in Britain and, over time, in other countries to which the British legal system was extended. Hence, Ireland, Australia, New Zealand, Nigeria, the US and Canada, for example, all have common law legal systems – albeit influenced to an extent by continental code-based legal systems in the latter two countries. Under the common law system, judges in the higher courts apply legal principles based on the rationale applied by judges in previous cases involving similar facts and points of law – this is known as 'following precedent'. Judges in the lower courts are obliged to follow the precedents set in the High Court and / or Supreme Court, while the High Court must apply the precedents set in the Supreme Court. Judges in the High Court may differentiate the rationale they apply in a particular case from that applied in a previous High Court case – this is known as 'distinguishing' a precedent judgment. The inherent ability of the common law to evolve new legal principles derived from those established in previous cases gives it an organic quality, enabling it to adapt to developments in society and in social mores. However, the common law always must be interpreted and applied in a manner consistent with the *Constitution*.

Legislation

Legislation, also referred to as statute law, is law made by the legislature – the Oireachtas. As set out in the *Constitution*, legislation must be approved by both Dáil Éireann and Seanad Éireann, and then signed into law by the President, before it becomes law. A piece of legislation that has been proposed (usually by the Government) but has not yet passed through this procedure is called a Bill; once it has passed successfully through the legislative process, it is called an Act. A Committee system operates in both the Dáil and Seanad Éireann to facilitate the detailed scrutiny of the provisions of a Bill prior to its approval by either House of the Oireachtas.

A form of secondary legislation, known as a statutory instrument (SI) can be passed – usually by a Government Minister or State body – under the authority given to that Minister or body by an Act. This enabling legislation, as it is sometimes called, enables the Minister or body to give effect to an over-arching objective of an Act, EU Directive or EU Regulation. Section 3 of the *European Communities Act, 1972* gives a general power to Ministers to make SIs giving domestic effect to EU legislation. Broadly speaking, SIs are concerned with implementing the detail of a piece of legislation.

EU law

Ireland ratified the Treaty of Rome in 1973, thereby becoming part of the community of states then referred to as the European Economic Community (EEC) and now known as the European Union (EU). A constitutional referendum was held in 1972, which in addition to allowing Ireland become a member of the EEC, the European Coal and Steel Community and the European Atomic Energy Community also allowed certain EEC (now EU) laws to have domestic effect in Ireland (see Article 29.4.10° of the *Constitution*).

The two principal forms of EU law that have effect in Ireland are EU Regulations and EU Directives. Regulations have a specific objective and automatically have direct binding effect in Member States, without the need for implementation by domestic legislation. Directives aim to harmonise certain areas of law across the EU (for example, copyright law) by setting out legislative objectives to be achieved by each Member State in that area of law within a specified time-frame.

EU Decisions are another form of EU law, which are directed at specific individual or state authorities in a Member State, requiring them to take or refrain from taking a certain action. Decisions are binding on the person or parties to whom they are addressed.

Other international treaties

As a sovereign State, Ireland can sign and become a party to any number of international treaties and conventions dealing with a range of matters, including copyright, extradition, child abduction and the international enforcement of judgments.

The provisions of such a treaty can have a strong moral effect in a signatory country, indicating certain principles to which the government of a country has subscribed by signing that treaty. For the provisions of a treaty to have direct legal effect under Irish law, however, its provisions must be incorporated into Irish law though the national legislative process.

An example of this is the *European Convention on Human Rights*, which was brought into existence by a community of states known as the Council of Europe (a separate organisation to the EU) in the aftermath of World War II. The *Convention* explicitly sets out, for example, the rights of freedom of expression (Article 10) and individual privacy (Article 8). Ireland signed the *Convention* in 1953 but it was not until 2003, with the passing of the *European Convention on Human Rights Act*, that the provisions of the *Convention* were given direct effect under Irish law. The Act requires every organ of the State to carry out its functions in a manner "compatible with the State's obligations" under the *Convention* (section 3(1)). This requirement includes the legislature and the Courts. The Courts are obliged to take "due account" of decisions of the European Court of Human Rights when considering cases involving the interpretation of rights set out in the *European Convention on Human Rights* (section 4).

See also

Q3   How is the Irish courts system structured?

> **www.citizensinformation.ie** – for a copy of the Irish Constitution and a useful explanation of the legislative process.
> **www.europa.eu** – for an explanation of the EU law-making process.
> **www.irishstatutebook.ie** – for an index and the texts of Acts of the Oireachtas and of Statutory Instruments.

Q2   What is the difference between civil law and criminal law?

Irish courts have the authority – referred to as the 'jurisdiction' – to adjudicate on both civil and criminal law cases.

Civil law

The civil law is concerned primarily with adjudicating on private disputes between one or more individuals or legal entities and others. A person who believes they have been wronged by another can bring a claim in the civil courts – referred to as a civil action or a civil suit (hence the term 'to sue'). Examples of civil actions include breach of contract cases, negligence cases (for example, medical negligence resulting in physical injury) and defamation cases.

The plaintiff (the person making the claim through the courts) will seek:

- A ruling by the judge that they have been wronged by the defendant; *and*

- A court order that the defendant pay a sum of money to compensate them for the harm or damage they have suffered as a result of that wrongdoing.

Pending a final determination on whether she / he has been wronged, the plaintiff occasionally may seek a judicial order requiring the defendant to do or refrain from doing something until the trial of the action. This is known as either an interim or an interlocutory injunction. Permanent injunctions occasionally may be made after the trial of an action has concluded.

In a civil case, a case must be proved on the balance of probabilities. This is known as the civil law burden of proof.

The financial compensation the judge orders to be paid is referred to as an 'award of damages'. The amount of damages can be assessed under several different headings. In debt collection cases, the plaintiff is not awarded damages but is given a judgment in their favour for the amount found to be due to them by the debtor.

A judge in a civil court is not entitled to convict the wrong-doer or to sentence them to a term of imprisonment. A judge has power, however, to send a person who is refusing to comply with a civil court order to prison until such time as they comply with the court order. Such refusal is known as civil contempt.

Criminal law

The criminal law is concerned primarily with the State maintaining social order by prosecuting wrong-doers who have intentionally or recklessly broken the criminal law, thereby harming not only the victim of the crime but also, by that action, harming society as a whole. A judge in a criminal court has authority to convict an offender found guilty of a crime and to impose a punishment on them by way of a fine and / or a term of imprisonment.

The victim of a crime is not the person who brings a criminal prosecution; the State – acting through a State legal officer known as the Director of Public Prosecutions (DPP) – brings the prosecution against an accused person. The victim may be the person who reports the crime and who gives evidence at the trial of the offence but it is the State that prosecutes the case against the accused.

In a criminal case, the State must prove beyond reasonable doubt that the accused has committed the offence with which they are charged. This is known as the criminal law burden of proof.

There are situations where both a criminal law and civil law case may be brought arising from the same incident. A common example is where a road traffic accident results in both a criminal prosecution (for example, for dangerous driving) as well as a civil claim for damages for personal injuries and car damage caused by the accident. In such situations, the criminal prosecution usually is concluded before the civil action is heard.

Public law and private law

Another categorisation of different types of law is public law and private law. Broadly speaking, public law is the law relevant to the interaction of individuals or private entities with the State (which can encompass both civil and criminal law cases) whereas private law is the law relevant to the interaction of private individuals and private entities with each other.

See also

Q1   What are the sources of Irish law?

Q3   How is the Irish courts system structured?

Q9   What are damages and how are they assessed?

www.dppireland.ie – Office of the Director of Public Prosecution.

Q3 How is the Irish Courts system structured?

The basic structure of the Irish courts is a four-tier system, with an additional appeal court for criminal law cases. The courts range from the District Court (relatively minor cases) to the Circuit Court (more extensive jurisdiction in both civil and criminal cases), to the High Court (the highest court of first instance) and finally to the highest appeal court, the Supreme Court.

The *Constitution* requires that justice be administered in courts "established by law" (Article 34.1). Article 34 requires that the law provide for the establishment of a High Court of first instance and a court of final appeal known as the Supreme Court. The current Irish courts system was established by the *Courts (Establishment and Constitution) Act, 1961*.

A court of first instance is a court in which the initial trial of a case can take place, prior to any appeal or reference of that case to a higher court. The District Court, the Circuit Court and the High Court are all courts of first instance.

District Court decisions may be appealed to the Circuit Court, and Circuit Court decisions to the High Court. The District Court may refer a question on the interpretation of a particular law to the High Court. Decisions of the High Court can be appealed to the Supreme Court on points of law only, which means the Supreme Court determines whether the law was correctly interpreted or applied in a High Court case. The Supreme Court does not determine issues of fact that arose in a case in a lower court; it decides only whether the law as applied to the determination of that case was correctly applied.

There is a Court of Criminal Appeal (three judges, no jury), to which convictions and sentences of the Circuit Criminal Court and the Central Criminal Court may be appealed. Decisions of the Special Criminal Court also may be appealed to the Court of Criminal Appeal. The Court of Criminal Appeal does not re-hear the criminal trial; it reviews only to the extent required by the grounds of appeal the original trial and decides whether the law was correctly interpreted or applied at the trial.

There is a judge-only Court of Civil Appeal in the English courts system at a level equivalent to that of the Irish Court of Criminal Appeal. It hears civil rather than criminal law appeals. While the establishment of an Irish Court of Civil Appeal is under consideration, none has been established to date and a constitutional referendum to provide for such a court may be required.

Special Criminal Courts, presided over by three judges without a jury, were provided for by the *Offences against the State Act, 1939* and are permitted by Article 38.3 of the *Constitution*. Such courts may be established when deemed necessary by the Government. A Special Criminal Court last was established in 1972, to try paramilitary and firearms offences associated with politically-motivated violence in Northern Ireland. It remains in place today, hearing cases associated with firearms and drug-related crime where there is a fear that a jury trial may not be effective because of potential intimidation of jury members.

Quasi-judicial bodies established by law in accordance with Article 37 of the *Constitution*, but with more limited powers than those held by judges in courts, are active principally in the areas of industrial relations and employment law (the Labour Court, the Employment Appeals Tribunal and the Equality Tribunal), consumer law (the Small Claims Court) and landlord and tenant law (the Rent Tribunal). Although sometimes referred to as courts, these bodies are not judicial courts.

Military tribunals, which try cases involving members of the military in accordance with military law, are constitutionally provided for by Article 38.4.

See also

Q4　　What is the role of the District Court?
Q5　　What is the role of the Circuit Court?
Q6　　What is the role of the High Court?
Q7　　What is the role of the Supreme Court?
Q8　　What cases are heard by a jury?

www.courts.ie

Q4 What is the role of the District Court?

The District Court is a court of summary jurisdiction, meaning cases are heard by a judge sitting alone without a jury. Cases are said to be tried 'summarily' in the District Court.

The District Court hears both civil and criminal cases; this is referred to as the court exercising its civil / criminal jurisdiction.

Civil law jurisdiction

The civil law jurisdiction of the District Court includes:

- Contract, tort, landlord and tenant, consumer and debt collection cases up to a maximum award of damages or order for judgment of €6,348.69.

- Certain family law cases, including safety, barring, child custody, access and maintenance orders (maximum €500 per week for a spouse, maximum €150 per week for each child).

- Certain types of licensing applications, including the granting of pub licence renewals, restaurant licences, special exemptions and occasional licences.

Criminal law jurisdiction

The criminal law jurisdiction of the District Court includes:

- Preliminary hearings on charges of indictable offences (offences liable to jury trial): Preliminary hearings relating to serious criminal charges are heard in the District Court before the case is sent forward for trial to the appropriate higher court for trial by jury. Evidence of arrest, charge and caution on all criminal charges is given by the State to the District Court.

- Indictable offences where the accused agrees to summary (no jury) trial: This procedure usually is adopted where the offence is a relatively minor one and the accused is willing to have the matter dealt with summarily in the District Court.

- Indictable offences where the accused pleads guilty and is sent forward to the Circuit Criminal Court for sentencing.

- Summary offences: Where legislation specifies that particular offences be tried summarily in the District Court.
- District Court bail applications.

The maximum prison sentence that may be imposed in the District Court in respect of any one offence is 12 months, although the imposition of consecutive sentences may mean that a convicted person receives a longer aggregate sentence up to a maximum of two years.

Location
The District Court sits at locations throughout Ireland. The country is divided into 25 Districts, plus the Dublin Metropolitan District, with one or more District Court judges assigned to each District. There are several locations at which the District Court sits in each District, according to a schedule of sittings. The Dublin Metropolitan District Courts and Cork City District Court sit continuously during Law Terms.

Note that the District Court hearing a criminal case against a child (under 18) is called the Children Court and may sit in any District Court location.

See also
Q3   How is the Irish Courts system structured?
Q5   What is the role of the Circuit Court?
Q6   What is the role of the High Court?
Q7   What is the role of the Supreme Court?
Q8   What cases are heard by a jury?

Q5   What is the role of the Circuit Court?

The Circuit Court hears both civil and criminal cases; this is referred to as the court exercising its civil / criminal jurisdiction.

Civil law jurisdiction
The civil law jurisdiction of the Circuit Court includes:

- Contract, tort, landlord and tenant, defamation, consumer and debt collection cases: The Court may award damages or give an order for judgment on a debt up to the value of €38,092.14 (€50,000 in defamation cases).
- Appeals from District Court decisions.
- Family law cases: Judicial separation and divorce cases; protection, barring, child custody, access and maintenance orders.
- Licensing law: Including the grant of new pub licences and hotel licences.

All civil cases are heard by judges only, without the involvement of the jury.

Criminal law jurisdiction
The criminal law jurisdiction of the Circuit Court includes:

- Trial of serious criminal charges on indictment (jury trial). However, murder, rape, aggravated sexual assault, treason, genocide and piracy are excluded from the jurisdiction of Circuit Criminal Court and are tried instead by the Central Criminal Court.
- Appeals from District Court convictions and / or sentences (heard by judge only, no jury).

Location
Ireland is divided into eight Circuits, with one judge assigned to each Circuit, except for Dublin and Cork to which more judges are assigned. The Circuit Court sits at designated locations on each Circuit, according to

a schedule of sittings. In Dublin and Cork, the Circuit Courts sit continuously during the Law Terms.

Appeals
Appeals of decisions made by the Circuit Criminal Court may be made to the three-judge Court of Criminal Appeal. The appellant may appeal either the conviction and sentence or the sentence only. The Court of Criminal Appeal does not re-hear a criminal trial but determines whether the law was correctly applied at the original trial.

See also
Q3   How is the Irish Courts system structured?
Q4   What is the role of the District Court?
Q6   What is the role of the High Court?
Q7   What is the role of the Supreme Court?
Q8   What cases are heard by a jury?

Q6   What is the role of the High Court?

The High Court hears both civil and criminal cases. When the High Court exercises its jurisdiction to hear criminal trials, it is called the Central Criminal Court.

A dedicated arm of the High Court – the Commercial Court – hears high-value commercial cases and intellectual property claims. An application must be made to the Commercial Court to have a case accepted for hearing by that Court.

Civil law jurisdiction

The civil law jurisdiction of the High Court includes:

- Family law cases, including judicial separation, nullity and divorce applications.
- Breach of contract, tort, landlord and tenant, defamation, negligence, consumer and debt collection cases.
- Appeals from Circuit Court decisions.
- Injunction applications.
- Judicial review applications by which an individual or other entity seeks to have the actions of a State body or private organisation reviewed on the grounds that the body or organisation acted in a way that exceeded or derogated from its lawful powers.
- Rulings on the constitutionality of a piece of legislation or part of a piece of legislation.
- Rulings on questions on the correct interpretation of a legal rule or principle raised by a judge in the District Court – this is known as a 'case stated'.

Note that, in the High Court:

- Most civil cases are heard by a judge only, without a jury.
- Some civil cases are heard by a judge sitting with a jury – the most common of these are defamation trials.

- On occasion, three judges sitting together may be designated to hear a case – for example, a ruling on the constitutionality of a piece of legislation.
- While it can hear cases of any value, civil cases usually are brought in the High Court only where the plaintiff is seeking in excess of €38,092.14 (€50,000 in defamation cases) by way of damages.
- Bail applications may be heard, where the charge is one of murder or, on appeal, where the District Court has refused to grant bail.

Criminal law jurisdiction
The High Court, when trying criminal law offences, sits as the Central Criminal Court and tries the following offences on indictment (a jury trial): murder, rape, aggravated sexual assault, treason, genocide and piracy.

Location
The High Court sits continuously during the Law Terms in Dublin. It also sits on scheduled dates to hear certain types of case, such as personal injury actions, in designated venues throughout Ireland. When sitting as the Central Criminal Court, the Court sits in Dublin and also on occasion in court venues outside Dublin.

Criminal appeals
Appeals of decisions by the Central Criminal Court may be made to the three-judge Court of Criminal Appeal. The appellant may appeal either conviction and sentence or sentence only. The Court of Criminal Appeal does not re-hear a criminal trial but determines whether the law was correctly applied at the original trial.

See also
Q3   How is the Irish Courts system structured?
Q4   What is the role of the District Court?
Q5   What is the role of the Circuit Court?
Q7   What is the role of the Supreme Court?
Q8   What cases are heard by a jury?

Q7   What is the role of the Supreme Court?

The Supreme Court is the ultimate appeal court in the Irish court system. It considers whether the legal rules and principles relevant to a particular case have been correctly interpreted and / or applied in a lower court. The Supreme Court makes decisions on points of law, leaving the matter of making findings of fact to the trial courts.

The Supreme Court considers appeals arising at both civil law and criminal law, although the extent to which findings of the Court of Criminal Appeal are appealed to the Supreme Court is limited.

The Supreme Court usually sits with three judges hearing a case but, on occasion, depending on the importance of the point of law at issue in the appeal, it may sit with five or even seven judges. Save in cases concerning the constitutionality of a piece of legislation, all the judges hearing a case may give a reasoned explanation of their decision by way of a written judgment, whether theirs is a minority or majority view of the court.

The Supreme Court, on appeal from the High Court, may be asked to decide on the constitutionality of a piece of legislation either in whole or in part.

The Supreme Court has a unique constitutional role in the consideration of the constitutionality of proposed legislation referred to it by the President under Article 26 of the *Constitution*. This is a power granted to the President, following consultation with the Council of State, to refer all or part of a legislative Bill directly to the Supreme Court for a ruling on its constitutionality. At least five judges must hear such a case and only one judgment may be issued by the court.

The Supreme Court has an explicit power under section 13 of the *Defamation Act, 2009* to replace the amount of damages awarded to a plaintiff in a defamation case with an amount that the Supreme Court "considers appropriate".

Location
The Supreme Court sits in the Four Courts, Dublin.

See also

Q3   How is the Irish Courts system structured?
Q4   What is the role of the District Court?
Q5   What is the role of the Circuit Court?
Q6   What is the role of the High Court?
Q8   What cases are heard by a jury?

Q8   What cases are heard by a jury?

Everyone charged with a criminal offence in Ireland has a right under Article 38.5 of the *Constitution* to be tried by a jury. There are three exceptions to this provision:

(i) The summary trial of minor offences in the District Court.

(ii) Offences tried by the Special Criminal Court.

(iii) Offences tried by military tribunals.

Some minor indictable offences (offences liable to be tried before a jury) can be tried summarily in the District Court, subject to certain conditions, including the consent of the accused. However, serious criminal charges are tried before a jury in either the Circuit Criminal Court or the Central Criminal Court.

Note that the right to a jury trial applies only to the trial, not to an appeal hearing. Accordingly, if a trial is heard before a jury in the Circuit Criminal Court and appealed to the Court of Criminal Appeal, the appeal will be heard by a judge-only court with no jury.

A jury comprises 12 people. On occasion, a juror may be discharged or become unavailable during a criminal trial but the trial may proceed nonetheless.

In a criminal trial, a jury decision is required to be unanimous unless, having deliberated for a reasonable period of time (two hours minimum) without reaching a unanimous verdict, the trial judge agrees to accept a majority verdict. Ten of the jurors (of whom there must be at least 11 in total) must agree with the verdict (section 25, *Criminal Justice Act, 1984*). A jury is concerned only with making a finding of the guilt or otherwise of the accused. Once an accused is convicted – or acquitted – the jury has no further role in the proceedings. Sentencing is carried out by the judge alone.

There is no equivalent constitutional requirement that civil trials be heard by juries as there is in respect of criminal trials. Breach of contract and debt collection cases always have been heard by judges sitting without a jury. Trial by jury in other civil law cases was the norm until 1971, when jury trials in the Circuit Court were abolished (section 6, *Courts Act, 1971*). Civil jury trials continued to take place in the High Court until 1988, when they were abolished in the majority of categories of civil trial (section 1, *Courts Act, 1988*). Jury trials were not abolished in defamation claims, however, so defamation cases in the High Court continue to be heard by a jury.

In High Court civil jury trials, including defamation trials, at least nine of the jurors must agree on the verdict (section 95, *Courts of Justice Act, 1924*). In such cases, the jury makes findings both on liability and also on the amount of damages to be awarded to the plaintiff.

See also
Q3   How is the Irish Courts system structured?
Q4   What is the role of the District Court?
Q5   What is the role of the Circuit Court?
Q6   What is the role of the High Court?

Q9 What are damages and how are they assessed?

The term 'damages' describes the financial compensation awarded by a court in favour of a successful plaintiff, and against the defendant, in a civil law claim. If the defendant does not pay the award of damages, the plaintiff may need to take a separate legal action to enforce the award.

Damages fall broadly into four categories and an overall award of damages can include an element of any or all of them:

- General damages: Awarded to compensate for the general pain, distress, and upset felt by the plaintiff as a result of the wrong done to them by the defendant. This amount is not quantifiable by reference to any mathematical formula and varies from case to case.

- Special damages: A figure put on the quantifiable expenses or loss that the plaintiff has incurred, or will incur, as a result of the wrong done to them by the defendant – for example, medical expenses, loss of earnings for an individual or loss of business for a trading company.

- Punitive (or exemplary) damages: Damages awarded by a court by way of indicating the court's particular disapproval of the actions of the defendant in relation to the wrong that was done to the plaintiff. There is an element of deterrence of both the defendant and others against future similar wrongdoing inherent in an award of punitive damages.

- Aggravated damages: Additional damages may be awarded in respect of the intensification of the injury caused to the plaintiff by the behaviour or motivation of the defendant, whether in respect of the original wrongdoing or in the manner in which the defence of the claim was conducted.

There are entire books written about this subject alone and extensive case law on the topic. It is important to understand that damages are assessed on a case-by-case basis, taking into consideration the particular circumstances of each case; there is no 'rate card' for damages at civil law generally nor under defamation law.

In most civil claims (for example, for personal injuries sustained in a road accident), the amount of damages awarded is decided by the judge hearing the case. However, in a High Court defamation action, damages are assessed by the jury, with the judge giving directions to the jury on the matter of damages as required by section 31(2) of the *Defamation Act, 2009*, in respect of claims made arising from publications made on or after 1 January 2010.

See also
Q8   What cases are heard by a jury?
Q51   How are damages assessed in a defamation case?

Q10   How is the right to freedom of expression protected under Irish law?

The right to freedom of expression is explicitly protected by:

- The 1937 *Constitution*.
- The *European Convention on Human Rights* (ECHR).
- The *International Covenant on Civil and Political Rights*, which incorporates the rights set out in the *Universal Declaration of Human Rights* of 1948.

The 1937 *Constitution*

Article 40.6.1°(i) guarantees liberty for the exercise of the "right of citizens to express freely their convictions and opinions". Inherent in this right is the right to communicate the facts on which those convictions and opinions are based. "It therefore appears to me that the right ... guaranteed by Article 40 of the *Constitution* is a right to communicate facts as well as a right to comment on them", said Judge Barrington in *Irish Times Ltd v Ireland [1998] 1 IR 359* at page 405. In the same judgment (page 405), Judge Barrington also recognised that the right extends to those who control "organs of public opinion", thereby acknowledging the right to freedom of expression of the media.

Judge Fennelly's judgment in *Mahon v Post Publications [2007] IESC 15* indicates the high level of protection that the Irish courts give to the right to freedom of expression. At paragraph 51 of his judgment, he stated, "The right of a free press to communicate information without let or restraint is intrinsic to a free and democratic society". Significantly, in the same judgment at paragraph 43, he says that the "right of freedom of expression extends the same protection to worthless, prurient and meretricious publication as it does to worthy, serious and socially valuable works".

However, the right to free expression of convictions and opinions is not absolute. It is qualified, not only by considerations of "public order, morality and the authority of the State" (Article 40.6.1° (i)), but also by the need to respect and uphold other constitutionally-protected rights such as the protection of reputation, the right to privacy and the right to a fair trial.

Irish constitutional law requires that any restriction on the right to freely express convictions and opinions must be proportionate to the objective sought to be achieved by that restriction. This principle of proportionality is reflected also in Article 10 of the *European Convention on Human Rights*.

The *European Convention on Human Rights*

The right to freedom of expression is set out in Article 10 of the ECHR, which includes the statement, "This right shall include freedom to hold opinions and to receive and impart information and ideas without interference by public authority and regardless of frontiers".

However, the exercise of the right is not absolute. Article 10.2 sets out a three-part test for the imposition of any restrictions, which must be:

- Prescribed by law, *and*
- Necessary in a democratic society, *and*
- For the purposes of one of the stated aims expressed in Article 10.2, as being "... in the interests of national security, territorial integrity or public safety, for the prevention of disorder or crime, for the protection of health or morals, for the protection of reputation or the rights of others, for preventing the disclosure of information received in confidence, or for maintaining the authority and impartiality of the judiciary".

The *European Convention on Human Rights* was incorporated into Irish domestic law by the *European Convention on Human Rights Act, 2003*.

The *International Covenant on Civil and Political Rights* and the United Nations *Universal Declaration of Human Rights*

The United Nations (UN) was established as an international organisation in 1945, at the end of World War II. In 1948, the UN General Assembly adopted the *Universal Declaration of Human Rights* (UDHR), Article 19 of which states, "Everyone has the right to freedom of opinion and expression; this right includes freedom to hold opinions without interference and to seek, receive and impart information and ideas through any media and regardless of frontiers".

An international treaty committing signatory states to upholding the rights set out in the UDHR – the *International Covenant on Civil and Political Rights* (ICCPR) – was opened for signature in 1966. Ireland signed the ICCPR in 1989 but has not incorporated it directly into Irish domestic law. In the case of *Kavanagh v Governor of Mountjoy Prison, 2001 IEHC*, the High Court held that the ICCPR does not confer rights on individuals that can be legally enforced through the Irish courts.

Article 19.3 of the ICCPR also recognises that there may be restrictions imposed on the exercise of the right to freedom of expression but these restrictions are limited: "The exercise of the rights provided for in paragraph 2 of this article carries with it special duties and responsibilities. It may therefore be subject to certain restrictions, but these shall only be such as are provided by law and are necessary: (a) For respect of the rights or reputations of others; (b) For the protection of national security or of public order (*ordre public*), or of public health or morals". In effect, the ICCPR is a moral touch-stone for the interpretation of civil rights law before the Irish courts. Furthermore, the provisions of the ECHR, which was incorporated into Irish domestic law in 2003, are similar, to a significant extent, to the provisions of the ICCPR.

Case law
Mahon v Post Publications [2007] IESC 15
The Tribunal of Inquiry chaired by Judge Alan Mahon sought an order restricting the publication of any material designated confidential by the Tribunal, pending disclosure of that material at a public sitting of the Tribunal. The order was refused by the High Court, and on appeal by the Supreme Court, on the grounds that, if granted, it would be too wide in its effect and would amount to a disproportionate restriction on the right to freedom of expression. The judgment of Judge Fennelly in the Supreme Court asserted the importance of not restricting the exercise of the right to freedom of expression other than in a manner permitted by both the *Constitution* and by Article 10.2 of the ECHR.

He stated at paragraph 43 of his judgment that, "The right of freedom of expression extends the same protection to worthless, prurient and meretricious publication as it does to worthy, serious and socially valuable works. The undoubted fact that news media frequently and implausibly invoke the public interest to cloak worthless and even offensive material does not affect the principle". At paragraph 51, he stated, "Clearly, the *Constitution* unequivocally guarantees both the right to express convictions and opinions and the right to communicate facts or information. These rights are inseparable. It matters little, at least for present purposes, which Article of the *Constitution* expresses the guarantee. The right of a free press to communicate information without let or restraint is intrinsic to a free and democratic society".

See also

Q11   How is the right to good name and reputation protected under Irish law?

Q70   How is privacy protected under Irish law?

www.bailii.org – selected judgments from the jurisdictions of England, Scotland, Northern Ireland and the Republic of Ireland.
www.courts.ie/judgments – selected judgments of the Irish High Court, Court of Criminal Appeal and Supreme Court.
www.echr.coe.int – official Council of Europe website for the ECHR.
www.ihrc.ie – website of the Irish Human Rights Commission.
www.irishstatutebook.ie – texts of Irish Acts and Statutory Instruments.
www.un.org – official United Nations website.

DEFAMATION LAW

Q11   How is the right to good name and reputation protected under Irish law?

The protection of reputation against unjust attack is a civil right protected under Irish and international law. The right is referred to in:

- The 1937 *Constitution*.
- The *European Convention on Human Rights* (ECHR).
- The *International Covenant on Civil and Political Rights* (ICCPR), which protects the rights set out in the *Universal Declaration of Human Rights* (UDHR) of 1948.

The law of defamation is the means by which legal redress in the case of unjust attack against reputation is provided for by the State.

The 1937 *Constitution*

Article 40.3.1° contains a guarantee by the State to defend and vindicate the personal rights of the citizen. Article 40.3.2° requires the State, by its laws, to protect and vindicate in particular certain personal rights, including the right to "good name". The law that fulfils this Constitutional obligation is the law of defamation.

Defamation law, in effect, strives to find a constitutionally-acceptable balance between the exercise of the right to freedom of expression guaranteed under Article 40.6.1° (i) of the *Constitution* and the obligation to protect and vindicate reputation provided by Article 40.3.2°.

The *European Convention on Human Rights*

The right to freedom of expression is set out in Article 10 of the ECHR, but the exercise of the right is not absolute. Article 10.2 sets out a three-part test for the imposition of any restrictions, which must be:

- Prescribed by law, *and*
- Necessary in a democratic society, *and*
- For the purposes of one of the stated aims expressed in Article10.2, as being "... in the interests of national security,

territorial integrity or public safety, for the prevention of disorder or crime, for the protection of health or morals, *for the protection of reputation* or the rights of others, for preventing the disclosure of information received in confidence, or for maintaining the authority and impartiality of the judiciary" *(italics added)*.

Thus, in Article 10.2, the ECHR explicitly acknowledges the protection of the reputation of others as a legitimate basis on which to impose restrictions on the right to freedom of expression. The ECHR was incorporated into Irish domestic law by the *European Convention on Human Rights Act, 2003*.

Note that the ECHR was drafted by the Council of Europe, a separate organisation from the European Union and any of its institutions, albeit that most Council of Europe member states are also members of the EU (Switzerland being a notable exception). There is close co-operation between the Council of Europe and the EU in the area of human rights protection.

The *International Covenant on Civil and Political Rights* and the United Nations *Universal Declaration of Human Rights*

The United Nations (UN) was established as an international organisation at the end of World War II in 1945. In 1948, the UN General Assembly adopted the UDHR, Article 19 of which states, "Everyone has the right to freedom of opinion and expression; this right includes freedom to hold opinions without interference and to seek, receive and impart information and ideas through any media and regardless of frontiers".

An international treaty committing states to upholding the rights set out in the UDHR – the *International Covenant on Civil and Political Rights* (ICCPR) – was established in 1966. Although Ireland signed the ICCPR in 1989, it has not been incorporated directly into Irish domestic law. The High Court held in the case of *Kavanagh v Governor of Mountjoy Prison [2001] IEHC 77* that the ICCPR does not confer legally-enforceable rights on individuals in the Irish courts. In effect, the ICCPR is a moral touch-stone for the interpretation of civil rights law before the Irish courts. Furthermore, the provisions of the ECHR, which was incorporated into

Irish domestic law in 2003, are similar, to a significant extent, to the provisions of the ICCPR.

Article 19.3 of the ICCPR recognises that there may be restrictions imposed on the exercise of the right to freedom of expression although these restrictions are limited: "The exercise of the [freedom of expression] rights provided for in paragraph 2 of this article carries with it special duties and responsibilities. It may therefore be subject to certain restrictions, but these shall only be such as are provided by law and are necessary: (a) For respect of the rights or reputations of others; (b) For the protection of national security or of public order (*ordre public*), or of public health or morals".

See also

Q10   How is the right to freedom of expression protected under Irish law?

> **www.bailii.org** – selected judgments from the jurisdictions of England, Scotland, Northern Ireland and the Republic of Ireland.
> **www.courts.ie/judgments** - selected judgments of the Irish High Court and Supreme Court.
> **www.echr.coe.int** – official Council of Europe website for the ECHR.
> **www.ihrc.ie** – website of the Irish Human Rights Commission.
> **www.irishstatutebook.ie** – texts of Irish Acts and Statutory Instruments.
> **www.un.org** – official United Nations website.

Q12 What is defamation?

Defamation law is the area of law concerned with protecting and rectifying injury done to a person's reputation by the publication of a statement that tends to damage their good name and reputation.

The Defamation Act, 2009 provides a statutory definition of both a 'defamatory statement' and the 'tort of defamation'. Section 2 defines a defamatory statement as one that "… tends to injure a person's reputation in the eyes of reasonable members of society …". Section 2 also specifies (non-exhaustively) the different forms in which a statement may be made, including statements made orally or in writing, by images, sounds, gestures, by broadcast, on the Internet and by electronic communications.

Section 6(2) states, "The tort of defamation consists of the publication, by any means, of a defamatory statement concerning a person to one or more than one person (other than the first-mentioned person), and 'defamation' shall be construed accordingly". A tort is a wrong done by one person to another that gives rise to an entitlement for the person who has been wronged to apply to the civil courts for redress, usually by way of an award of damages.

Section 6(2) of the 2009 Act requires that the defamatory publication must be made to at least one person other than the person about whom the statement is made. It is not unheard of for a claim to be made where a defamatory statement has been published to only one person other than the subject of the statement.

Defamation is part of the civil law. Since the 2009 Act became law, defamation is exclusively a civil law matter.

See also
Q2   What is the difference between civil law and criminal law?
Q11 How is the right to good name and reputation protected under Irish law?
Q13 Is it possible to be prosecuted for defamation or blasphemy?

Q13   Is it possible to be prosecuted for defamation or blasphemy?

All forms of criminal libel, with the exception of blasphemous libel, were abolished by section 35 of the *Defamation Act, 2009*.

Over the years, four forms of criminal defamation offence evolved at common law: defamatory libel, seditious libel, obscene libel and blasphemous libel. Three of these offences – defamatory libel, seditious libel and obscene libel – were abolished by the 2009 Act. Furthermore, the statutory punishments for all forms of criminal libel, including blasphemous libel, contained in the *Defamation Act, 1961* were abolished with the repeal of the 1961 Act by section 4 of the 2009 Act.

Thus, criminal libel was consigned to the legal history books, with the exception of blasphemous libel, which already had an uncertain status under Irish common law. Furthermore, as there was no longer any statutory provision for the punishment of blasphemy, the Minister for Justice was advised that this could lead to the State being in dereliction of a constitutional obligation; the same Article of the *Constitution* that protects the right to freedom of expression also contains a final paragraph that states: "The publication or utterance of *blasphemous*, seditious, or indecent matter is an offence which shall be punishable in accordance with law" *(italics added)*.

While it would have been preferable to hold a constitutional referendum to amend Article 40.6.1°(i) to remove the reference to the publication of blasphemous material being an offence, for a variety of reasons and as a supposedly short-term measure pending a constitutional referendum on the issue, the government of the day introduced a statutory offence of blasphemy in the *Defamation Act, 2009*.

Accordingly, an offence of publishing or uttering blasphemous material was introduced by section 36 of the 2009 Act. It is an indictable offence (trial by jury). No term of imprisonment can be imposed on conviction; a punitive fine may be imposed, subject to a maximum of €25,000.

Blasphemy is described in the 2009 Act (section 36(2)) as the publication or utterance of "matter that is grossly abusive or insulting in relation to matters held sacred by any religion, thereby causing outrage among a substantial number of the adherents of that religion" with intent to cause such outrage by such publication or utterance.

Section 36(3) provides that it shall be a defence to a charge of blasphemy for a defendant to prove that "a reasonable person would find genuine literary, artistic, political, scientific, or academic value in the matter to which the offence relates".

There has been extensive criticism, both nationally and abroad, of the introduction of a criminal offence of blasphemy in Ireland. To the date of writing, there have been no prosecutions under these sections of the 2009 Act.

Note that, by contrast with Irish and English law, criminal prosecutions for libel are the norm by way of response to a defamatory publication under the laws of continental European legal systems – for example, in Austria and France.

See also
Q12   What is defamation?
Q14   What do the terms libel and slander mean?

Q14   What do the terms libel and slander mean?

The terms 'libel' and 'slander' formerly described two forms of the tort (civil wrong) of defamation.

Libel described a defamatory statement published in permanent form, such as a newspaper article, a photograph or a magazine. A broadcast defamatory statement was designated a libel under section 15 of the now-repealed *Defamation Act, 1961*.

Slander described a defamatory statement published in transient form, such as a verbal statement made in a pub or a verbal allegation of theft made in front of other shoppers in a department store.

Slightly different procedural rules applied to cases involving slander and to cases involving libel. Those distinctions were abolished by the *Defamation Act, 2009*, section 6(1) of which states: "The tort of libel and the tort of slander − (a) shall cease to be so described, and (b) shall, instead, be collectively described, and are referred to in this Act, as the 'tort of defamation'". The same procedural rules now apply to all defamation cases, regardless of the form in which that publication is made.

In colloquial terms, the words 'defamation', 'libel' and 'slander' tend to be used interchangeably. It is likely that this usage will continue, despite the abolition by the 2009 Act of the legal distinction between them.

See also
Q12   What is defamation?
Q13   Is it possible to be prosecuted for defamation or blasphemy?

Q15   What is a publication under defamation law?

For the purposes of defamation law, a publication is the communication of a statement by one person (A) about another person (B) to one or more people (C, etc) other than the subject of the statement.

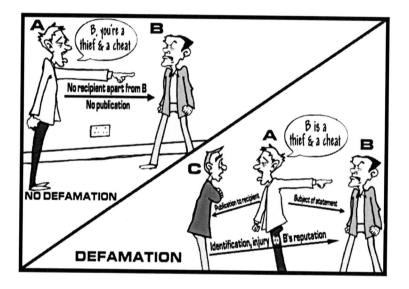

If the statement is communicated only by A to B and there is no communication of the statement about B to C, etc, then there is no publication under defamation law.

A defamatory publication can be by "any means" (see section 6(2) of the *Defamation Act, 2009*), including by letter, email, telephone, website or other Internet posting, radio and television broadcast, photograph, film, sound recording, book and newspaper. This list is not exhaustive; neither is the definition of "statement" set out in section 2 of the 2009 Act.

The publication does not need to be for commercial purposes to constitute a defamatory publication. A defamatory publication can be made in a private context, such as in a private letter or email or even in a conversation involving several people in a pub. It is rare, but not unheard of, for defamation actions to arise from statements made in communications such as private letters or conversations. The contents of such letters or conversations usually remain private unless the person who receives the letter or takes part in the conversation communicates its content to other third parties. For example, an email from A to C containing a statement about B may be defamatory. While published to C, it may never come to the attention of B so, for purely practical reasons, it does not give rise to a defamation action. However, if C forwards the email to third parties (D, etc) and B becomes aware of its contents, both C and A may find themselves liable for publishing a defamatory statement. Similarly, a statement made directly by A to B about B in an email may be disparaging and untrue but, in most circumstances, will not amount to a publication. However, if A copies that email (by way of the 'cc' or 'bcc' function) to any third party (C, D, etc), A becomes a publisher of the contents of that email for the purposes of defamation law.

The explanations above are subject to any protection from liability for defamation afforded to certain publications by the law of qualified privilege discussed elsewhere in **QUICK WIN MEDIA LAW IRELAND**.

The *Defamation Act, 2009* provides a 'saver clause' for situations where there is unintentional publication of what was intended to be a private communication. Section 6(4) can be invoked where a statement about B is communicated by A to B, and also to C, in circumstances where A did not intend that the statement would be published to C. Furthermore, it must not have been "reasonably foreseeable" that, in communicating the statement to B, it would be published also to C. Marking correspondence 'Private' or 'For attention of addressee only', where a letter or email contains information that could be defamatory about the person to whom it is addressed, were it to be seen by a third party, may assist the sender in showing to a court that they did not intend that the correspondence would be published to a third party. Section 6(4), at the time of writing, is untested in the Irish courts.

See also
Q12 What is defamation?

Q16   Who is a publisher under defamation law?

The term 'publisher' has a far broader meaning under defamation law than in colloquial speech.

Anyone involved in the process of the publication of a defamatory statement potentially can be regarded as a publisher. This includes the author of a book, as well as the publishing company that publishes the book; the journalist who writes a newspaper article; the editor, producer or presenter of a radio or television show; the independent television production company that produces a television show; the company that owns a newspaper, a radio station or television station in which or by which a defamatory statement is carried. An interviewee or contributor to a radio show, television show or newspaper article also can be held liable if that show or article contains a defamatory statement made by them.

While one or more defendants – each of whom may have played a different role in the publication of the same defamatory statement – may be sued by a plaintiff, in practice defamation actions tend to be brought against the defendant most likely to be a good 'mark' for damages. This means that owners of publishing outlets tend to be sued, rather than the individual employees involved in the publication process. However, journalists are often named as defendants in defamation proceedings, along with the newspaper that published the allegedly defamatory article; independent production companies tend to be named as defendants, along with the television station that broadcast an allegedly defamatory programme; and occasionally, presenters of, or contributors to, allegedly defamatory radio or television broadcasts are sued, as well as the broadcasting station that produced and transmitted the item.

Where an employee of a media outlet (for example, a journalist) is sued in her / his own name, it is a matter for the employer organisation to decide whether it will indemnify its employee's liability (pay for any costs or damages incurred in the name of the employee) for defamation. In practice, media organisations generally indemnify the liability of their employees in such circumstances.

Even if a contributor on a radio or television show makes a defamatory statement, in circumstances where the radio or television station had no advance knowledge of, or control over, the making of the statement, the broadcasting station is regarded at law as a publisher of that statement. This rule creates particular hazards in live broadcast situations – especially where the limited comfort of a time-delay mechanism is not available to the broadcaster.

As a result of their role in the publication of a defamatory statement, those who sell or distribute a defamatory publication potentially are exposed to liability for such a publication. This includes a bookshop owner or newspaper vendor, as well as an Internet service provider. The law provides a defence for such individuals and businesses, however, in the form of both the 'innocent publication' defence provided by section 27 of the *Defamation Act, 2009* and the 'hosting' defence provided by the *Electronic Commerce Regulations* of 2003 (which incorporated the *Electronic Commerce Directive, 2000* into Irish domestic law). These defences are discussed elsewhere in **QUICK WIN MEDIA LAW IRELAND.**

See also

Q15 What is a publication under defamation law?
Q19 Who is liable for a defamatory publication made online?
Q20 What is innocent publication?
Q39 Can employers be held liable for defamatory publications made by their employees?

Q17   Can a business sue for defamation?

Section 12 of the *Defamation Act, 2009* allows a body corporate both to sue and to be sued for defamation. The section also specifically states that a body corporate is entitled to sue for damages for defamation whether or not it has suffered, or is likely to suffer, financial loss as a result of the defamatory publication.

A body corporate is a legal entity established in accordance with, or by, law that allows a group of individuals to carry on a specific common activity as a distinct single legal 'person' with rights and obligations at law, even though that person is not a natural person – for example, a limited liability company. As a body corporate, a limited liability company can sue for defamation, as can a public liability company. A trading entity such as a partnership or sole trader is not a body corporate.

UK case law suggests that corporate bodies that fulfil a public service role should not be entitled to sue for defamation, as to do so would tend to discourage public debate on matters of public importance. However, section 12 of the Irish 2009 Act does not make any such exception to the entitlement of corporate bodies to sue for defamation. The availability of the new 'fair and reasonable publication' defence under section 26 of the 2009 Act will make it unlikely that a responsibly-written article about the activities of a State body would result in liability for defamation of that body, given that there is usually a strong public interest element in any publication scrutinising a State body. In practice, State bodies do not sue for defamation, although this observation does not apply equally to officials or employees of State bodies who may be identified or identifiable by a publication.

A limited liability company or partnership is entitled to use a business name that may be different from the name of the company or individuals carrying on that business. When making or responding to a defamation complaint, it is important to ascertain precisely the identity and legal status of the individual or entity making or responding to the claim. The Companies Registration Office (CRO) website (**www.cro.ie**) maintains a searchable register of limited companies, as well as a register of business names. Although all businesses using a business name are legally obliged to register that name with the CRO, compliance with this requirement is not universal.

Case law

Derbyshire County Council V Times Newspapers Ltd [1999] UKHL 6
A UK case in which the House of Lords held that a county council was not entitled to sue for damages for defamation on the grounds that to allow such an action to proceed could inhibit the public discussion of matters of public interest.

See also

Q12   What is defamation?
Q34   What is the fair and reasonable publication defence?

www.cro.ie – Companies Registration Office website.

Q18   What can a business do to protect its website from a defamation claim?

Below is a non-exhaustive list of suggested steps that a business can take to manage and minimise the defamation risk posed by having a website:

1. Draft a clear protocol, to be notified to all employees, that:
   - (i) Identifies exactly who may make changes to, or post material, on the website – and who may not.
   - (ii) Sets out an approval or clearance procedure for material to be posted on the website.
   - (iii) Sets out clearly the required notification procedure (for example, to a designated manager or editor) for defamation complaints.
   - (iv) Sets out the procedures that must be followed on receipt of a complaint of defamation – including temporary or permanent disablement of website access to the item complained of, consultation with a senior manager and / or a legal advisor, and communication with the journalist or researcher responsible for the item.

2. Do not permit user-generated content (UGC) to be posted by third parties on the website without taking prior legal advice, including advice on:
   - (i) The legal risks inherent in permitting UGC on the website.
   - (ii) Whether to moderate UGC postings.
   - (iii) The terms and conditions on which a UGC facility will be offered to third-party users of the website.

   Such terms and conditions ought to include:
   - (i) A requirement that no material that is defamatory or otherwise infringes the legal rights of others or is obscene or offensive may be posted.
   - (ii) A statement of the website's moderation policy.
   - (iii) A statement of the website's notification and take-down policy, giving contact details for notifications of any material that is unlawful or otherwise offends the terms and conditions of use.

(iv) A disclaimer of the company's liability for unlawful or offensive postings or postings otherwise in breach of the terms and conditions.

(v) A disclaimer of liability for the contents of any links on the site.

(vi) A requirement that the terms and conditions must be accepted by third parties posting UGC on the website.

3. Do not re-publish data (for example, articles, client or customer reviews of the providers of goods and services) sourced from other websites without taking prior legal advice on the implications of this practice. As well as posing a defamation risk, data protection and copyright issues may be raised by copying and re-using such data.

4. Ensure that employees are made aware of the basic elements of defamation law – especially those responsible for website postings. Awareness of defamation risk and managing that risk is a team effort.

5. Take specialist legal advice in relation to archiving articles, broadcasts or postings that are the subject of a defamation claim or complaint – either the removal of allegedly defamatory postings or at least notification to online archive users of any defamation challenge to an archived story or item may be advisable.

Case law

Flood v Times Newspapers Ltd [2010] EWCA Civ 804

The Times newspaper in England published an article stating that an internal police investigation was underway in relation to allegations of corruption made against a police officer working in the Extradition Unit of the Metropolitan Police Service. The allegations were that the officer was selling information to various Russian businessmen. The officer, Detective Sergeant Gary Flood, was named and details of the allegations were published. Flood sued for damages for defamation. It was held in the High Court that the public interest defence applied to the publication of the article both in *The Times* newspaper and as part of *The Times'* online archive. However, it was held that, once the newspaper had been informed of the outcome of the investigation exonerating Detective Sergeant Flood and confirming no criminal charge or disciplinary action would be taken against him, the public interest defence ceased to apply to the defendant's online archive version of the article and the defendant was liable for defamation from that time onwards. The newspaper had failed to publish online a correction of the original article once notified of the outcome of the investigation.

On appeal, the High Court's substantive finding was reversed, in that the public interest defence, in circumstances where the newspaper had not sought to investigate further the truth or otherwise of the allegations before publishing them, was held not to apply to either the original newspaper publication or the publication of the allegations online.

What is clear from the rationale in both the High Court and Court of Civil Appeal judgments, however, is that including a correction or qualification of the information on the online archive version of the article once the newspaper had been made aware of the outcome of the police investigation into the allegations would have been an indicator of 'responsible journalism' from the point of view of the defendant's reliance on the public interest defence in respect of the online archive publication.

See also

Q19   Who is liable for a defamatory publication made online?
Q33   What is the public interest defence?
Q42   Does defamation law apply to social networking sites?
Q43   What can a business do to protect its social networking site from a defamation claim?

Q19 Who is liable for a defamatory publication made online?

The law of defamation applies equally to online publication as it does to any other form of publication. Section 2 of the *Defamation Act, 2009* includes a statement published on the Internet as a statement for the purposes of the Act. The publisher of a defamatory statement online can be held liable at law for that publication.

If the person or company having control of a website resides or has a place of business in Ireland, they can be sued for damages for defamation in Ireland in respect of defamatory material that they place on that website. Thus, the same care taken by publishers to avoid defamation in other media is required to avoid defamation online.

Tracing individuals who post defamatory statements online often can pose challenges. Even if traceable, such individuals may not have substantial assets and, therefore, may not be a good 'mark' for damages in a defamation claim. In addition, because of the international nature of the Internet, issues of court jurisdiction and enforceability of any award of damages also can arise. For these reasons, Internet Service Providers (ISPs), rather than original publishers, have been targeted in defamation actions in the past.

A level of protection from defamation liability for ISPs (along with similar protection from liability in respect of other unlawful content) is provided by the EU *Electronic Commerce Directive (Directive 2000/31/EC)*, which was incorporated into Irish law by SI 68 of 2003 (the *Electronic Commerce Regulations*). The Directive applies to Information Society Services (ISS), defined as "any service normally provided for remuneration, at a distance, by electronic means and at the individual request of a recipient of services". The *Electronic Commerce Regulations* use the term "intermediary service provider" to describe a provider of an ISS for the purposes of the defences referred to below and refer to an ISS as a 'relevant service'.

Three defences for defamation liability are available to an intermediary service provider under the *Electronic Commerce Regulations*:

- The 'mere conduit' defence is available to a provider that enables the transmission of information *via* the Internet (see Regulation 16).
- The 'caching' defence is available to a provider that temporarily stores information in order to render the process of onward transmission *via* the Internet more efficient (see Regulation 17).
- The 'hosting' defence is available to a provider that stores information, which may be defamatory, although the provider is neither aware of the defamatory material nor aware of facts or circumstances from which the defamatory nature of the material may be apparent (see Regulation 18).

The caching and hosting defences are available only if the intermediary service provider has acted expeditiously to remove the information or disable access to it on obtaining actual knowledge of the defamatory material (both caching and hosting) or awareness of facts or circumstances from which the defamation is apparent (hosting only). This means that failure to take down or disable access to defamatory material, once the defamatory nature of that material has been notified to the intermediary service provider, can render the provider liable for defamation.

From a complainant's point of view, notifying an intermediary service provider (for example, notification to the ISP or the administrator of an online forum) of the presence of defamatory material on a site or forum is the first step in trying to have that defamatory material removed or access to it disabled. Websites that provide information about the registrants of domain names (for example, the 'who is' search facility on **www.networksolutions.com**) may be helpful in tracing the person or entity to be notified in this regard if a contact or administrator's email address is not provided on a website.

From the point of view of online service providers, the extent and range of individuals or businesses regarded as intermediary service providers of 'relevant services' entitled to avail of the hosting defence has not yet been considered extensively in the Irish courts. Subject to the *caveat* that the law on this point is still evolving, the hosting defence is the defence that is potentially of assistance to owners and operators of websites that permit the posting of user-generated content (third-party postings). Accordingly, on being made aware that a posting may be defamatory, prompt action should be taken – usually to remove or disable access to the item pending resolution of the complaint or claim.

The issue of whether to moderate content posted by third-party users of a site should be made with the benefit of legal advice. Moderation whereby third-party postings are scrutinised in advance by the website-owner and selected for publication on the website potentially renders the website-owner liable for any defamatory content in those postings. On the other hand, moderation whereby postings that are posted directly onto a website by third-party users and then 'de-selected' from publication by a moderator probably means that the website-owner will be entitled to make the 'hosting defence' if the site is deemed to be a 'relevant service' for the purposes of the *Electronic Commerce Regulations*. However, the extent to which this argument will be successful has yet to be tested before the Irish courts. In practice, sites such as online forums and message boards tend to be moderated in the 'de-selection' sense outlined above on a basis that varies from systematic and regular to occasional and spasmodic. The question of what constitutes "actual knowledge" or awareness of "facts or circumstances from which that unlawful activity is apparent" (both relevant factors to the hosting defence) has not been explored in any depth by Irish case law to date. It is significant to note that Article 15 of the *Electronic Commerce Directive* of 2000 precludes EU Member States from imposing any legal obligation on intermediary service providers to monitor information stored or transmitted by them or an obligation to 'seek facts or circumstances indicating illegal activity'.

It is not advisable for a website-owner to modify in any way third-party postings to render them non-defamatory; to do so is to assume clearly the role of a publisher and potentially precludes a website-owner or operator from relying on the hosting defence under the *Electronic Commerce Regulations*.

The 'innocent publication' defence created by section 27 of the *Defamation Act, 2009* also offers a defence that, depending on the circumstances of the publication, potentially could be availed of by ISPs and other intermediary service providers, although its application as yet is untested in the Irish courts. The innocent publication defence hinges primarily on the defendant being able to prove that they were not the author, editor or publisher of the statement (see exclusions from being categorised as such in section 27(2)) and that they took "reasonable care" in relation to the publication. The extent of this duty of "reasonable care" is not clearly defined and therefore open to interpretation by the courts.

Much online content accessed in Ireland is generated by Internet users based in the US, which operate under a different defamation regime to that which pertains in Ireland and England. US defamation law generally affords a higher degree of protection to statements published about public figures than provided by Irish and UK law. Such statements are protected, even if untrue, provided their publication is not motivated by malice (interpreted as knowledge of the falsity of the statement or recklessness as to whether it is false or not – see *New York Times v Sullivan 376 US 254 (1964)*). Further, section 230 of the US *Communications Decency Act, 1996* provides statutory protection from liability for defamation for ISPs and online service providers in the US. It is important for Irish publishers to be aware of this jurisdictional factor and not to rely on the content of US-based websites or blogs as an indicator of statements that will withstand scrutiny under Irish defamation law.

Case law
Godfrey v Demon Internet Ltd [1999] EWHC QB 244
An early UK Internet defamation case in which an ISP, Demon Internet, was held to be the 'publisher' and, therefore, liable for a defamatory publication online as and from the date it was made aware of the existence of the defamatory posting on a Usenet Newsgroup carried by it. Demon did not remove the defamatory posting until 10 days after it had been notified by the plaintiff of the presence of the material on the newsgroup. The case pre-dated the *Electronic Commerce Directive of 2000*, which was incorporated into UK law in 2002.

Bunt v Tilley and Others [2006] EWHC QB 407
This was a UK case, in which the alleged operators of websites on which defamatory statements were published were sued, along with three ISPs providing the Internet services on which these websites were maintained. The presiding judge held that the three ISPs could not be held to be publishers of the statements and, therefore, that the cases against them should be struck out.

Mulvaney v Betfair [2009] IEHC 133
An Irish High Court case, in which it was held that the owner of a website featuring user-generated content in the form of an online chat-room was entitled to avail of the hosting defence under Regulation 18 of the *Electronic Commerce Regulations*. This judgment was made on foot of an application for an interim ruling on whether the website in question, which was concerned with on-line betting, was entitled to avail of the *Electronic Commerce Regulations* hosting defence; it was not a final ruling on whether the hosting defence would succeed in that particular case. At the time of writing, the decision is under appeal to the Supreme Court.

See also
Q15   What is a publication under defamation law?
Q16   Who is a publisher under defamation law?
Q18   What can a business do to protect its website from a defamation claim?
Q20   What is innocent publication?
Q42   Does defamation law apply to social networking sites?
Q43   What can a business do to protect its social networking site from a defamation claim?

Q20   What is innocent publication?

Innocent publication is a defence created by section 27 of the *Defamation Act, 2009*. It replaces the former common law defence of 'innocent dissemination' abolished by the 2009 Act, as well as the former 'unintentional defamation' defence provided for by section 21 of the *Defamation Act, 1961*, and similarly abolished by the *Defamation Act, 2009* (section 4).

It is important to note that this defence is *not* available to broadcasters where a contributor to a live programme makes a statement that is defamatory, even in circumstances where the broadcaster did not know or expect the statement to be made and had taken reasonable care in respect of the broadcast (for example, briefing the contributor before going on air). The broadcaster always is regarded as the publisher of the defamatory statement and can be held liable for that defamatory publication. Here, Irish law differs from English law, which offers a defence to broadcasters in such circumstances under section 1(3)(d) of the UK *Defamation Act, 1996*.

A three-step test to avail of the innocent publication defence is set out in section 27(1) of the 2009 Act. The defendant must prove that they:

- Were not the editor, author or publisher of the statement.
- Took reasonable care in relation to the publication.
- Did not know or have reason to believe that they were contributing to a publication that would give rise to an action for defamation.

Section 27(2) exempts certain categories of person from being regarded as an editor, author or publisher of a defamatory statement for the purposes of the section. These exemptions apply, for example, to printers and newspaper vendors (section 27(2)(a)), as well as to cinemas and record shops (section 27(2)(b)). A further significant category of exemption in section 27(2)(c) applies to a person who was "responsible for the processing, copying, distribution or selling only of the electronic medium or was responsible for the operation or provision only of any equipment, system or service by means of which the statement would be capable of being retrieved, copied, distributed or made available". At the time of writing, it remains to be seen the extent, if any, to which this section may provide a defence to a website-owner on whose website a defamatory posting is made by a third party.

Section 27(3) sets out matters to which the court must have regard when deciding whether a person took reasonable care in relation to the publication or had reason to believe they were contributing to the publication of a defamatory statement. These are:

- The extent of the person's responsibility for the content of the statement or the decision to publish it.
- The nature or circumstances of the publication.
- The previous conduct or character of the person.

This "reasonable care" test is one for the court to assess. At the time of writing, no cases have been decided on the section 27 defence. It is likely, based on existing case law on the former common law defence of innocent dissemination, that a commonsense standard will be applied rather than a standard that would put unfeasible demands on, for example, printers or book-sellers to read every word of every publication before going to print or putting a book on their shelves for sale.

See also

Q16   Who is a publisher under defamation law?
Q18   What can a business do to protect its website from a defamation claim?
Q19   Who is liable for a defamatory publication made online?

Q21   What is the single publication rule?

The single publication rule, as introduced into Irish law by section 11 of the *Defamation Act, 2009,* provides that only one defamation action may be brought by a plaintiff in respect of all publications of the same defamatory statement to two or more recipients, whether those individuals receive the statement at the same time or not (section 11(3)).

Prior to the *2009 Act,* under common law, in theory a separate defamation action could be brought in respect of every publication of a defamatory statement, publication taking place when the statement was made to and received by any individual person. So, for example, a newspaper publisher providing a person with a back-issue of a newspaper containing a defamatory article about the plaintiff 17 years after its original publication was regarded as a fresh publication of the article (*Duke of Brunswick v Harmer (1849) 14 QB 154*).

While in practice, in the Irish courts, single defamation actions have been brought in respect of multiple publications, the common law position posed serious issues for online publishers – for instance, of newspaper archives. This was because each Internet 'hit' by an individual Internet user on an archive potentially could be regarded as a separate act of publication and thus potentially could give rise to a separate defamation action. In effect, section 11 means that an online archive is deemed published only once, regardless of how many times it is accessed by Internet users. Accordingly, its publication online can give rise to only one defamation action.

Furthermore, the limitation period, within which a defamation action may be brought in respect of an online publication, is addressed in the *2009 Act.* The period commences when the statement in question is first made publicly available ("capable of being viewed or listened to") online (section 11(3B), *Statute of Limitations, 1957,* as inserted by section 38(1) (b) of the *2009 Act*).

As a saver provision, section 11(2) entitles a court to permit more than one defamation to be brought in respect of a multiple publication where "the interests of justice so require".

Case law

Loutchansky v Times Newspapers [2001] EWCA Civ 1805
This was a UK case arising from two defamation actions brought by a Russian businessman against Times Newspapers. The first action arose from the original publication of articles in *The Times* newspaper on 8 September and 14 October 1999. The second action was based on the continued availability of the articles on the Times Online archive, without amendment or qualification, despite the newspaper having been notified of the defamation claim. Times Newspapers sought to have its defence amended to plead that Loutchansky was out of time to bring his second action. Times Newspapers maintained that the limitation period should run from the date of original posting of the articles online and not from any later date on which the archive was accessed by an Internet user. Times Newspapers' attempt to have the court accept a single publication rule in respect of Internet publication failed.

See also
Q16   Who is a publisher under defamation law?
Q18   What can a business do to protect its website from a defamation claim?
Q19   Who is liable for a defamatory publication made online?
Q53   How long after a publication is made does a plaintiff have to bring a defamation claim?

Q22   How can someone be identified in a defamatory publication?

For a statement to be defamatory, the subject of the statement must be identified or sufficiently identifiable to recipients of the statement to render the statement defamatory. Section 6(3) of the *Defamation Act, 2009* states: "A defamatory statement concerns a person if it could *reasonably be understood* as referring to him or her" (italics added). This element of 'reasonableness' is important when it comes to a court deciding whether or not a plaintiff has been identified.

The intention of the publisher is not relevant to the issue of identification; there can be situations where an individual or business entity is inadvertently identified and the publisher is not even aware of that individual's or that entity's existence.

Identification can be:

- Direct and explicit: A publication can identify a name or corporate entity, such as a limited liability company, by name or image.

- Indirect: A publication may give sufficient elements of information about a person or business that falls short of giving their name but is sufficient to enable them to be identified by the recipients of the publication. While not a legal term, this form of identification can be described as 'jigsaw identification', in that sufficient pieces of the identification 'puzzle' are published to enable recipients to identify the person who is the subject of the statement. A person's voice, on occasion, can be a factor in identifying them, particularly if combined with other information that also tends to identify them.

- Innuendo: A statement may be expressed in such a way that the plaintiff can show that she / he was identifiable to some or all of the recipients of the publication by reason of other information in the knowledge of those recipients that enabled them to identify her / him. Another form of innuendo is when information is presented in a publication in a manner that falsely (even if inadvertently) links that information to identifiable individuals. If a newspaper article or television programme discusses, for example, the prevalence of drug-taking or sexually-transmitted disease among young people, and the item is illustrated by images of identifiable young people to whom that information may not necessarily relate, those identified individuals may be able to maintain that they have been defamed. The test will be whether the statement published could 'reasonably be understood' to the individuals depicted in the publication and this will vary from case-to-case depending on the circumstances and content of the publication. The lines of distinction between 'indirect identification' and 'identification by innuendo' are often unclear and not readily discernible.

- Class or group: Reference may be made in a publication to a class or group of people that, depending on the circumstances, could reasonably be understood as identifying one or more members of that class or group. Section 10 of the 2009 Act specifically addresses this form of identification, stating: "Where a person publishes a defamatory statement concerning a class of persons, a member of that class shall have a cause of action under this Act against that person if – (a) by reason of the *number of persons* who are members of that class, or (b) by virtue of the *circumstances* in which the statement is published, the statement could reasonably be understood to refer, in particular, to the member concerned" (italics added). Class identification can take place, for example, where a lobby group or an association is referred to in a publication. Despite the lack of explicit reference to them, certain individuals with responsibility for running that organisation may be identifiable by reference to how many people are involved in running the organisation and / or the circumstances of the publication. Whether they have been identified will be decided on a case-by-case basis. Under section 10, such individuals would need to be able to show in a defamation action that the publication in question could reasonably be understood to have referred to them in particular. For publishers, there can be occasions where defamation risk is lessened by being more specific, rather than less, concerning the identity of the subject of a publication. On occasion, spreading the potential identification of the subject of a publication across a wider category of individuals can increase, rather than decrease, the risk of a defamation claim being made.

Case law
Bradley v Independent Star Ltd, Unreported, High Court (The Irish Times, 23.02.06)
Two brothers claimed they had been identified and defamed by articles in the *Irish Daily Star* newspaper. Photographs of two men with their faces blurred were published along with a nickname, "Fat Heads", stating that the two men depicted were engaged in gangland crime. The jury found, in all the circumstances, that the plaintiffs had not been identified in the article. Having failed to prove identification, the plaintiffs' claim failed.

See also
Q12   What is defamation?
Q16   Who is a publisher under defamation law?
Q23   Can a publisher be held liable if they inadvertently defame someone?
Q26   Can a publisher be held liable for defamation as a result of a hidden meaning?
Q38   Can a defamation action be brought in respect of someone who is dead?

Q23 Can a publisher be held liable if they inadvertently defame someone?

The intention (or lack of it) to defame someone on the part of the publisher is irrelevant to their liability for defamation. The test is whether the statement could reasonably be understood to refer to the plaintiff. Whether the publisher was even aware of the plaintiff's existence is irrelevant to the publisher's liability.

Section 6(3) of the *Defamation Act, 2009* states: "A defamatory statement concerns a person if it could reasonably be understood as referring to him or her". The section makes no reference to the subjective motivation of the publisher in identifying a person.

It makes no difference to liability for defamation whether the publisher has been deliberate, reckless or careless in identifying the subject of the publication or simply identifies that person by accident. However, the publisher's explanation of how the inadvertent identification occurred may be a factor taken into account in assessing damages, since the court is obliged to have regard to all the circumstances of the case in making an award of general damages (section 31(3) of the 2009 Act). Nonetheless, the intention of the publisher is not a factor that the court is explicitly obliged to consider under section 31(4) of the 2009 Act (specific factors to which the court must have regard when assessing general damages).

Inadvertent defamation can take place where a radio interviewer agrees to use a false name for an interviewee and the false name identifies another person. When using false names for interviewees or contributors, it is recommended that this be made clear to viewers, readers and listeners.

Inadvertent defamation also can take place when the name of a wrongdoer is mistakenly published alongside a photograph of someone with the same name but who has not been engaged in that wrongdoing.

Occasionally, a court report inadvertently and incorrectly identifies a person as having been convicted of a crime – for example, by publishing the incorrect address for the convicted person or publishing information about the convicted person that leads to the identification of someone else. This may be entirely accidental but can result in a defamatory publication. Usually, the most practical response is to publish a corrected version of the report as quickly as possible to limit the damage done to the innocent person's reputation. If a defamation claim is made or threatened, an offer of amends made under section 22 of the 2009 Act may be considered.

See also

Q16   Who is a publisher under defamation law?
Q20   What is innocent publication?
Q22   How can someone be identified in a defamatory publication?
Q24   Who can be held liable for a defamatory publication?
Q35   Does offering a right of reply avoid liability for defamation?
Q45   What is malicious falsehood?
Q62   What is an offer of amends?

Q24   Who can be held liable for a defamatory publication?

The publisher of a defamatory publication can be held liable for defamation and ordered to pay damages to the plaintiff in a defamation action.

However, the term 'publisher' has a far wider meaning under defamation law than it does in everyday language. The law regards a very wide range of individuals and entities engaged in the publication process as publishers.

A publisher can be anyone who contributes to the process of publication of a defamatory statement. This includes the author of a book, as well as the publishing company that publishes the book; the journalist who writes a newspaper article; the editor, producer or presenter of a radio or television show; the company that owns a newspaper, a radio station or television station; the contributor or interviewee on a radio or television show. Effectively, anyone who is involved in the process of publishing a defamatory statement potentially is liable at law.

See also
Q15   What is a publication under defamation law?
Q16   Who is a publisher under defamation law?
Q23   Can a publisher be held liable if they inadvertently defame someone?

Q25   Is it possible to insure against defamation liability?

Media liability policies are available to companies in respect of liabilities arising from the publication of the *content* they produce. This is often referred to as 'errors and omissions' (E&O) insurance. Note that, within the insurance industry, the term 'E&O insurance' may cover a range of liabilities beyond liability arising solely from media content; accordingly, the term 'media liability' is used below.

Standard media liability policies provide cover in respect of four principal categories of liability:

- Defamation or malicious falsehood.
- Infringement of intellectual property rights.
- Breach of confidence or infringement of privacy.
- Misuse of confidential information or information the use of which is restricted by statute.

Larger companies, such as major book publishers and broadcasting organisations, usually maintain an ongoing, multi-annual policy of insurance in respect of the entirety of their print publication or broadcast output. These policies are subject to arrangements agreed between the publisher and the insurance company for pre-publication checking and clearance of content. What is essential is that such policies continue to be renewed each year so that they are in place when a claim is made as indemnity is offered to media liability policyholders on a 'claims made' basis. This means that the insured is required to have insurance in place at the date *on which the claim is made* rather than the date on which the publication occurred.

The norm in the audio-visual production industry, however, is for separate policies of media liability insurance to be put in place for each production. Most TV and radio production policies are put in place for a period of three to five years after they take effect. Media liability policies usually are set up to take effect on the date of first publication /

broadcast, although some commissioning broadcasters require that such policies take effect from an earlier date. Independent producers should identify early on in the commissioning negotiation process whether a policy of media liability insurance is required in respect of a production and, if so, when it must take effect.

With the reduction of the limitation period for defamation claims to one year by section 38 of the *Defamation Act, 2009* (with a possible extension up to two years), any defamation claims are likely to arise within the duration period of the policy. If a production is likely to be re-published outside the period of the policy (for example, on foot of a licence sale to an overseas television station), an extension of the term of the policy may be required. Care should be taken to make sure that liability in all territories and distribution media in which or through which the production is published are covered by the policy.

It is important to note that the standard package of policies for film, television or radio productions does not include media liability insurance; such insurance must be applied for separately.

When a radio, television or audio-visual producer is putting a media liability policy in place, consideration should be given to potential exposure to privacy claims. It is not a pre-requisite for a privacy claim that publication should have taken place; an actionable infringement of privacy may take place during the course of production of a film or television programme. If a production, by its nature, risks encroaching on the privacy of an individual (for example, observational documentaries in which members of the public are filmed), there may be merit in putting the policy in place from the first day of filming.

One feature of media liability insurance is that the excess or 'deductible' on the policy (the amount of the claim the insured is liable to pay itself before the insurance indemnity takes effect) can be quite significant. It is important to check this amount when obtaining a quote.

Media liability insurance, including its duration and territorial extent, should be considered early in the planning process for a production. It is best to use an insurance broker with experience in this area of insurance. These can found through a Google search.

Q26   Can a publisher be held liable for defamation as a result of a hidden meaning?

A hidden meaning or 'innuendo' in a published statement can give rise to a defamation action. The hidden meaning may be implicit in the statement itself, such as in the case of *Campbell v Irish Press (1955) ILTR 105*, in which the publication of a review of a snooker exhibition that stated "the table told lies" gave rise to a defamation claim by the organiser of the competition. He maintained successfully that he was identifiable as the person who organised the exhibition and that the innuendo in the review was that he was incompetent in how he had organised the event.

Section 31(5) states: "For the purposes of *subsection (4)(c)*, a defamatory statement consisting of words that are innocent on their face, but that are defamatory by reason of facts known to some recipients only of the publication containing the defamatory statement, shall be treated as having been published to those recipients only". Thus, although the circulation of the publication may be limited to people who, only because of particular information available to them, will have spotted the hidden defamation, the publication still is defamatory. In such circumstances, the defamatory statement is regarded as having been published to that limited group of people. A published statement that has a meaning hidden to all but a few of those who read or view it fulfils the definition of the tort of defamation set out in section 6(2) of the 2009 Act.

Section 31 (4) (c) of the *Defamation Act, 2009* provides that the extent of circulation of the defamatory statement must be considered by the court in assessing defamation damages.

See also
Q12   What is defamation?
Q23   Can a publisher be held liable if they inadvertently defame someone?

Q27   What is the truth defence?

A publication is defamatory if it "tends to injure a person's reputation in the eyes of reasonable members of society" (section 2 of the *Defamation Act, 2009*). A publisher may avoid being held liable for defamation if he / she can prove that the statement was true.

Section 16 of the 2009 Act provides for a defence known as the 'defence of truth', a statutory form of the old common law defence known as the 'defence of justification', which was abolished by section 15 of the 2009 Act.

It is important to be aware that, where the truth of facts contained in a publication is at issue in a defamation case, the law presumes the facts were false; it is for the publisher to prove they were true. This is known as 'the presumption of falsity'. It remains in place after the enactment of the *Defamation Act, 2009*. Thus, when making the truth defence, the onus is on the defendant publisher to prove that what they published was true. The plaintiff is not required to adduce any evidence in relation to the veracity of the statement published, although they may choose to do so.

A prudent publisher, prior to publication, will make sure that, if required to prove the truth of what was published, she / he will be able to bring sufficient evidence to prove that truth. Where it is proved in a defamation claim that the publisher knew that what was published was untrue, or was reckless as to whether it was true, the publisher is at risk of having additional damages by way of punitive damages being awarded against them (section 32(2)(c)).

Mere hearsay evidence, such as evidence by a journalist that a third party gave her / him information that the journalist believed to be true, is not sufficient to prove the truth of a statement; direct evidence from someone with first-hand knowledge of the facts at issue is required. Where a journalist has given a commitment to maintain the confidentiality of their source, calling such direct evidence may not be possible. Other witnesses may need to be called to give that evidence instead.

Prior to publication, a publisher must consider whether the witnesses to be called to prove the truth are likely to be reliable or credible – or even available to give evidence to the court. A witness who lives abroad may not respond to a witness summons to appear before an Irish court, although she / he may agree voluntarily to give evidence.

The publisher may produce documentation to prove the truth of what was published. Such documentation must be authentic and credible. It may be difficult to obtain original documentation. The defendant publisher may need to seek a court order for the discovery (disclosure) of documents, either by the plaintiff or by a third party who holds the relevant documentation. However, the defendant publisher may be refused an order for discovery if they have not set out the particulars of their truth defence to a sufficient extent to enable the court to conclude that the defendant genuinely has such a defence and, by seeking discovery of documents, is not simply seeking discovery in order to find a basis on which to prove the truth of what they have published.

Journalists and researchers should keep research notes, so that they have basic information, such as names and contact details of potential witnesses, in case a publication or broadcast gives rise to a defamation claim. In this regard, remember that the limitation period for defamation claims is one year, with a possible extension to two years, after the date of publication (section 38).

Pleading the truth defence effectively means endorsing the defamatory statement; it means the publisher is standing over what was published and asserting it was true. This potentially exposes the plaintiff's reputation to further injury, unless the truth of the statement is proved. Should the truth defence fail, court disapproval of the manner in which the case was defended may be reflected in the award of additional damages known as 'aggravated damages' (section 32(1)).

Section 16(2) of the 2009 Act is important for publishers who have made several allegations against a plaintiff in the statement complained of and who are making the truth defence. Its effect is that the defence of truth will not fail simply because each and every allegation cannot be proved by the defendant; if the 'sting' of the defamatory publication is largely attributable to the matters that the defendant succeeds in proving to be true, then the fact that the defendant fails to prove every single allegation will not necessarily deprive them of the benefit of the truth defence.

Case law

McDonagh v Sunday Newspapers t/a The Sunday World, High Court, 28.02.08 (The Irish Times, 29.02.08)
The plaintiff sued over a newspaper article that labelled him a "drug king" and asserted that he had engaged in money-lending and drug importation. The defendant newspaper proved that the plaintiff had criminal convictions and was a tax-evader. The defendant failed to prove however, that the plaintiff was a drug-dealer and a loan-shark. The plaintiff was awarded €900,000 in damages by the jury. An appeal by the newspaper to the Supreme Court is pending at time of writing. In an interim judgment in this case earlier (*[2005] IESC 183*), the High Court declined to make an order for discovery against Mr McDonagh on the grounds that the newspaper's defence, at that point in time, did not disclose sufficient particulars of the defence of justification (truth) being made. Accordingly, the judge could not assess at that time whether the documents sought were necessary to back up the newspaper's justification defence or were sought merely in order to be able to make such a defence.

Cooper-Flynn v RTÉ and Others, High Court, 23.03.2001 (The Irish Times, 24.03.01)
Beverley Cooper-Flynn TD sued RTÉ, journalist Charlie Bird and interviewee James Howard, as a result of broadcasts asserting that, in a previous employment with National Irish Bank, she had sold certain insurance policies to bank customers to facilitate tax avoidance by those customers. The defendants did not succeed in proving that such a policy had been sold to Mr Howard but succeeded in proving that such policies had been sold by Ms Cooper-Flynn to other individuals with the aim of tax evasion. The defence of justification succeeded, despite the fact that not all the allegations made in the broadcasts had been proved. In the Cooper-Flynn case, RTÉ had sought discovery of documents relevant to its defence of justification (now known as the truth defence) from

National Irish Bank, and succeeded in obtaining disclosure of those documents (*Cooper-Flynn v RTÉ [2000] 3 IR 344*).

See also

Q12   What is defamation?
Q29   What is the honest opinion defence?
Q32   Is consent a defence to a defamation action?
Q33   What is the public interest defence?
Q34   What is the fair and reasonable publication defence?

Q28   What is the presumption of falsity?

There is a common law presumption in defamation cases that what the defendant publisher has published is untrue. This presumption places the onus of proving the truth of the statement on the publisher. This is a reversal of the position that usually applies in civil law claims whereby the plaintiff must prove that they have been wronged by the defendant; in a defamation case, where the truth of the publication is at issue, the defendant publisher must prove that what they published was true and, thus, that they have *not* wronged the plaintiff.

The presumption of falsity has been criticised on the grounds that it has a chilling effect on publications made in the public interest, such as allegations of corruption or impropriety on the part of public officials or politicians in the discharge of their duties. However, the availability of the 'fair and reasonable publication' defence provided for by section 26 of the *Defamation Act, 2009* can offer an alternative to a publisher who is not in a position to make out a truth defence in a defamation action.

The presumption of falsity was considered by the Legal Advisory Group on Defamation, which reported to the Minister for Justice in 2003. The Group's report (available on **www.justice.ie**) recommended no change to the law on presumption of falsity, subject to the verifying affidavit procedure provided for by section 8(1) of the 2009 Act being introduced. The Group also was conscious of the potential of its proposed 'fair and reasonable publication' defence to offer an alternative to a publisher who was not in a position to make a defence of truth successfully.

See also
Q12   What is defamation?
Q27   What is the truth defence?
Q34   What is the fair and reasonable publication defence?
Q58   What is a verifying affidavit?

Q29   What is the honest opinion defence?

The right to express opinions is an integral element of the right to freedom of expression.

The *Constitution* protects the right of citizens to "express freely their convictions and opinions" (Article 40.6.1°(i)). In *Irish Times Ltd v Ireland [1998] 1 IR 359*, Judge Barrington stated at page 405, "A constitutional right which protected the right to comment on the news but not the right to report it would appear to me to be a nonsense. It therefore appears to me that the right of citizens 'to express freely their convictions and opinions' guaranteed by Article 40 of the Constitution is a right to communicate facts as well as the right to comment on them".

In *Lingens v Austria (E.Ct.H.R. 08.07.86, Application no. 9815/82)*, the European Court of Human Rights observed that the right to freedom of expression secured by Article 10 of the *European Convention on Human Rights* "is applicable not only to 'information' or 'ideas' that are favourably received or regarded as inoffensive or as a matter of indifference, but also to those that offend, shock or disturb. Such are the demands of that pluralism, tolerance and broadmindedness without which there is no 'democratic society' ..." (paragraph 41 – quoting in turn from *Handyside v UK (E.Ct.H.R. 07.12.76, Application no. 5493/72)*).

The defence of honest opinion is relevant to critiques and reviews of matters of public interest and other matters held out for public scrutiny – for example, reviews of films, plays, books or restaurants as well as the discussion of political, social and economic affairs.

Prior to the implementation of the *Defamation Act, 2009*, common law provided a defence known as the 'defence of fair comment'. This defence allowed a publisher to defend a defamation claim on the basis that a publication was an expression of an honestly-held opinion, which opinion was based on facts. The use of the word 'fair' in the title of the defence was misleading, as the defence was predicated not on the fairness, but on the honesty, of the opinion. The common law defence of fair comment was abolished by section 15 of the 2009 Act and replaced by section 20 with a similar, but statutory, form of the defence entitled the 'defence of honest opinion'.

The essential elements of the new statutory form of the defence are:

- The statement must have been expressed on a matter of public interest.

- The statement must have been one of opinion rather than fact.

- The statement of opinion must have been based on fact or allegations of fact.

- The facts on which the opinion was based must have been clear to the recipient.

- The opinion must have been honestly held.

It is important for the publisher to be able to show that she / he *believed* that the facts on which the opinion was based were true. Furthermore, the publisher must be able to *prove* that the facts on which the opinion was based were true (see section 20(3)).

If the publisher, let us say for illustration purposes a radio station, is not the same as the contributor who expressed the opinion, then the radio station must be able to show that they believed that the contributor believed in "the truth of the opinion" (see section 20(2)(a)). This reference in the Act to 'the truth of the opinion' is unhelpful; an opinion is not susceptible to being proved to be true, being by its nature a subjective and evaluative statement. It remains to be seen how the courts will interpret section 20. In practical terms, publishers who publish the opinions of contributors, interviewees and commentators should be satisfied that the opinions expressed by those contributors are genuinely-held opinions expressed in good faith and based on demonstrable facts.

Section 20 makes daunting reading, particularly for those previously unfamiliar with law. The following paragraphs set out practical observations based on the provisions of section 20 and section 21. Section 20 sets out the new defence of honest opinion; section 21 provides guidance to courts in distinguishing between statements of fact and statements of opinion.

The facts on which an opinion is based must be specified in the publication containing that opinion. Alternatively, in circumstances where the viewers / listeners / readers might reasonably be expected to know the facts on which the opinion is based, the person expressing the opinion should make some general reference to those facts (see section 20(2)(b)(i)). Accordingly, if an opinion is expressed on a matter that is the subject of a current news story, it may not be necessary to specify precisely the facts on which the opinion is based if those facts are broadly referred to in the statement containing the opinion and the wider public could reasonably be expected to know those facts.

Sub-sections 20(2)(b)(ii) and 20(3)(b) are concerned with situations where the allegations of fact on which an opinion is based attract either absolute privilege or qualified privilege. A defendant publisher is required to prove the truth of those allegations of fact. If they cannot do so, they still may avail of the honest opinion defence if the opinion expressed could not reasonably be understood as implying that the allegations of fact were true and also that the defendant did not know or could not reasonably have been expected to know at the time of the publication that the allegations of fact were untrue. As with the greater part of section 20, these provisions are challenging to interpret in practical terms. In practice, opinions expressed on reports of privileged statements, the contents of which cannot be proved by the publisher to be true, should be expressed in precautionary terms to avoid endorsing, through those opinions, the truth of the allegations made in those privileged statements.

Whether a statement should be construed as a statement of fact or opinion is a matter for the court to decide. In a High Court case, it is for the judge to determine whether the statement is *capable* of being construed as a statement of opinion; however, it is a matter for the jury to decide whether the statement was *actually* one of opinion or fact. If the statement is found to be one of opinion, the jury also decides whether a defence of honest opinion should succeed.

Some terminology does not lend itself to clear interpretation as either fact or opinion; simple examples of everyday words that could fall into this category are 'scam' and 'dodgy'. Avoiding the use of ambiguous terminology can lessen the risk of defamation, as can making clear that a statement is intended to be one of opinion not of fact. The extent to which a statement was subject to a qualification or disclaimer or use of 'cautionary words' is one of the factors set out in section 21 as relevant for consideration when a court is distinguishing between a statement of fact and a statement of opinion.

Two other factors specifically set out in section 21 are the extent to which the statement is capable of being proved and the extent to which the statement is likely to have been "reasonably understood" as one of opinion rather than as an allegation of fact.

The defence of honest opinion as outlined in section 20 of the *Defamation Act, 2009* does not lend itself readily to clear interpretation. For those engaged in the business of publication, the most practical approach to take would be:

- To bear in mind the core components of the defence as outlined above.

- To make clear where opinions are expressed that they are intended to be understood as opinions, not statements of fact.

- To avoid, where possible, language that could render a statement liable to be regarded as one of fact rather than opinion.

Case references
Convery v Irish News [2008] NICA 14
This case was brought in the courts of Northern Ireland. The defendant newspaper published a review of a meal eaten in the plaintiff's restaurant in Belfast. The restaurateur sued for damages for defamation arising from the review and was awarded £25,000. The defendant newspaper appealed the finding to the Northern Ireland Court of Civil Appeal on the grounds that the trial judge had not properly directed the jury in relation to the fair comment aspect of the newspaper's defence (re-stated under Irish law in 2009 in statutory form as the defence of honest opinion). The

Court of Appeal held that the trial judge had misdirected the jury by failing to identify certain aspects of the article as comment rather than fact — for example, the statement that the chips served were "pale, greasy and undercooked". The defendant newspaper was successful in its appeal and a re-trial was ordered.

British Chiropractic Association v Singh [2010] EWCA Civ 350
The defendant is a science writer who wrote of the British Chiropractic Association (BCA) in the *Guardian* newspaper's Comment and Debate page: "The British Chiropractic Association claims that their members can help treat children with colic, sleeping and feeding problems, frequent ear infections, asthma and prolonged crying, even though there is not a jot of evidence. This organisation is the respectable face of the chiropractic profession and yet it happily promotes bogus treatments".

In a pre-trial hearing, Judge Eady in the High Court in London found that the statements comprised statements of fact, not of comment and that the defendant would be obliged to prove the truth of those statements at the trial of the action. On appeal by the defendant, the Court of Civil Appeal held that the statements comprised statements of opinion, not fact. The BCA subsequently discontinued its action. The Court of Civil Appeal was influenced in its decision by the public interest served by scientific debate uninhibited by fear of defamation action.

Associated Newspapers v Burstein [2007] EWCA Civ 600
The *Evening Standard* newspaper published a review of an opera on the subject of a suicide bomber. The review contained the following statement: "But I found the tone depressingly anti-American, and the idea that there is anything heroic about suicide bombers is, frankly, a grievous insult". The composer and co-writer of the libretto, Mr Burstein, sued for defamation on the grounds that the review portrayed him as a terrorist sympathiser who applauded the actions of suicide bombers. In an application for summary judgment by the defendant (for dismissal of the action on the grounds that the statement clearly comprised fair comment), the judge held that, while the meaning of the review could be such that it was fair comment, the matter should be decided by a jury. The Court of Civil Appeal overturned this decision on the grounds that the

review clearly comprised fair comment and gave judgment in favour of the defendant newspaper.

See also

Q12   What is defamation?
Q27   What is the truth defence?
Q28   What is the presumption of falsity?
Q30   What is absolute privilege and when does it apply to a publication?
Q31   What is qualified privilege and when does it apply to a publication?
Q32   Is consent a defence to a defamation action?

Q30   What is absolute privilege and when does it apply to a publication?

The law recognises that, as a matter of public policy and in the public interest, certain statements should be capable of being made without the people making such statements being deterred from doing so for fear of incurring liability for defamation. The protection afforded by the law for the making of such statements is known as 'privilege' and such statements are said to 'attract privilege'.

Two forms of privilege exist. One is 'absolute privilege', which offers absolute protection to the statement, regardless of the motivation of the person making the statement. The other is 'qualified privilege', in respect of which the good faith of the person making the statement is relevant to the defence. This is the core distinction between the two forms of privilege defence available at law.

Absolute privilege is provided for under the *Constitution* (Articles 13.8, 15.12 and 15.13), the common law and by statute. The common law on absolute privilege, as it stood up to the *Defamation Act, 2009* taking effect, was not affected by the passing of the 2009 Act. The absolute privilege provided for court reporting by the *Defamation Act, 1961* was abolished along with the repeal of the 1961 Act by the 2009 Act. The absolute privilege discussed here is the absolute privilege provided by section 17 of the 2009 Act. Section 17 consolidated and re-stated the law on absolute privilege that applied prior to the 2009 Act coming into force. Section 17 also expanded the range of statements to which the absolute privilege defence will apply.

Section 17 sets out 23 categories of statement that attract absolute privilege. Those likely to be most frequently encountered by the media include:

- Statements made by TDs and / or Senators in both the Dáil and / or Seanad (section 17(2)(a)).
- Statements made in the European Parliament by MEPs (section 17(2)(c)).

- Statements made in proceedings before quasi-judicial bodies (for example, the Employment Appeals Tribunal), subject to those statements being connected with those proceedings (section 17(2)(h)).

- A fair and accurate report of proceedings heard in public before, or a decision made public by, a Republic of Ireland or Northern Irish court (section 17(2)(i)).

- Statements made in proceedings before an Oireachtas Committee (section 17(2)(l)), subject to the qualification that, if a person giving evidence is directed by the Committee to cease giving such evidence, any further such evidence they may give will not attract absolute privilege. The person giving such evidence may rely on the defence of qualified privilege only if sued for defamation as a result of giving that further evidence (see section 11(2) of the *Committees of the Houses of the Oireachtas (Compellability, Privileges and Immunities of Witnesses) Act, 1997*).

- Statements made in the course of proceedings before a Tribunal of Inquiry set up under the *Tribunals of Inquiry (Evidence) Acts, 1921 – 2004* and any report of such Tribunal (section 17(2)(n) and (o). The privilege afforded to statements made in the course of Tribunal proceedings applies only to statements that are "connected with those proceedings" (section 17(2)(n)).

- Statements contained in the course of proceedings before or in a report of a Commission of Investigation set up under the *Commissions of Investigation Act, 2004* (section 17(2)(p) and (q)). The privilege afforded to statements made in the course of Commission proceedings will apply only where the statement made is "connected to those proceedings" (section 17(2)(p)).

- Statements made in the course of a coroner's inquest or a decision or verdict given at or during a coroner's inquest (section 17(2)(r)).

- Statements made in the course of an inquiry conducted on the authority of a Government Minister, the Government, the Oireachtas, either House of the Oireachtas or an Irish Court (section 17(2)(s)). Reports of such inquiries also attract absolute privilege (section 17(2)(u)).

It should be noted that it is the original statements that attract absolute privilege under section 17 of the 2009 Act; media reports of such statements attract qualified privilege under section 18 of the Act. There are two exceptions to this:

- Fair and accurate court reports by the media (Republic of Ireland and Northern Irish courts – see section 17(2)(i)) will attract absolute privilege.

- Fair and accurate court reports of proceedings before or judgments of international courts to which Ireland is a party (for example, the European Court of Justice, the European Court of Human Rights) will attract absolute privilege – see section 17(2)(k).

Article 15.12 of the *Constitution* explicitly provides that "official reports and publications of the Oireachtas or of either House thereof and utterances made in either House wherever published shall be privileged". The judgment in *Attorney General v Hamilton [1993] IR 250* indicates that the absolute privilege attaching to statements made in either House of the Oireachtas by virtue of Article 15.12 extends to newspaper reports of such statements. However, the form of privilege applicable to such reports under section 18 of the 2009 Act is qualified privilege. While this distinction may give rise to academic discussion, in practical terms, so long as a media report of statements made in either House of the Oireachtas is fair, accurate and made in good faith, it will attract sufficient privilege to protect the publisher from liability for defamation.

Note that it is for the defendant in a defamation action to prove that the statement in respect of which she / he is sued was a statement that attracted absolute privilege under section 17 of the 2009 Act.

Any reader wishing to familiarise themselves thoroughly with the extent of the absolute privilege afforded to publications by section 17 is recommended to consult the full text of the 2009 Act. Only the most commonly-occurring categories of publication that attract statutory absolute privilege are outlined here.

See also

Q16   Who is a publisher under defamation law?

Q31   What is qualified privilege and when does it apply to a publication?

Q33   What is the public interest defence?

Q34   What is the fair and reasonable publication defence?

Q31   What is qualified privilege and when does it apply to a publication?

The law recognises that, as a matter of public policy and in the public interest, certain statements should be capable of being made without the people making such statements being deterred from doing so for fear of incurring liability for defamation. The protection afforded by the law for the making of such statements is known as 'privilege' and such statements are said to 'attract privilege'.

Two forms of privilege exist. One is 'absolute privilege', which offers absolute protection to the statement, regardless of the motivation of the person making the statement. The other is 'qualified privilege', in respect of which the good faith of the person making the statement is relevant to the defence. This is the core distinction between the two forms of privilege defence available at law.

Qualified privilege is provided for by the common law and by statute. The common law relating to qualified privilege, as it stood up to the *Defamation Act, 2009* taking effect, was not affected by the passing of the 2009 Act. The qualified privilege provided for certain media reports by section 24 of the 1961 Act was abolished as part of the total repeal of the 1961 Act by the 2009 Act. The qualified privilege discussed here is that privilege provided by section 18 of the 2009 Act. Section 18 consolidated and re-stated the law on qualified privilege that applied prior to the 2009 Act coming into force. Section 18 also expanded the range of statements to which the qualified privilege defence will apply.

Section 18(2) and 18(7) effectively re-state the general principles of the common law of qualified privilege by providing that qualified privilege will apply to a statement if the person who made the statement can show that:

- They had a legal, moral or social duty or interest in communicating the information contained in the statement, *and*
- The person(s) to whom they communicated the statement had a corresponding duty or interest in receiving that information.

In common law form, this has been the defence traditionally been relied upon in circumstances where, for example, employee A in a company suspects that employee B has been stealing company property and reports these suspicions to a senior manager so that the matter can be investigated. This defence continues to exist both at common law and under section 18 of the 2009 Act. Section 19(2) provides a 'saver clause' for a publisher who mistakenly believed that the person to whom the publication was made had the necessary interest in receiving the communication.

Section 18, sub-sections (3) and (4), extends statutory qualified privilege to specific published reports. These sub-sections must be read in conjunction with Schedule 1 to the Act. Schedule 1 sets out the categories of report that attract qualified privilege under section 18. In turn, Schedule 1 is divided into two parts. The categories of report set out in Part 2 attract qualified privilege, subject to what is known as 'a right of explanation or contradiction'. This is explained in more detail below.

The most commonly-occurring categories of report listed in Schedule 1, Part 1 that attract qualified privilege under section 18 (3) are *fair and accurate* reports of:

- Any matter to which absolute privilege applies under section 17 of the Act (excluding certain court reports that attract absolute privilege under section 17) (paragraph 1).

- Reports of public proceedings before, and decisions made public by, the courts of any State other than the Republic of Ireland and Northern Ireland (these reports attract absolute privilege under section 17) (paragraph 2).

- Public proceedings in any house of any legislature – including subordinate or federal legislatures – of any state other than the Republic of Ireland (paragraph 4).

- Public proceedings of any body set up on the authority of a Government Minister, the Government, the Oireachtas or either House of the Oireachtas or an Irish court to conduct a public inquiry on a matter of public importance (paragraph 5).

- Public proceedings of an international organisation of which Ireland or the Irish Government is a member or the proceedings of which are of interest to the Irish state (paragraph 8).

In addition, any determination of the Press Ombudsman or Press Council, and any statement published by a newspaper or periodical of such a determination where this is done pursuant to and in accordance with a direction of the Press Ombudsman or Press Council, will attract qualified privilege (paragraphs 14, 15 and 16).

The categories of report set out in Schedule 1, Part 2 attract qualified privilege, subject to a right on the part of a person who believes they have been defamed by such a report to request the publisher to publish *a reasonable statement by way of explanation or contradiction.* If it is proved that the publisher failed to grant such request or granted it in a manner that was not adequate or reasonable having regard to all the circumstances, then the publisher will lose this form of qualified privilege defence.

The most commonly-occurring categories of report listed in Schedule 1, Part 2 that attract qualified privilege under section 18(4) are *fair and accurate* reports of:

- Proceedings at any public meeting held in the Republic of Ireland or any other EU State, where the meeting is held for a lawful purpose and for the discussion of a matter of public concern (paragraph 2).
- Proceedings at a general meeting of any company or association established by or under statute or incorporated by charter (paragraph 3) – this provision relates to general meetings of corporate bodies such as limited liability companies and statutory bodies.
- Proceedings at a local authority or Health Service Executive meeting or meetings of corresponding bodies in any other EU state (paragraph 4).
- A press conference held by or on behalf of a body to which Schedule 1, Part 2 applies (for example, a local authority, limited

liability company, Health Service Executive) or by the organisers of a public meeting described in Schedule 1, Part 2, paragraph 2 (see above) to give an account of that meeting (paragraph 5).

Note that it has not been determined to date by the Irish courts whether press releases made available to the media in conjunction with press conferences held by the organisers of a public meeting will attract qualified privilege in accordance with paragraph 5 of Schedule 1, Part 2. The UK House of Lords in *Turkington and others v Times Newspapers Ltd [2000] UKHL 57* held that statutory qualified privilege under broadly corresponding Northern Ireland legislation applied to the publication of the contents of a press release where, in the view of Lord Bingham of Cornhill, "It seems clear that the press release was treated by the Committee [organising the press conference] as read even though not read aloud". Unless a similar finding is made by an Irish court, it cannot be assumed conclusively by journalists that qualified privilege under section 18(4) will extend to publishing the contents of a press release where the press release contains a statement that was not made at the press conference in respect of which it was issued.

There is an important over-riding requirement in respect of reports attracting qualified privilege under section 18(3) and 18(4) that the statements made in those reports are *of public concern* and their publication is *for the public benefit*. Furthermore, the publication of those statements must not be "prohibited by law" (see section 18(5)(a)).

The defence of qualified privilege will fail if the plaintiff in a defamation action proves that the defendant publisher was motivated by malice in publishing the statement the subject of the action (section 19(1)). Note that such malice will not be presumed on the part of the defendant publisher; it must be proved by the plaintiff that the defendant acted out of malice in publishing the statement.

Any reader wishing to familiarise themselves thoroughly with the extent of the qualified privilege afforded to publications by section 18 is recommended to consult the full text of the 2009 Act. Only the most commonly-occurring categories of publication that attract statutory qualified privilege are outlined here.

See also

Q16   Who is a publisher under defamation law?
Q30   What is absolute privilege and when does it apply to a publication?
Q33   What is the public interest defence?
Q34   What is the fair and reasonable publication defence?
Q63   What is the Press Council and what does it do?

Q32   Is consent a defence to a defamation action?

It is a defence to a defamation action for the defendant publisher to prove that the plaintiff consented to the publication of certain statements or allegations made about them. The burden of proof is on the defendant publisher to prove consent.

This defence previously existed at common law and was given statutory form by section 25 of the *Defamation Act, 2009*, which reads: "In a defamation action it shall be a defence, to be known as the 'defence of consent' for a person to prove that the plaintiff consented to the publication of the statement in respect of which the action was brought".

This defence can be availed of, for example, where allegations of wrong-doing have been made against an individual, that individual willingly consents to giving an interview to respond to those allegations and, of necessity, the allegations are repeated in the publication to enable the interviewee to respond to them.

However, a refusal or failure by a person to avail of a right to reply or to respond to a journalist's queries in the course of investigating a story – even one clearly in the public interest – cannot be construed as consent to publication. Section 26 of the 2009 Act sets out the defence of fair and reasonable publication. Section 26(3) specifically states: "The failure or refusal of the plaintiff to respond to attempts by or on behalf of the defendant, to elicit the plaintiff's version of events, shall not –

(a) constitute or imply consent to the publication of the statement, or

(b) entitle the court to draw any inference therefrom".

Accordingly, a journalist should be wary of drawing conclusive inferences from a failure or refusal of the subject of an investigation to reply to queries, as to do so could jeopardise any fair and reasonable publication defence made in the event that the publication gives rise to a defamation claim.

Where the subject of an investigation or news story agrees to be interviewed on a controversial topic, giving advance notice of the specific nature of the matters that a journalist – whether print or broadcast – wishes to raise with the subject in interview will assist in making a consent defence, where relevant. Similarly, recording in writing the fact that those matters were specified to the subject of the investigation (for example, an email to the proposed interviewee or a contemporaneous note of a telephone conversation with them) also may assist in making a consent defence, if that defence is relevant. Whether the defence succeeds will depend on the circumstances of the particular case. The 2009 Act does not specify how consent to publication must be proved.

See also

Q29   What is the honest opinion defence?

Q33   What is the public interest defence?

Q34   What is the fair and reasonable publication defence?

Q35   Does offering a right of reply avoid liability for defamation?

Q33   What is the public interest defence?

This common law defence (also known as the 'Reynolds defence') emerged from the common law qualified privilege defence in a UK defamation case in the House of Lords in 1999, *Reynolds v Times Newspapers Ltd [1999] UKHL 45.*

Common law qualified privilege can be invoked where the person communicating a statement has a duty or interest in communicating it and the person to whom it is communicated has a corresponding interest in receiving it. The effect of the House of Lords findings in *Reynolds* was to recognise that this duty / interest correlation applies to the media in circumstances where there is a sufficiently high level of public interest in the story and responsible journalism has been applied to the evaluation, investigation and writing of it. The House of Lords found that the nature, status and source of the material published and the circumstances of the publication needed to be taken into account in deciding whether there was a sufficient level of public interest in the publication to merit the protection of the defence.

Lord Nicholls set out the factors that he believed should be considered in determining whether the required level of public interest in the publication existed. They have become known as 'the Nicholls tests' or 'the Reynolds factors' and amount, in practice, to the test of responsible journalism. Using Lord Nicholls' words, they are:

1.   The seriousness of the allegation. The more serious the charge, the more the public is misinformed and the individual harmed if the allegation is not true.

2.   The nature of the information, and the extent to which the subject matter is a matter of public concern.

3.   The source of the information. Some informants have no direct knowledge of the events. Some have their own axes to grind, or are being paid for their stories.

4.   The steps taken to verify the information.

5. The status of the information. The allegation may have already been the subject of an investigation that commands respect.

6. The urgency of the matter. News is often a perishable commodity.

7. Whether comment was sought from the plaintiff. He / she may have information others do not possess or have not disclosed. An approach to the plaintiff is not always necessary.

8. Whether the article contained the gist of the plaintiff's side of the story.

9. The tone of the article. A newspaper can raise queries or call for an investigation. It need not adopt allegations as statements of fact.

10. The circumstances of the publication, including the timing.

Initially, the Nicholls tests tended to be applied in a quite rigorous manner by the UK courts. The decision of the House of Lords in *Jameel v Wall Street Journal [2006] UKHL 44* permits a more expansive and holistic approach. In *Jameel*, the Nicholls tests were regarded as guidelines for the assessment of the degree of public interest in a publication and the level of responsible journalism applied to it rather than as criteria to be strictly and serially fulfilled before the public interest defence can apply.

The public interest defence was referred to with approval by the judges in two Irish High Court cases, *Hunter v Gerald Duckworth & Co. Ltd [2003] IEHC 81* and *Leech v Independent Newspapers [2007] IEHC 223*, thereby assimilating the public interest defence into Irish common law. The status of the common law public interest defence under Irish law following the 2009 Act coming into effect is uncertain for reasons connected with a largely academic discussion as to whether it should be regarded as a form of common law qualified privilege defence or as a stand-alone defence in a category of its own. In practical terms, the new statutory fair and reasonable publication defence created by section 26 of the *Defamation Act, 2009* is the form of this defence that will be pleaded by publishers in Irish defamation cases. The relevance of the public interest defence and the UK case law referred to here is that it is likely that existing UK case law on the public interest defence will be quoted and relied on by litigants in Irish courts where a defence of fair and reasonable publication is made, pending the development of a body of Irish case law on the statutory form of that defence provided by section 26 of the 2009 Act.

Case law

Reynolds v Times Newspapers Ltd [1999] UKHL 45

Former Irish Taoiseach Albert Reynolds sued Times Newspapers Ltd (TNL) and two of its journalists for defamation arising out of an article carried in the UK edition of *The Sunday Times* in November 1994. The article asserted that Mr Reynolds had misled the Dáil in a speech shortly before his resignation as Taoiseach. The initial finding in the London High Court was that he had been defamed but he was awarded only nominal damages of one penny. Both Reynolds and TNL appealed to the Court of Civil Appeal – Reynolds on the question of damages, TNL on the issue of its entitlement to the defence of common law qualified privilege. TNL appealed the latter issue to the House of Lords. While the House of Lords' finding did not exonerate TNL from liability, it brought about the emergence of a defence for publishers that became known as the 'public interest' or 'Reynolds' defence.

Galloway v Telegraph Group Ltd [2006] EWCA Civ 17

Labour MP George Galloway successfully sued for damages for defamation arising from four articles published in the *Daily Telegraph* alleging that Galloway had sought money from Saddam Hussein's regime in Iraq in the context of oil-for-food contracts and used it for personal enrichment. The story was based on documents found by a *Telegraph* journalist in damaged Iraqi government buildings in Baghdad in 2003 and the newspaper pleaded both a public interest and fair comment (honest opinion) defence. Upholding the finding of the trial court, the UK Court of Civil Appeal agreed that the *Telegraph* had "embraced the allegations [against Mr Galloway] with relish and fervour", had not been neutral and could have made further inquiries to verify the story before publication. Mr Galloway was awarded £150,000 in damages, which was upheld on appeal.

Jameel v Wall Street Journal [2006] UKHL 44

The European edition of the *Wall Street Journal* published a story that the central banking authority of Saudi Arabia, at the request of US law enforcement agencies, was monitoring bank accounts associated with named Saudi businessmen, including the plaintiff, to prevent those accounts being used to funnel funds, wittingly or unwittingly, to terrorist organisations. Mr Jameel and one of his companies sued for damages for defamation. At the trial, the presiding judge declined to allow the public interest defence to be put to the jury, holding that it did not apply in the circumstances. The *Wall Street Journal* appealed this aspect (among others) of the trial judge's decision to the Court of Civil Appeal and, ultimately, to the House of Lords. The House of Lords reached a different conclusion to both the trial judge and the Court of Appeal, holding that the public interest defence applied to the publication of the story in all the circumstances of the case. Of Lord Nicholls' tests in the *Reynolds* case, Lord Bingham of Cornhill observed (paragraph 33 of his judgment), "He [Lord Nicholls] intended these as pointers which might be more or less indicative, depending on the circumstances of a particular case, and not, I feel sure, as a series of hurdles to be negotiated by a publisher before he could successfully rely on qualified privilege". He continued later in the same paragraph, "Weight should ordinarily be given to the professional judgment of an editor or journalist in the absence of some indication that it was made in a casual, cavalier, slipshod or careless manner".

Leech v Independent Newspapers (Ireland) Ltd [2007] IEHC 223
Lewd and false allegations were made about the plaintiff by a caller to a live phone-in radio show. The radio station later apologised to the plaintiff for the broadcast. The defendant newspaper published a report of the incident. The plaintiff sued the newspaper for damages for defamation. At the start of the trial, the trial judge gave a preliminary ruling on questions raised concerning the public interest defence. He held that: (i) a public interest defence could be made under Irish common law; (ii) once a public interest in the publication had been established, it must be considered whether the steps taken to gather and publish the information were responsible and fair; (iii) in considering whether the publisher's conduct was fair and responsible, the court must have regard to the practical realities of news-gathering and the fact that news is "a perishable commodity". In a later ruling, the judge declined to allow a defence of public interest to be put to the jury on the grounds that no evidence had been given by any witness for the defendant newspaper to

substantiate its public interest defence. The jury ultimately found that the plaintiff had not been defamed by the article in question. At time of writing, the case is under appeal to the Supreme Court.

See also

Q28 What is the presumption of falsity?
Q29 What is the honest opinion defence?
Q31 What is qualified privilege and when does it apply to a publication?
Q34 What is the fair and reasonable publication defence?

Q34   What is the fair and reasonable publication defence?

The 'fair and reasonable publication' defence is an important new defence provided for by section 26 of the *Defamation Act, 2009*. In effect, it is a statutory form of the common law 'public interest' or 'Reynolds' defence, which emerged at UK common law in the case of *Reynolds v Times Newspapers Ltd [1999] UKHL 45.*

The fair and reasonable publication defence offers a defence to publishers in circumstances where their publication was in the public interest and responsibly reported but they are not in a position to prove the truth of what was published. Thus, its inclusion in the 2009 Act somewhat eases the strictures imposed on reporting and current affairs investigation by the common law presumption of falsity.

While there is wide latitude given to the court (the jury in a High Court jury trial) to reach its own conclusions as to whether the fair and reasonable publication defence should succeed in the circumstances of any particular case, section 26 sets out four broad criteria, each of which must be fulfilled in order for the defence to succeed. The first two concern the public interest aspect of the defence. Section 26(1)(a) requires the defendant to prove that the statement was published:

- In good faith; and
- In the course of, or for the purpose of, the discussion of a subject of public interest, the discussion of which was for the public benefit.

Section 26(1)(b) and (c) are concerned with the fairness and reasonableness aspects of the publication. These sub-sections require the defendant to prove that, in all of the circumstances of the case:

- The manner and extent of publication of the statement did not exceed that which was reasonably sufficient, and
- It was fair and reasonable to publish the statement.

Section 26(2) requires the court to take into account whatever matters it "considers relevant" when determining whether it was fair and reasonable to publish the statement in question, including all or any of 10 factors set out in the sub-section. In summarised form, these factors are:

1. The extent to which the statement referred to the performance by the plaintiff of her or his public functions.

2. The seriousness of any allegations made in the statement.

3. The context and content (including language used) of the statement.

4. The extent to which a distinction was drawn between suspicions, allegations and facts.

5. The extent to which exceptional circumstances necessitated publication of the statement on the particular day it was published.

6. The extent to which a statement published in a periodical (newspaper or magazine) which is a member of the Press Council adhered to the *Press Council Code of Practice* and the determinations of the Press Ombudsman and Press Council.

7. The extent to which a statement published in a periodical (newspaper or magazine) which is *not* a member of the Press Council adhered to standards and criteria equivalent to those described at point 6 above.

8. The extent to which the publication gave the plaintiff's version of events and gave this version similar prominence to the statement giving rise to the action.

9. If the plaintiff's version of events was not given, the extent to which a reasonable attempt was made to get and publish a response from her / him.

10. The attempts made and means used to verify assertions and allegations made about the plaintiff.

While not identical, these 10 considerations reflect the substance of the 'Nicholls tests' applicable to the public interest defence at common law. For this reason, it is likely that the UK case law on the public interest defence will be referred to in Irish courts where the fair and reasonable publication defence is pleaded, particularly pending the development of a body of case law on the new defence in Irish courts.

News journalists and editors in the print media, in particular, are advised, in the light of sub-sections 26(2)(f) and (g) (see points 6 and 7 above), to keep themselves informed of determinations of the Press Ombudsman and Press Council. These are published on the Press Council website **www.presscouncil.ie**.

Some individuals in public or business life adopt a policy of declining to comment on media queries and may be unlikely to give a response or comment to a media inquiry. Prudent practice, nonetheless, is to give an opportunity to comment to such individuals where an investigation or news story concerning them is underway, even if the journalist is aware in advance that a response is highly unlikely. Keeping records of attempts made to contact the subject of an investigation – especially one who fails to respond – may be useful as evidence of attempts being made to obtain and publish a response from that person. As explained above, making such attempts is a factor relevant to making a defence of fair and reasonable publication.

At time of writing, no cases have been defended at full trial on the basis of the fair and reasonable publication defence.

See also

Q28   What is the presumption of falsity?
Q29   What is the honest opinion defence?
Q32   Is consent a defence to a defamation action?
Q33   What is the public interest defence?
Q63   What is the Press Council and what does it do?
Q81   Do celebrities and politicians have the same rights of privacy as private citizens?

Q35 Does offering a right of reply avoid liability for defamation?

No, this is an over-simplified and inaccurate assumption, albeit one that is commonly held in the media. However, offering a right of reply can have a significant bearing on the determination of defamation cases where a fair and reasonable publication defence is being made.

Offering a right of reply also can be a relevant factor in the determination of any complaint or investigation by the Broadcasting Authority of Ireland into whether a broadcaster has complied with its regulatory obligation to be fair and impartial in its treatment of current affairs and matters of public controversy and debate.

Section 26(2) of the *Defamation Act, 2009* is concerned with the 'fair and reasonable publication' defence in a defamation action and, in particular, the extent to which a publisher gave a plaintiff's version of events in the publication concerned (sub-section (2)(h)) and / or made reasonable attempts to obtain and publish a response from the plaintiff (sub-section (2)(i)). In this context, therefore, giving a right of reply will be an important factor in making a defence of 'fair and reasonable publication'.

There is no statutory indication of how much notice should be given to the subject of a proposed publication for the purposes of providing a reply to media queries. A degree of common sense, reasonableness and fairness should be applied.

Publishers need to take care not to misrepresent the position of a person who has been asked for a right of reply but who does not avail of this opportunity. There is a distinction to be made between 'declining to reply' and simply giving no response at all. In the interests of fairness and accuracy, this distinction should be honoured in publishing a story or article where no reply has been made by an individual or business to a media query.

Section 26(3) concerning the fair and reasonable publication defence states: "The failure or refusal of a plaintiff to respond to attempts by or on behalf of the defendant, to elicit the plaintiff's version of events, shall not – (a) constitute or imply consent to the publication of the statement, or (b) entitle the court to draw any inference therefrom". This means that a journalist or other publisher is at risk, from the point of view of making a fair and reasonable publication defence, if they draw inferences from the failure or refusal of a person to avail of a right to reply.

Some individuals in public or business life adopt a general policy of declining to comment on media queries and may be unlikely to give a response or comment to a media inquiry. Prudent practice, nonetheless, is to give an opportunity to comment to such individuals where an investigation or news story concerning them is underway, even if the journalist is aware in advance that a response is highly unlikely. Keeping records of attempts made to contact the subject of an investigation – especially one who fails to respond – may be useful as evidence of attempts being made to obtain and publish a response from that person.

Note that a post-publication 'right of reply' may be sought by a complainant in the context of a complaint to the Compliance Committee of the Broadcasting Authority of Ireland arising from the content of a radio or television broadcast.

See also

Q34   What is the fair and reasonable publication defence?

Q63   What is the Press Council and what does it do?

Q64   What is the Broadcasting Authority of Ireland and what does it do?

Q65   What regulatory requirements apply to broadcast programme content and advertisements?

Q66   How does the Broadcasting Authority of Ireland secure compliance by broadcasters with regulatory obligations and codes?

Q81   Do celebrities and politicians have the same rights of privacy as private citizens?

Q36   Can texts be defamatory?

A text message is an electronic communication and therefore 'a statement' for the purposes of defamation law (see the definition of "statement" in section 2 of the *Defamation Act, 2009*).

Text messages are most likely to give rise to the risk of defamation proceedings when they are sent to radio stations and read out on air. Listener interaction *via* text messaging is now an integral part of much radio programming. Typically, texts are sent to a dedicated telephone number connected to the station's computer system. Both the mobile phone number from which the text has been sent and the listener's text message show up on a screen and can be read by the producer and presenter or forwarded by the producer to a screen visible to the presenter. If the contents of a listener's text constitute a defamatory statement, reading out that text on air is a re-publication of the defamatory statement for which both the broadcaster and the original author of the text message can be held liable. In practical terms, the radio station owner will be the best 'mark' for damages in the event of a successful defamation claim and, therefore, will be the most likely to be sued. Furthermore, the radio station also will be more readily traceable as a publisher than the original author of the text.

Listeners' texts sent to a radio station can range from the capricious to the malicious. Radio producers and presenters must be constantly vigilant to ensure that, in re-publishing the contents of text messages by way of broadcast, they are not inadvertently defaming either the purported sender of the text or any person referred to in that text.

Care needs to be taken to ensure that all texts are read and screened prior to being read out on air. Avoiding the use of surnames of individuals referred to in listeners' texts can help to lessen the risk of inadvertent defamation. Even restricting reference to first names only can lead to identification of an individual referred to in a potentially defamatory text if other identifying factors are included in the text, such as the locality in which they reside and / or the nature of the business in which they are engaged. Those responsible for screening texts in a radio station need to be familiar with issues of identification in defamation law and to make prudent judgment calls as to whether certain texts should be read out on air, in full or partially-edited form.

Referring on air to the death of someone who, in fact, has not died can cause distress to the individual concerned and their family, as well as causing embarrassment to a radio station. Malicious or misinformed texts sometimes can give rise to such a scenario. However, such references are highly unlikely to give rise to an action for defamation as, in most circumstances, there will be no adverse effect on the reputation of the person whose death has been mistakenly referred to on air.

See also
Q15   What is a publication under defamation law?
Q16   Who is a publisher under defamation law?
Q22   How can someone be identified in a defamatory publication?
Q23   Can a publisher be held liable if they inadvertently defame someone?
Q24   Who can be held liable for a defamatory publication?
Q26   Can a publisher be held liable for defamation as a result of a hidden meaning?
Q37   Can emails be defamatory?
Q38   Can a defamation action be brought in respect of someone who is dead?
Q40   Can repeating a story sourced from another media outlet be defamatory?
Q41   Does using the word 'alleged' avoid liability for defamation?

Q37   Can emails be defamatory?

An email is a publication for the purposes of defamation law. The *Defamation Act, 2009* makes clear that a publication of a defamatory statement may be "by any means" (section 6(2)) and that a "statement" includes a statement published on the Internet, as well as an electronic communication (section 2).

The speed, ease and relative informality of email communication can undermine the appreciation by those who send emails that their communications are publications to which the law of defamation applies. Bear in mind that it is often, although not invariably, possible for emails that have been deleted to be retrieved from hard drives. Pressing the Delete button does not necessarily destroy the contents of an email; potentially, it can be retrieved and disclosed at a later date from the hard drive of the sender or recipient or an Internet Service Provider providing the email account.

The issue of defamation by email needs to be considered from two points of view: that of the individual email user and that of an employer whose employees use email facilities provided by the employer.

Individual user considerations
An individual user should be aware:

- Of the need to exercise caution in copying emails concerning the principal addressee to others by way of 'cc' or 'bcc' functions, where the contents of the email potentially would be defamatory of the principal addressee were they to be read by a third party.

- That forwarding an email they have received and which contains defamatory material is a re-publication of that defamatory statement for which they, as well as the person who originated the email, potentially can be held liable under defamation law.

- That it is not a defence in itself under defamation law to plead that what was written or circulated by email was "only a joke".

Employer considerations

An employer providing email facilities for use by employees needs to ensure that they have in place a clear email usage policy indicating the purposes for which work-place emails may – and may not – be used. Such a policy should include a requirement:

- That all reasonable care be taken by employees to ensure emails sent from workplace email addresses do not defame any person or breach the intellectual property, privacy or other rights of any third party or contain material that is otherwise unlawful.

- That no email sent from a workplace email address contains material that is obscene or offensive.

If the employer also implements a policy of monitoring or spot-checking work-place emails, this needs to be made clear to all employees.

Employers should ensure that emails sent from a company email address carry a disclaimer notice that includes:

- An expression of intent that the email is for the attention of the addressee only.

- A request that the sender of the email be notified by return email of any misdelivery.

- A request that a misdelivered email be deleted by the recipient.

- A caution against further dissemination where an email has been sent in error to someone other than the intended addressee.

- A disclaimer that opinions expressed in the email are those of the author and not necessarily those of the employer company.

Employers should take legal advice on the wording of the policies and disclaimers referred to above. There may be other matters relevant to a particular employer that usefully could be included in such a disclaimer notice – for example, where an employer organisation is a prescribed body under Freedom of Information legislation.

A defamation settlement in the High Court, believed to be the first email defamation case to come before the Irish courts, attracted considerable media attention in May 2010. A college lecturer sued two of his colleagues and their mutual employer, Galway Mayo Institute of Technology, for defamation arising from the contents of an attachment to an email that was forwarded on to third parties by his two colleagues (*Casey v Elwood and Ors, The Irish Times, 15 May 2010*).

See also
Q15   What is a publication under defamation law?
Q19   Who is liable for a defamatory publication made online?
Q36   Can texts be defamatory?
Q39   Can employers be held liable for defamatory publications made by their employees?

Q38   Can a defamation action be brought in respect of someone who is dead?

Prior to the *Defamation Act, 2009*, an individual's right to recover damages for defamation ceased to exist on their death. Similarly, a defamation action being taken against them could not be continued after they had died. That position has been modified by section 39 of the *Defamation Act, 2009*.

Section 39(2) (by amending section 7 of the *Civil Liability Act, 1961*) provides that, where a person had a cause of action for defamation vested in her / him immediately before their death, that cause of action survives for the benefit of their estate. This means that, if a defamatory statement is published before the person identified in that defamatory statement dies, the legal representatives of their estate are entitled to issue proceedings for defamation after the individual's death, subject to the statutory limitation period for bringing that action. If a person has been defamed and has issued defamation proceedings within the statutory limitation period and prior to their death, the legal representatives of their estate are entitled to proceed with that claim and bring it to conclusion after the individual's death.

The category of damages that may be awarded to the defamed person's estate in such circumstances is restricted, however, to special damages. Section 39(2) (by amending section 7 of the *Civil Liability Act, 1961*) excludes general damages, punitive damages and aggravated damages from the damages that the estate of a deceased person may recover in a defamation claim, leaving only special damages to be awarded.

This provision allows for the recovery by the estate of any loss of income or other quantifiable financial losses suffered by the deceased as a result of the defamation, the value of which would otherwise have comprised part of the deceased's estate on their death.

The right of action conferred by section 39(2) does not confer a right to recover damages in the defamation action for hurt feelings or distress caused by a defamatory publication to family members or others close to the deceased.

Where a defamatory publication is made after the death of the person identified in the defamatory statement, neither their family nor the legal representatives of their estate have any right to claim damages for defamation arising from that publication. The right of action provided for by section 39(2) of the 2009 Act applies only in respect of publications made before the death of the individual concerned (where the right of action for defamation "vested" in the individual "immediately before" their death – see section 39(2)(a)).

Section 39(3) (by amending section 8 of the *Civil Liability Act, 1961*) allows a person who has been defamed to take or continue a defamation action against the estate of the person who defamed them after that person has died, subject to the statutory limitation period for bringing such an action. The damages recoverable by the plaintiff in such circumstances, however, are confined to special damages only.

While the publication or broadcast of a reference to or announcement of the death of someone who has not actually died can cause distress to the individual concerned and their family, generally it will not give rise to a defamation action. Such an announcement is highly unlikely to affect adversely the reputation of the person whose death has been publicised erroneously.

See also
Q9   What are damages and how are they assessed?
Q22   How can someone be identified in a defamatory publication?
Q51   How are damages assessed in a defamation case?
Q53   How long after a publication is made does a plaintiff have to bring a defamation claim?

Q39   Can employers be held liable for defamatory publications made by their employees?

Defamatory publications by employees can be made by various means, including letter, email, press release, ezine, social media posting and newspaper article. An employer potentially can be held liable for defamatory publications made by their employees.

As a general legal principle, an employer can be held liable for the wrongful act of their employee if that wrongful act was carried out in the course of the employee's employment. This 'vicarious liability' can extend not merely to acts specifically authorised by the employer but also to acts implicitly authorised by the employer. Whether an authorised action was carried out by an employee but in such a manner that it should be regarded as outside the range of actions for which the employer should be held vicariously liable will depend on the circumstances of each case.

In most defamation cases, the issue of vicarious liability does not arise because a company that runs a media outlet such as a radio station, for example, is a joint-publisher, along with the reporter or radio presenter who made a defamatory broadcast. More often than not it is only the broadcasting organisation or newspaper proprietor that is sued for damages, to the exclusion of any individual who also may have contributed to the publication.

Even if an employer is not aware of a defamatory publication made by an employee in the course of their work, the employer is at risk of being held vicariously liable for that publication. Such situations could arise, for instance, in respect of emails sent from workplace computers, use of social media by an employee on behalf of the company or participation by an employee in online forum discussions in the course of their work.

To manage this risk, employers need to have internal policies in place that set out guidelines and ground rules for employees who are using various forms of media either in the course of their work or for private purposes but using workplace computers. The complexity and contents of these policies will vary from one business to another, depending on factors such as the nature of the work carried out by that business, the number of employees working there and the management structure of the business. Where employees write advertising copy, blog, use social media or issue press releases on behalf of a company, an internal copy clearance mechanism may need to be included in such a policy.

A clear in-house policy relating to email, social media and other forms of publication serves a three-fold purpose:

- It creates a risk management mechanism in respect of defamation and other legal risk such as liability for breach of copyright.

- From a human resource management and disciplinary point of view, both the employer company and its employees are aware of the extent and nature of the publication activity that is or is not permitted either on behalf of the company or for private purposes using workplace computers.

- An employer company can refer to the policy to defend a claim of vicarious liability for an employee's defamatory publication on the grounds that the publication was not made in accordance with the employer's internal Internet usage / publication policy. Whether such a defence will be successful will depend on the circumstances of each specific case.

Depending on the circumstances, the principle of vicarious liability can also extend to liability for the acts of contractors. Accordingly, contractors who use email, social media or other Internet-based media in the course of their work for a contracting company also should be made aware of any relevant internal policies of the company to which they are providing services.

In the retail sector, employers potentially can be held vicariously liable for any defamatory statements made by employees in the course of handling incidents of suspected shop-lifting. Employees or contractors engaged in the prevention and detection of shop-lifting should receive specialist training in how to handle such situations in a manner that minimises exposure to defamation risk.

See also

Q40   Can repeating a story sourced from another media outlet be defamatory?

It is well-established at common law that repeating, by way of re-publication, a defamatory statement is in itself a defamatory publication. Therefore, the repetition by a publisher of a story, which was originally published by another, is a defamatory publication for which the repeating publisher can be held liable.

For example, a radio show that repeats, by way of a review of the morning's newspapers, a defamatory statement contained in one of those newspapers can be held liable for the further publication of that defamatory statement. This principle applies whether the original publisher is referenced in the re-publication. This principle also applies regardless of the status of the original publisher, whether an international news service or a regional newspaper, and regardless of whether it was sourced online or otherwise.

A journalist or broadcaster who has concerns that a news item or information sourced from another media outlet could be defamatory ought to make further inquiries about the story before deciding whether to re-publish it.

Care also needs to be taken to ensure that advertisements carried for other publications (for example, radio advertisements for Sunday newspapers) do not repeat in full or in part defamatory statements that may be made in those publications.

It will not be a defence to a defamation action taken against a publisher who re-publishes a defamatory statement to assert that the defamatory statement originated from another media outlet.

An original publisher is at risk of being held liable for defamation if their original publication is re-published by a secondary publisher. This issue was most recently considered in the Irish courts in the case of *Hunter v Gerald Duckworth & Co [1999] IEHC 56*. In that case, both the UK-based publisher and the author of a booklet were sued in the Irish courts for defamation arising from the sale of the booklet in Ireland. The court endorsed a pre-existing common law rule (see *Speight v Gosnay (1891) 60 LJQB 231*) in holding that the author of the book had published the manuscript of his book by supplying it to his publisher in London for publication as a booklet. He could be sued for damages for defamation in Ireland arising from its contents as its re-publication by way of sale as a booklet in Ireland, in the circumstances, was the natural and probable consequence of his publishing the manuscript in the UK. Note that, at time of writing, this case has not yet come to full trial, so no determination has been made on the liability or otherwise of the defendants for defamation.

See also
Q15   What is a publication under defamation law?
Q16   Who is a publisher under defamation law?
Q20   What is innocent publication?
Q36   Can texts be defamatory?
Q37   Can emails be defamatory?

Q41   Does using the word 'alleged' avoid liability for defamation?

Formulating a statement as an allegation rather than as a statement of fact, of itself, does not provide protection to the publisher from liability for defamation. The reputation of the person referred to in the statement can be tarnished by the mere association of their name with an allegation of involvement in an activity, such as, for example, fraud or marital infidelity.

If a publisher can prove the truth of an allegation she / he has published, they may be able to make a defence of truth to any defamation claim brought against them arising from that publication. If she / he is not in a position to make a truth defence, it may be open to them to defend the publication on the basis of a 'fair and reasonable publication' defence. Formulating a statement as an allegation can be an important factor in making a fair and reasonable publication defence. Created by section 26 of the *Defamation Act, 2009*, this defence can be availed of by a publisher where they can show there was a public interest in publishing a statement, that the statement was published in good faith and that it was fair and reasonable to publish it in the circumstances. The issue of publishing allegations is addressed in three out of the 10 considerations listed in section 26(2) that the court is obliged to take into account if it considers them relevant to the case before the court:

- "the seriousness of any allegations made in the statement" (section 26(2)(b)).
- "the extent to which the statement drew a distinction between suspicions, allegations and facts" (section 26(2)(d)).
- "the attempts made, and the means used, by the defendant to verify the assertions and allegations concerning the plaintiff in the statement" (section 26(2)(j)).

Thus, although appearing in only three out the 10 considerations listed, the use of the word 'alleged' or 'allegations' in a publication can be relevant to defending that publication, should it give rise to a defamation claim.

Another area of defamation law where the publication of allegations may not attract liability for defamation is where qualified privilege applies. For example, a communication by an employee in a workplace to a line manager of allegations or suspicions of theft of company property by another employee can attract protection from liability under the qualified privilege defence.

In the context of court reports, allegations or charges made in civil or criminal proceedings against an individual who has not yet been found liable for an alleged wrongdoing or guilty of a crime should not be reported as statements or findings of fact pending the final determination of the court on those issues; they must be reported as allegations only pending the determination of the court on the questions of fact that will determine liability or guilt. Fair and accurate court reports (Republic of Ireland and Northern Ireland courts) attract absolute privilege under section 17 of the 2009 Act.

In summary, merely using the word 'alleged' or 'allegation' to preface a statement made in a publication will not protect the publisher from liability for defamation for that statement. There are circumstances, however, where the law will protect a publisher of allegations (as opposed to statements of fact) from liability for defamation, even where the publisher cannot prove the truth of those allegations.

See also
Q22   How can someone be identified in a defamatory publication?
Q27   What is the truth defence?
Q30   What is absolute privilege and when does it apply to a publication?
Q31   What is qualified privilege and when does it apply to a publication?
Q33   What is the public interest defence?
Q34   What is the fair and reasonable publication defence?

Q42   Does defamation law apply to social networking sites?

The *Defamation Act, 2009* specifies that a defamatory statement can be made "by any means" (section 6(2)) and further includes statements made by Internet and by electronic communication in the definition of "statement" for the purposes of the Act. Irish defamation law clearly applies to statements made on social networking sites (SNS).

Most SNS-providers operate self-regulating policies relating to defamation, breach of copyright and offensive content. Their terms and conditions of use include a requirement that site-users must not post material that is defamatory, unlawful or offensive.

Liability of users

A user of an SNS who posts defamatory material on the site can be held liable for that defamatory posting. If the user making the posting is an Irish business, or an employee of an Irish business who makes the posting in the course of their employment, then the business potentially can be held liable and sued for damages for defamation – as can the employee in their personal capacity.

In practice, tracing individual SNS-users in order to sue them for damages in many instances can be difficult, depending on the extent to which they are identifiable and their geographical location. So, it is to the site-provider or the Internet service provider that facilitates the posting that aggrieved individuals may look for redress for defamation. The question of the liability (if any) of an SNS account-holder on whose profile page a defamatory posting is made by a third-party has not yet been clarified by Irish case law.

Liability of intermediary service providers

The *Electronic Commerce Regulations, 2003* (SI 68 of 2003) provide defences for "intermediary service providers" when they are sued for damages in respect of unlawful activity – including defamation – on any "relevant service" they provide.

The Regulations implement the provisions of the EU *Electronic Commerce Directive* (*Directive 2000/31/EC*). The Directive (referring back to definitions in previous *Directives* (*98/34/EC* and *98/84/EC*)) states that the term "information society service" covers "any service normally provided for remuneration, at a distance, by means of electronic equipment for the processing (including digital compression) and storage of data, and at the individual request of a recipient of a service". This definition is referred to in the *Electronic Commerce Regulations* as a "relevant service".

It is clear from both the *Directive* (see Recital 18) and existing case law (such as it is) that the term "information society service" will be given a wide interpretation. Both the *Directive* and the *Electronic Commerce Regulations, 2003,* in setting out the defences available to information society services (ISS), use the term "intermediary service providers" to indicate ISS providers.

The question not yet clearly established, pending further case-law on the subject, is exactly who will be regarded as an intermediary service provider of a "relevant service" for the purposes of relying on the defences provided by the *Electronic Commerce Regulations*. It is clear that an Internet service provider, such as eircom or UPC, can avail of the defences. It also seems that social networking service providers, such as Facebook or Twitter, would be able to avail of the defences. In *Mulvaney v Sporting Exchange t/a Betfair [2009] IEHC 133,* the High Court held that the 'hosting defence' provided by the Regulations could be availed of by a business that provided chat-room facilities on its website. That decision is currently under appeal to the Supreme Court but the rationale on this particular point can be regarded as a helpful guideline. What has not been explored by case-law to date is whether, for example, a business that sets up a profile page on Facebook could avail of the 'intermediary service provider' defences, if sued for damages arising from a defamatory posting made by a third-party on that page. A precautionary approach for such users – usually businesses – is to manage defamation risk as if they were an intermediary service provider of a "relevant service".

The defences provided by the Regulations are:

- The 'mere conduit' defence.
- The 'caching' defence.
- The 'hosting' defence.

These defences are explained in detail at **Q19**. What is important for intermediary service providers is to act expeditiously on being notified of, or becoming aware of, the defamatory nature of a posting on a social networking site by taking down the posting or disabling access to it. The question of moderation of postings and its effect on the availability of the 'hosting' defence also is considered at **Q19**.

It should be noted that Internet law in the US contrasts with EU law in respect of liability for defamatory statements online. By virtue of section 230 of the US *Communications Decency Act, 1996,* online service providers ("provider or user of an interactive computer service") in the US are protected from being held liable for defamatory material posted by third parties on services provided or facilitated by them; no 'take down' or 'disabling access' requirements apply as they do under the 'hosting' and 'caching' defences provided for by EU law and the Irish *Electronic Commerce Regulations, 2003.*

See also

Q15   What is a publication under defamation law?
Q19   Who is liable for a defamatory publication made online?
Q39   Can employers be held liable for defamatory publications made by their employees?
Q43   What can a business do to protect its social networking site from a defamation claim?
Q84   What is copyright?
Q91   What steps can a copyright-owner take to protect their copyright online?

Q43 What can a business do to protect its social networking site from a defamation claim?

Many companies now use social networking sites (SNS) as part of their business promotion activities and to interact online with clients and customers.

Where employees use SNS on behalf of the company or the company's clients, a clear internal SNS usage policy should be put in place which includes reference to the following:

- Who is entitled to use and post material on SNS used by the company?

- What restrictions apply to the type of material employees may place on the company's SNS page or post on the company's behalf to an SNS account?

- Any in-house copy clearance procedures that apply, including clearance procedures for graphics, logos and audio / audio-visual material posted or used on the company's SNS pages or accounts.

- Procedures for obtaining authorisation from clients to use SNS on a client's behalf.

- Any in-house education programmes or materials available to raise awareness of defamation and intellectual property law.

As a matter of employment law and HR management, any restrictions or guidelines that apply to access to SNS for personal use during work hours or from workplace personal computers should also be clearly specified to employees.

It can be useful if Facebook or similar SNS pages set up by a company or business on its own or a client's behalf include a simple set of user conditions as part of the company's profile page requiring third parties making posts on the page not to post:

- Defamatory material.

- Material in breach of the intellectual property rights of any third party.

- Material in breach of the privacy rights of or any obligation of confidentiality towards any third party.
- Material otherwise unlawful, obscene or offensive.

In addition, the notice of conditions can usefully:

- Require users to notify the company if they become aware of defamatory, unlawful or offensive postings on the page, and
- Disclaim liability for any defamatory or otherwise unlawful postings.
- Disclaim liability for the contents of any links on the page.

The decision to moderate third-party postings to an SNS page should be taken with the benefit of legal advice. Moderation by way of selecting third-party messages for posting to an SNS page potentially could be regarded as publication on the part of the moderator, due to the editorial function inherent in selecting that message for publication. On the other hand, moderation either by systematic or occasional scrutiny of messages already posted to an SNS page and 'de-selection' of certain messages by removing them arguably is a different form of editorial intervention and ought not to have the effect of rendering the moderator liable for any defamatory statements contained in those messages.

At the time of writing, these questions in respect of SNS postings have not been explored by Irish case law. Therefore, it is possible only to speculate on the rationale that might be applied were such points to be considered by the courts. It is worthwhile noting that Article 15 of the *Electronic Commerce Directive* of 2000 precludes EU member states from imposing any legal obligation on intermediary service providers relying on the defences provided by the Directive to monitor information stored or transmitted by them or to seek facts or circumstances indicating illegal activity on the services they provide.

On being specifically notified by a third party of a defamatory posting on the SNS page or account maintained by a business or individual, prudent practice is to print a hard copy or save a screen-shot of the posting before deleting it. If a complaint of defamation is made at a later stage, the hard copy or screen-shot may be relevant in establishing the fact of and / or content of the posting if that is in dispute. Removing the posting expeditiously, after obtaining actual knowledge of it from a third party, maximises the potential to rely on the hosting defence provided for by the Directive and set out in Regulation 18 of the *Electronic Commerce Regulations* (SI 68/2003) (see **Q19**).

Section 27 of the *Defamation Act, 2009* offers another potential defence to an SNS service provider and possibly, although this cannot be stated with any certainty, an individual or entity that maintains an SNS profile page on which defamatory material is posted by a third party. It is a new defence at the time of writing and as yet untested in the courts. Accordingly, its scope only can be speculated upon rather than asserted with any authority. The innocent publication defence hinges primarily on the defendant not being the author, editor or publisher of the statement (see exclusions from being regarded as such in section 27(2)) and proving that she / he took "reasonable care" in relation to the publication. The extent of this duty of "reasonable care" is not defined and therefore open to interpretation by the courts.

See also

Q19   Who is liable for a defamatory publication made online?

Q20   What is innocent publication?

Q39   Can employers be held liable for defamatory publications made by their employees?

Q70   How is privacy protected under Irish law?

Q82   What is intellectual property?

Q83   How are intellectual property rights protected by legislation?

Q84   What is copyright?

Q91   What steps can a copyright-owner take to protect their copyright online?

Q44 Can an apology be construed as an acknowledgment of liability in a defamation action?

Since the *Defamation Act, 2009* took effect, the fact that a defendant publisher made an apology for the publication of a statement cannot be treated in a defamation action as an admission of liability that she / he published a defamatory statement.

Section 24(1) re-states the pre-2009 Act position that a defendant may give evidence in mitigation of damages of the fact that they made, or offered, an apology to the plaintiff. This apology or offer of apology must have been made as soon as practicable after the plaintiff made their complaint or after they brought the defamation action, whichever was earlier.

The defendant, under the 2009 Act, is obliged to give written notice to the plaintiff of her / his intention to give such evidence in mitigation of damages. They must do this, either at the time they file their defence in the relevant court office or when they deliver their defence to the plaintiff (section 24(2)). This was also the position under the *Defamation Act, 1961* (now repealed).

Making an apology, prior to the 2009 Act, was tantamount to an acknowledgment by the defendant publisher that they would be found liable for damages for defamation. However, section 24(3) of the 2009 Act provides that an apology made by the defendant does not constitute an express or implied admission of liability by the defendant and is not relevant to the determination of liability in the action.

Lawyers acting for defamation litigants should note that SI 511 of 2009 (*Rules of the Superior Courts (Defamation), 2009*) and SI 486 of 2009 (*Circuit Court Rules (Defamation), 2009*) amend the *Rules of the Superior Courts* and the *Circuit Court Rules* respectively to allow a notice of intention to plead an apology in mitigation of damages to be made by inclusion of a statement to this effect in the defendant publisher's defence.

It is important to note that section 24(1), which allows a defendant publisher to plead the fact of an apology or offer of apology in mitigation of damages, requires not only that the apology was made or offered but also that it was actually published or offered to be published "in such a manner as ensured that the apology was given the same or similar prominence as was given to that statement ...".

Although, under the 2009 Act, an apology cannot be construed as an admission of liability in a defamation action, publishers should consult with their legal advisors prior to making any apology. The making or offering of an apology can be central to the defence strategy in a defamation action, particularly if an 'offer of amends', as provided for by sections 22 and 23 of the Act, has been made.

Care needs to be taken that the publication of an apology does not in itself defame another person. When apologising for comments made by a third-party interviewee in an article or radio broadcast, the publisher may risk defaming that interviewee in apologising for their statement. Such apologies should be made either with the assent of the interviewee or, where proceedings have issued, read out in court, in which case the apology will attract the protection of privilege.

See also

Q30   What is absolute privilege and when does it apply to a publication?
Q35   Does offering a right of reply avoid liability for defamation?
Q62   What is an offer of amends?

Q45 What is malicious falsehood?

A false statement may be published concerning a person, their business or their products that causes or is likely to cause them economic loss, even though the statement does not injure their reputation in the sense that reasonable people would not tend to think less of them as a result of what was published. On such occasions, the person may be able to sue for malicious falsehood.

The core elements of the common law tort of malicious falsehood were expressed in statutory form by section 42 of the *Defamation Act, 2009*. Furthermore, provisions relating to pecuniary damage in malicious falsehood actions contained in section 20 of the now-repealed *Defamation Act, 1961* were re-stated in section 42.

Section 42(1) requires that the plaintiff in a malicious falsehood action prove the following three elements of the claim:

- The statement was untrue;
- The statement was published maliciously; and
- The statement referred to the plaintiff, his or her property or his or her office, profession, calling, trade or business.

Section 42(2) requires the plaintiff in a malicious falsehood action to prove further that:

- She / he suffered special damage (being quantifiable financial loss, such as loss of turnover or profits); or
- The publication of the statement was calculated to cause and was likely to cause financial loss to the plaintiff in respect of his or her property or his or her office, profession, calling, trade or business.

If a publication is made that inadvertently contains a false statement about a person's product or business, the most effective way of making clear that the motivation was not malicious and was not calculated to cause financial harm to that person is usually to publish a correction as soon as possible after the false statement is brought to the publisher's attention.

An example of a publication that potentially could give rise to a malicious falsehood action is the malicious or reckless publication of a statement that a person or company has ceased trading when in fact they had not. If the publication was made on foot of a genuine mistake made in good faith, then the necessary element of malice in the making of the publication was absent. Speedy publication of a correction, as soon as the mistake has been brought to the attention of the publisher, can be relied on as evidence of good faith and absence of malice in the making of the original publication.

Malicious falsehood is a form of civil wrong (tort) that can arise in different circumstances, depending on the nature of the publication giving rise to the claim, including:

- Slander of goods arising from untrue and damaging statements maliciously published about the plaintiff's goods (such as products manufactured by the plaintiff).
- Slander of title arising from untrue and damaging statements maliciously published about the plaintiff's title to land.

Sometimes, it can be difficult to distinguish whether a published statement amounts to defamation of the plaintiff or to a malicious falsehood; there have been occasions where both a defamation claim and a malicious falsehood claim have been brought arising from the same publication.

Case law
Kaye v Robertson [1991] FSR 62
A well-known actor in the UK suffered head injuries in a car accident. He was recuperating in hospital when he was visited by a reporter and photographer from the *Sunday Sport* newspaper. Mr Kaye's representatives sought and obtained an injunction against publication on the grounds of malicious falsehood and the injunction was upheld on appeal. The proposed interview and photographs falsely indicated to the reader that Mr Kaye had consented to the interview. It was, or ought to have been, clear to the journalist and his editor that Mr Kaye was not fit to give consent to the interview. Accordingly, the required element of recklessness, tantamount to malice, was established. Mr Kaye could have

sold his story to other newspapers. Accordingly, the value of his right to sell his story would be undermined by the publication and the necessary element of likelihood to cause financial loss to the plaintiff also was established. Note that, were this action to be brought in Ireland, it would more likely be brought as a breach of privacy claim. Nowadays, the claim made by Mr Kaye alternatively might be brought as a privacy claim in the UK in the light of developments of the law of confidence and privacy in that jurisdiction in the intervening years.

See also

Q23   Can a publisher be held liable if they inadvertently defame someone?
Q51   How are damages assessed in a defamation case?

Q46   Can someone with a criminal conviction sue for damages for defamation?

While the fact of a criminal conviction adversely affects the reputation of an individual, it would be inaccurate to suggest that a person with a criminal conviction could not sue for damages for defamation. The fact of a conviction does not mean that a person no longer has any reputation to be protected.

In *Hill v Cork Examiner [2001] IESC 95*, an individual with a criminal conviction for assault occasioning actual bodily harm had been awarded £60,000 in damages for defamation, the jury having found that he had been implicitly and incorrectly identified in a newspaper article as a sex offender. The trial court's finding was appealed by the defendant newspaper to the Supreme Court, which upheld the original finding and the award of damages made by the jury.

In February 2008, an award of €900,000 was made in favour of a Mr Martin McDonagh against the *Sunday World* newspaper, which had published an article referring to Mr McDonagh as a "Traveller drug king" (*The Irish Times*, 29.02.208). The jury found that the newspaper had succeeded in proving that the plaintiff was a tax-evader and had a criminal conviction. However, it did not succeed in proving that he was a drug-dealer or a loan shark, both allegations having been made in the article in question. At the time of writing, this case is under appeal to the Supreme Court.

In November 2010, a Circuit Court judge in Dublin held that a man serving a prison sentence for possession of child pornography had, despite the nature of his offence, a "residual" reputation capable of being damaged. The *Irish Daily Star Sunday* newspaper had published an article describing the plaintiff as the "secret shower buddy" of a notorious rapist. The judge made a correction order in favour of the plaintiff, who did not seek an award of damages (see *The Irish Times*, 04.11.2010).

Evidence of criminal convictions can be relevant both to the defence of a defamation action and to the making of a plea in mitigation of damages.

Section 43 of the *Defamation Act, 2009* allows evidence of the acquittal or conviction of any person by an Irish court and any findings of fact made during the criminal proceedings resulting in that acquittal or conviction to be admitted as evidence in a defamation action. However, temporal considerations need to be borne in mind. It may be that, since their conviction, the person referred to has rehabilitated themselves to the extent that their good name and reputation has been restored to a greater or lesser extent. Each case will be decided on its own merits.

Section 31(6)(a) of the 2009 Act permits a defendant publisher, found liable for defamation, to give evidence in mitigation of damages of "any matter that would have a bearing upon the reputation of the plaintiff". Such evidence could include evidence of a criminal conviction. However, such evidence in mitigation of damages can be given only with the leave of the court and if it "relates to matters connected with the defamatory statement".

See also

Q47   What approach will the courts take if a plaintiff does not deserve the reputation she / he seeks to vindicate?

Q51   How are damages assessed in a defamation case?

Q56   What is a correction order?

Q47   What approach will the courts take if a plaintiff does not deserve the reputation she / he seeks to vindicate?

Case law in the UK and Ireland has debated the extent to which defamation law will vindicate the reputation that a plaintiff ought to enjoy — by reference, for example, to past misdeeds of the plaintiff that may not be widely known — as opposed to the reputation she / he actually enjoys. More recent case law in the UK and Ireland endorses the view that the law will not protect a reputation that the plaintiff does not deserve to have. Accordingly, if the defendant publisher proves in a defamation action that the plaintiff has acted in a manner that indicates that she / he is not entitled to the reputation they seek to vindicate, the law will not protect that reputation or may only protect it to a limited extent (by limiting or reducing the damages awarded to the plaintiff).

In *Grobbelaar v Newsgroup Newspapers Ltd [2002] UKHL 40*, Bruce Grobbelaar, a former Liverpool FC goalkeeper, sued for damages for defamation arising from an article in the *Sun* newspaper alleging that he had 'fixed' matches in return for bribes. The jury at the trial found that Grobbelaar had been defamed and awarded him damages of £85,000. The finding was appealed to the Court of Civil Appeal, which quashed the jury's verdict, on the grounds that it was perverse in the light of the evidence given in the trial. That decision was appealed to the House of Lords. The jury's findings at the trial of the action had failed to identify clearly whether the 'sting' of the defamation lay in the allegation that Grobbelaar had been willing to accept bribes (which was proved) or the allegation that he had deliberately let in goals (which was not proved). Accordingly, the House of Lords upheld the jury's finding of fact that Grobbelaar had been defamed. However, it substituted an award of £1 for the jury's award of £85,000, on the grounds that the proven fact that Grobbelaar had been willing to accept a bribe indicated that he did not deserve the reputation he sought to vindicate in the proceedings. Lord Bingham of Cornhill stated in his judgment: "The tort of defamation protects those whose reputations have been unlawfully injured. It affords little or no protection to those who have, or deserve to have, no reputation deserving of legal protection".

The *Grobbelaar* judgment was cited with approval by the Supreme Court in *Cooper-Flynn v RTÉ [2004] IESC 27*. In the course of his judgment, Chief Justice Keane stated: "I am satisfied that where, as here, evidence is before the jury of specific acts of misconduct which were relevant to that aspect of the plaintiff's reputation with which the defamation was concerned, there is no reason in principle why a defendant should not be allowed to rely on such evidence by way of mitigation of damages. Since the purpose of the law of defamation is to compensate a plaintiff for damage to his or her reputation, it would be singularly unsatisfactory if a jury were obliged to award anything other than nominal or contemptuous damages to a plaintiff whom they had found in effect not to be entitled to any reputation in the relevant area". Ms Cooper-Flynn's appeal for a re-trial of her action for defamation in which a jury found she had not been defamed by RTÉ was rejected in this case.

Accordingly, the Irish courts will take into account evidence of the reputation that the plaintiff deserves in the relevant sphere of their life as opposed to the reputation she / he actually enjoys, if there is a discrepancy between the two. However, the relevance of that evidence to the aspect of the plaintiff's reputation which she / he seeks to vindicate is crucial.

See also

Q46 Can someone with a criminal conviction sue for damages for defamation?
Q51 How are damages assessed in a defamation case?

Q48   Can satire be defamatory?

Satire can be defamatory. There is no 'just jesting' or 'only kidding' defence under Irish law. The test of defamation remains the same whether a publication is satirical or not. If the facts asserted in a satirical publication are not true and tend to injure the reputation of the person referred to in the publication, the publication potentially can be defamatory.

In 1988, two Belfast lawyers, Robert McCartney and Desmond Boal, were awarded £50,000 damages each in the Northern Ireland High Court. A light-hearted newspaper column had portrayed them as having "had words" over which of them had first spotted the remaining chocolate éclair in a bakery shop. It transpired that this anecdote was untrue. The newspaper accepted that it was untrue but argued – unsuccessfully – that the article was not defamatory (*The Irish Times*, 22.10.1988).

An *Irish Press* column in 1986 referred in a humorous manner to a Dublin solicitor, Patrick Madigan. It stated that Mr Madigan, having bought a hand-drawn map of Inishvickillane, an island owned by the then leader of the Fianna Fáil party, Charles Haughey, at a political fund-raising event, complained to Mr Haughey when he found it to be one of an edition of 300 such maps rather than the original he had thought it to be. The anecdote was found in the High Court in 1987 to be untrue and damages of £30,000 were awarded to Mr Madigan (*The Irish Times*, 21.11.1987).

In practice, the sharper the satire and more surreal the assertions of fact contained in a satirical publication, the less likely it is to give rise to a defamation action – even if it causes discomfort or offence to the person being satirised. Defamation risk tends to increase where lame or distasteful satire results in statements that will not be understood clearly by the reasonable recipient as satirical or which contain factual assertions merely masquerading as satire.

Political or social commentary expressed through satire tends to be tolerated in practice by those being satirised to quite a high degree, even where such satire is potentially defamatory. However, this is a practical dynamic, not a legal rule or principle.

The higher the public profile of the individual satirised, the higher their tolerance for being satirised is likely to be, whether that profile is attributable to their role in political or public life or to their celebrity status. Again, this is a practical observation and not a statement of legal principle. That level of tolerance will not necessarily extend, however, to their families or friends if the latter are not also in the public eye to the same extent as they themselves are. Particular caution, therefore, should be exercised in relation to satire that refers to family members or friends of high profile individuals who are being satirised.

In 2006, *The Dubliner* magazine published a purported image of Elin Nordegren-Woods, the then-wife of the golfer, Tiger Woods. The image had been manipulated to superimpose the head of Ms Woods onto the body of a nude model and was accompanied by an article indicating that similar images could be found on pornographic websites. The article had not been intended as a serious piece but gave rise to a defamation action that was settled in 2007 on payment of €125,000, which Ms Woods gave to a cancer research charity, and an extensive apology read out in court (*The Irish Times*, 8.2.2007).

See also

Q81 Do celebrities and politicians have the same rights of privacy as private citizens?

DEFAMATION COURT PROCEDURES

Q49   What does a plaintiff need to prove in a defamation claim?

A plaintiff seeking damages for defamation must prove the following:

- Publication: Where publication is in some permanent form (for example, newspaper publication or television broadcast), publication is usually self-evident and therefore both parties to the litigation accept in common ('common case') that the publication took place. Where the publication is in transient form (for example, words spoken at a meeting), witnesses may need to be called by the plaintiff to give evidence that they heard the words complained of being spoken about the plaintiff in order to prove that publication took place.

- Identification: If the plaintiff was explicitly referred to by name or image in the defamatory publication, the question of identification may be agreed by both parties to be self-evident and thus common case. If the plaintiff was not readily identifiable, or if identification was implicit or by innuendo (even if inadvertent on the part of the publisher), the plaintiff may need to call witnesses who identified the plaintiff from the publication, to prove identification. If disputed, the issue of identification ultimately will be decided as a finding of fact by the court (the jury in a High Court case).

- Meaning of the statement: The meaning of the statement giving rise to the proceedings is often clear and undisputed between the parties. However, the defendant may contend that the statement bore an alternative, non-defamatory meaning to that contended for by the plaintiff. The plaintiff must show the court that the statement bore the meaning or interpretation which she / he has put on it. The court (the jury in a High Court case) ultimately will determine the meaning to be attributed to the statement.

- The defamatory nature of the statement: A defamatory statement is one "that tends to injure a person's reputation in the eyes of reasonable members of society" (section 2, *Defamation Act,*

2009). The defamatory tendency of the statement usually is self-evident. However, if the tendency of the statement to injure the plaintiff's reputation is disputed, the plaintiff may call witnesses to give evidence that they thought less of the plaintiff because of the publication.

- Malicious motivation of defendant: Certain defences available to publisher defendants will not succeed if the plaintiff can prove to the court that the defendant was motivated by malice rather than good faith in publishing the statement in question. These defences include the defences of common law qualified privilege and statutory qualified privilege.

- Refusal to publish a statement or contradiction (statutory qualified privilege): Where a defence of statutory qualified privilege has been made under section 18 of the 2009 Act and the statement to which the action relates is one to which the right to require the publication of a statement of explanation or contradiction applies (see Schedule 1, Part 2 of the 2009 Act), the defence will fail if it is proved that the defendant was requested to publish a reasonable statement of explanation or contradiction but either failed to do so or failed to so in a manner that was adequate and reasonable taking all the circumstances into account (section 18(4) of the 2009 Act). Where relevant, therefore, this is a matter that must be proved by the plaintiff.

See also

Q12 What is defamation?
Q15 What is a publication under defamation law?
Q22 How can someone be identified in a defamatory publication?
Q31 What is qualified privilege and when does it apply to a publication?

Q50   How is it decided whether a statement has a defamatory meaning?

A published statement may be capable of bearing one or more meanings. Construed on the basis of one meaning, the statement may be defamatory; construed on the basis of another, it may not.

Whether a statement has a defamatory meaning will be decided by the court in a defamation action. In the Circuit Court, this will be decided by the trial judge alone. In the High Court, it is for the judge to decide whether a statement is reasonably capable of bearing the meaning contended for by the plaintiff; but it is for the jury to decide whether the statement in fact bears that meaning. It is also for the jury to determine whether that meaning is defamatory of the plaintiff.

Under section 14 of the *Defamation Act, 2009*, the court can dismiss a defamation action if it finds that the statement giving rise to the action was not "reasonably capable" of bearing the imputation pleaded by the plaintiff or, if it is reasonably capable of bearing that meaning, it is not reasonably capable of bearing a defamatory meaning. If such a ruling is sought in a defamation action in the High Court, it will be made by a judge alone without a jury. Section 34(2) of the 2009 Act entitles the court, should the defendant apply for such a ruling to be made, to dismiss a defamation action summarily (no jury) if the statement giving rise to the action is not "reasonably capable" of being found to have a defamatory meaning.

In *Quigley v Creation Ltd [1971] IR 269* at 272, Judge Walsh observed, "Basically, the question of libel or no libel is a matter of opinion and opinions may vary reasonably within very wide limits".

In 2002, well-known journalist John Waters contended in a defamation action against *The Sunday Times* that two paragraphs in an article that commented on a speech he had given at the Abbey Theatre bore the meaning that he was a bad father and someone who had behaved in an unfair and cowardly way by denying his audience at the theatre a right of reply. The newspaper, by contrast, contended that the paragraphs in question did not bear those meanings and that the article comprised robust, but not defamatory, commentary on the plaintiff's speech. The jury found that the article bore the meanings contended for by the plaintiff and that these were defamatory meanings. The jury awarded the plaintiff damages of €84,000 (*The Irish Times*, 24.2.2002).

The wide variation of opinion referred to by Judge Walsh in *Quigley v Creation Ltd* explains why the outcome of defamation proceedings can be notoriously difficult to predict. It also explains why the proprietors of publishing outlets and broadcasting organisations frequently opt to settle defamation proceedings based on commercial consideration of the legal costs that may be incurred in defending a defamation case where there is no reassurance of the likely outcome. Such settlements can be frustrating for journalists, who may feel that their impugned publication is defensible.

For publishers, journalists and reporters, using clear and unambiguous language in a story or other publication lessens the scope for the attribution of multiple meanings to a statement. The test for whether a statement has a defamatory meaning is an objective test carried out by the court; the subjective intention of the journalist or writer is not relevant to the determination of the meaning to be attributed to a statement.

See also

Q5   What is the role of the Circuit Court?
Q6   What is the role of the High Court?
Q27   What is the truth defence?
Q29   What is the honest opinion defence?

Q51 How are damages assessed in a defamation case?

In most civil cases in the High Court, the case is heard and damages are assessed by a judge alone. In High Court defamation actions, however, a case is heard and damages are assessed by a jury. In a Circuit Court defamation action, damages are assessed by the judge hearing the case.

There is provision in the *Defamation Act, 2009* for the award of damages by a judge alone in a High Court case where an application for 'summary relief' (judge sitting alone) is made under section 34 of the Act. The judge must be satisfied that the statement is defamatory and there is no defence that is reasonably likely to succeed.

There is no 'rate card' for damages in a defamation action. There is much judicial and academic discussion as to how the injury to a person's reputation should be reflected in financial terms when compared to the effect of, for example, a severe and permanently disabling physical injury suffered by a person in a car crash.

It can be argued that exceptionally high defamation awards can have a chilling effect on freedom of expression, such that the exercise of that right is unjustifiably curtailed. This argument was considered by the European Court of Human Rights in the cases of *Miloslavsky v United Kingdom* and *Independent News and Media PLC v Ireland* (see below).

Jury awards have been rising considerably in recent years in Ireland, the highest award to date being an award made in November 2010 of €10 million in favour of Donal Kinsella against his former employer, Kenmare Resources PLC (see *The Irish Times*, 18.11.2010). Prior to that, in June 2009, a jury awarded €1.87 million to Monica Leech against Independent Newspapers in respect of articles published about her in the *Evening Herald* (see *The Irish Times*, 25.06.2009). Both these awards, at the time of writing, are under appeal to the Supreme Court.

It is important to note that, in the cases referred to above, no substantive guidance was given to the jury by the presiding trial judges on the issue of damages. This was because the defamatory publications giving rise to those actions were made prior to the *Defamation Act, 2009* coming into effect. In respect of all defamation actions brought in respect of publications made on or after 1 January 2010 (the commencement date of the 2009 Act), the presiding judge in a High Court action is obliged, by virtue of section 31(2) of the Act, to give directions to the jury in relation to the matter of damages, although the decision on the actual amount to be awarded will be decided by the jury.

At the time of writing, a number of defamation actions continue to be tried in accordance with the pre-2009 Act procedures, by virtue of the date of publication of the statements giving rise to those actions. It will be some years before all cases before the courts are being tried in accordance with the procedures set out in the 2009 Act.

Section 31 of the 2009 Act contains specific provisions relating to the assessment of damages in a defamation action.

- Either party may make submissions to the court on the issue of damages (section 31(1)).

- The court must have regard to all the circumstances of the case (section 31(3)).

- The court is obliged to have regard to the following factors (among others) when making an award of damages (section 31(4)): the nature and gravity of the allegations made about the plaintiff; the means of publication of the statement; any offer of apology made by the defendant; and any evidence given concerning the plaintiff's reputation.

- Section 31(6) allows the defendant, with the leave of the court, to give evidence in mitigation of damages, about the plaintiff's reputation. The evidence must be relevant, however, to the matters contained in the defamatory statement.

- The defendant is entitled under section 31(6) to bring evidence about any other defamation action in which the plaintiff has already been awarded damages, if the other action was concerned with substantially the same allegations as were made in the defamatory statement the subject of the proceedings before the court.

- Special damages may be awarded in respect of the financial loss suffered by the plaintiff as a result of the publication of the defamatory statement (section 31(7)).

Section 32 is concerned with the award of aggravated and punitive damages:

- Aggravated damages may be awarded where the court finds that the defendant has conducted its defence in a manner that "aggravated the injury caused to the plaintiff's reputation by the defamatory statement" (section 32(1)). A defendant who makes the truth defence, but who fails to prove the truth of the defamatory statement, risks having aggravated damages awarded against them as the manner in which they defended the action may have caused further damage to the plaintiff's reputation.

- Power to award punitive damages is given to the court by section 32(2) where it is proved that the defendant intentionally published the statement about the plaintiff knowing it was untrue or being reckless as to whether or not it was true.

Case law
Independent News and Media and Independent Newspapers Ireland Limited v Ireland (E.Ct.H.R. 16.06.2005, Application no. 55120/00)
This case arose from an award of £300,000 in favour of politician Prionsias De Rossa in a defamation case brought against Independent Newspapers. The newspaper group claimed before the European Court of Human Rights that the very limited guidance given to juries in defamation actions in Ireland resulted in a breach of the newspaper's right to freedom of expression protected by Article 10 of the *European Convention on Human Rights*. The European Court of Human Rights found that, taking all the circumstances of this case into account, there had not been a breach of Article 10.

Tolstoy Miloslavsky v United Kingdom (E.Ct.H.R. 13.07.95, Application no. 18139/91)
An award of £1.5 million had been made in a UK defamation action brought by Lord Aldington, arising out of a pamphlet written by Count Tolstoy Miloslavsky, which stated that Aldington, when serving as a

British Army officer, had repatriated prisoners-of-war to certain death in Russia and Yugoslavia at the end of World War II. The European Court of Human Rights held that the amount of the award and inadequate guidance given to the jury on damages resulted in a violation of Count Tolstoy's Article 10 right to freedom of expression.

John v MGN Ltd [1995] EWCA Civ 23
A UK Court of Appeal case arising from a defamatory newspaper article about pop singer Elton John, which said he was on a "diet of death" and was spitting out food he had chewed in an effort to lose weight. Total damages of £350,000 awarded to Elton John against Mirror Group Newspapers were reduced by the UK Court of Civil Appeal to £75,000. The Court of Appeal considered and extended the guidance that can be given to juries in relation to defamation damages in UK courts.

See also

Q6   What is the role of the High Court?

Q7   What is the role of the Supreme Court?

Q9   What are damages and how are they assessed?

Q44 Can an apology be construed as an acknowledgment of liability in a defamation action?

Q47 What approach will the courts take if a plaintiff does not deserve the reputation she / he seeks to vindicate?

Q52 Can an award of damages for defamation be overturned by an appeal court?

Q52   Can an award of damages for defamation be overturned by an appeal court?

A plaintiff or defendant in a defamation action is entitled to appeal an award of damages to a higher court, subject to final appeal to the Supreme Court on a point of law.

In practice, few awards made in the Circuit Court are appealed to the High Court.

Section 13 of the *Defamation Act, 2009* expressly authorises the Supreme Court, on appeal from a High Court decision, to substitute the amount of damages awarded to a plaintiff with an alternative amount which it considers "appropriate".

Section 13 gives statutory authority to the Supreme Court to depart from its prior practice of declining to substitute its own award for a defamation award made by a jury. This provision may help to avoid the anomalous situation that arose in a defamation claim brought pre-2009 by businessman Denis O'Brien against Mirror Group Newspapers. Mr O'Brien was awarded £250,000 (€317,000) by a jury in 1999. The award was appealed to the Supreme Court and found to be "disproportionately high". The case was sent back to the High Court for assessment of damages by a different jury. That second jury in 2006 awarded Mr O'Brien €750,000 – considerably more than the original award (see *The Irish Times*, 24.11.06).

See also

Q5   What is the role of the Circuit Court?
Q6   What is the role of the High Court?
Q7   What is the role of the Supreme Court?
Q9   What are damages and how are they assessed?
Q51   How are damages assessed in a defamation case?

Q53 How long after a publication is made does a plaintiff have to bring a defamation claim?

In respect of publications that took place on or after 1 January 2010, a plaintiff has one year after the date of publication of a defamatory statement to bring an action in the courts claiming damages for defamation (the limitation period) (see section 38 of the *Defamation Act, 2009*). The plaintiff must issue civil proceedings in the relevant court office within the limitation period; it is not sufficient for the plaintiff merely to indicate an intention (for example, by solicitor's letter) to issue those proceedings.

It is possible for the one year limitation period to be extended by leave of the court up to a maximum of two years. The court may make this extension order where "the interests of justice" so require and the plaintiff would be more prejudiced by the order *not* being made than the defendant may be by it being made (see section 11(3A) of the *Statute of Limitations, 1957* as inserted by section 38(1) of the *Defamation Act, 2009*). The court must consider the reasons why the defamation action was not brought within the required one year period and the extent to which any relevant evidence no longer can be adduced by virtue of the plaintiff's delay in issuing proceedings.

A publication online (a blog, website posting or podcast) is deemed published on the date when it was first capable of being viewed or listened to on the Internet (see section 11(3B) of the *Statute of Limitations, 1957* as inserted by section 38(1)(b) of the *Defamation Act, 2009*).

It is advisable for publishers (including journalists and authors) to keep research records relating to published material for at least a year (and preferably two years) after the publication of a story or programme based on that research work. Such material may be required in order to defend a defamation case, as it may include the names and contact details of people who can testify as to the truth of an article or story that gives rise to a defamation action and / or documents on which that story is based.

It is important to be aware that, where a publisher re-publishes a defamatory statement – for example, by way of the re-publication of a newspaper article or the repeat broadcast of a television programme – the limitation period will start to run in respect of that re-publication from the date of such re-publication. While the limitation period may have expired in respect of the original publication, the re-publication will be regarded as a separate publication, triggering a fresh limitation period in respect of that separate publication.

See also

Q15   What is a publication under defamation law?

Q54   Can a plaintiff from abroad sue for defamation in the Irish courts?

A foreign national or person living abroad who has been defamed in Ireland – for example, by an article published in an Irish newspaper or a foreign newspaper with circulation in Ireland – can sue for damages in the Irish courts.

Two important considerations arise for such a plaintiff:

- What is the extent of any damages the plaintiff can claim in an Irish court?
- Will the plaintiff be able to enforce any award made against a foreign publisher by an Irish court?

What is the extent of any damages the plaintiff can claim in an Irish court?

If the defendant publisher of the defamatory statement is resident or established as a business in Ireland, the plaintiff can claim damages for all the injury done to her / his reputation by the publication, whether that injury was sustained in Ireland or elsewhere.

If the defendant publisher of the defamatory statement is not resident or established as a business in Ireland, the plaintiff is only entitled to claim damages in the Irish courts for the injury caused to her / his reputation in Ireland.

In 2007, a Ukrainian woman, Julia Kushnir, settled several defamation actions brought in Ireland claiming damages against a number of Irish newspapers. The actions were brought in respect of the injury caused to her reputation by articles published by those newspapers concerning the circumstances of the death of Irish politician, Liam Lawlor. Mr Lawlor died in a road accident in Moscow in 2005 and Ms Kushnir had been a passenger in the car in which he died (see *The Irish Times*, 07.11.2007).

In *Hunter v Gerald Duckworth & Co and Another [1999] IEHC 56*, the High Court affirmed the entitlement of an Irish plaintiff living in the UK to sue a

UK-domiciled author in the Irish courts for damages for the injury caused to the plaintiff's reputation in Ireland by a booklet published and written by the first and second named defendants respectively. As this case has not proceeded to a trial hearing at the date of writing, the issue of the defendant's liability (if any) has not been determined.

Will the plaintiff be able to enforce any award made against a foreign publisher by an Irish court?

The *1968 Brussels Convention on Jurisdiction and the Enforcement of Judgments in Civil and Commercial Matters* was incorporated into Irish domestic law by the *Jurisdiction of Courts and Enforcement of Judgments (European Communities) Act, 1988* and applies to judgements of courts in signatory countries to the *Convention*.

The 1968 *Brussels Convention* (Article 5.3) allows a plaintiff to sue a defendant publisher "in the place where the harmful event occurred". Where an action is brought claiming damages for defamation in the Irish courts in accordance with the provisions of the *Convention*, any award made in that action against an overseas publisher can be enforced through the courts of the defendant publisher's home country. This is the basis on which publishers based in the UK can be sued in the Irish courts for defamation and the plaintiff will be entitled to enforce that judgment through the UK courts, should the defendant publisher not pay the award made in the Irish courts.

Case law

Shevill and Ors v Presse Alliance S.A. ECJ Case C68/93, [1995] 2 AC 18
Shevill, a UK resident, brought a defamation action in the UK courts against a French newspaper publisher, *France Soir*, which had a circulation of 230 copies in the UK. The European Court of Justice (ECJ) was requested by the UK House of Lords for a ruling on the interpretation of Article 5(3) of the 1968 Brussels *Convention on Jurisdiction and the Enforcement of Judgments in Civil and Commercial Matters*, which entitles a claimant to bring an action in the jurisdiction "where the harmful event occurred". The ECJ held that, in a defamation case, a claim could be brought either in the jurisdiction in which the publisher was established (and damages for all injury to reputation, wherever suffered,

could be claimed) or in the courts of each jurisdiction in which injury to reputation had been suffered (and damages for injury suffered in each such jurisdiction only could be claimed).

Ewins v Carlton UK Television Ltd and Another [1997] IEHC 44
A television programme about IRA paramilitary activity was broadcast by UTV in Northern Ireland and viewed by an estimated 111,000 viewers in the Republic of Ireland. Ewins (and two other plaintiffs in related cases) were domiciled in the UK but brought defamation proceedings in the Irish courts. On foot of an application to determine certain jurisdictional issues raised by the defendants, it was held in the High Court that the plaintiff was entitled to bring his claim in the Irish courts but that the extent of any damages he could claim must be restricted to the injury sustained to his reputation in the Republic of Ireland.

Hunter v Gerald Duckworth & Co Ltd and Another [1999] IEHC 56
An Irish citizen residing in England brought defamation proceedings in Ireland against a UK publisher and author, alleging defamation. The booklet in question was published in the UK and sold in Ireland and the UK. In a pre-trial judgment on a jurisdictional issue raised by one of the defendants, it was held in the High Court that the publication (by way of distribution and sale) of the booklet in Ireland was the natural and probable result of the original publication of the booklet in the UK by the author. That original publication occurred when the author gave the manuscript to the publishing house on foot of a contract that permitted world-wide sales of the resulting book. Accordingly, the plaintiff was entitled to bring defamation proceedings against the author arising from the publication (by way distribution and sale) of the booklet in Ireland in the Irish courts. At the date of writing, this case has not been concluded.

See also

Q40   Can repeating a story sourced from another media outlet be defamatory?
Q55   Can a plaintiff from Ireland sue for defamation in foreign courts?

Q55   Can a plaintiff from Ireland sue for defamation in foreign courts?

Subject to the laws of overseas jurisdictions, an Irish citizen or person domiciled in Ireland can sue for damages for injury caused to their reputation outside Ireland by a defamatory publication in another jurisdiction.

It is only in common law jurisdictions (Ireland and the UK are the only European common law jurisdictions) that significant damages are likely to be payable under civil law in respect of injury to reputation. In other European countries, publications that cause injury to reputation are dealt with as a criminal law matter. While damages in these proceedings can be awarded in some jurisdictions (such as France), awards usually are significantly lower than the awards made to civil law plaintiffs in common law jurisdictions.

It is interesting to note that, in 2006, the owners of the *Telegraph* newspaper, brothers Sirs Frederick and David Barclay, brought criminal libel proceedings against Times Newspapers in a French court. The French court held that the Barclay brothers were entitled to bring their proceedings in France but ruled on a technical point against providing the 'right of reply' relief they sought from the court.

In the mid-1990s, a former Irish Taoiseach, Albert Reynolds, brought a defamation claim in the English courts against Times Newspapers Ltd, arising out of an article published in the English edition of *The Sunday Times* in November 1994. The case led to the emergence of what became known as the 'public interest defence', also referred to as the 'Reynolds defence'.

Under Article 5.3 of the *1968 Brussels Convention on Jurisdiction and the Enforcement of Judgments in Civil and Political Matters* – incorporated into Irish domestic law by *the Jurisdiction of Courts and Enforcement of Judgments (European Communities) Act, 1988* – a plaintiff in a defamation case is entitled to sue in respect of the wrong done to them "in the place where the harmful event occurred".

In practical terms, pursuing litigation in other jurisdictions is a costly exercise. The expense involved frequently acts as a disincentive for an Irish person to pursue defamation proceedings in other jurisdictions.

See also

Q1 What are the sources of Irish law?
Q33 What is the public interest defence?
Q54 Can a plaintiff from abroad sue for defamation in the Irish courts?

Q56   What is a correction order?

A correction order is a form of additional redress available to a plaintiff, where the court finds that she / he has been defamed. Introduced by section 30 of the *Defamation Act, 2009*, a correction order requires the defendant publisher to publish a correction of the defamatory statement that gave rise to the proceedings.

A section 30 correction order may be made where the statement giving rise to the claim is found to be defamatory and there is no defence to the action. The power of the court to make a correction order is discretionary – the term "may" is used in section 30(1) in relation to the court's power to make such an order rather than "shall".

The plaintiff must give the defendant at least seven days' advance notice before the trial of a defamation action of her / his intention to apply for a correction order and must inform the court of such intention at the trial itself (section 30(3)).

Under section 30(2), the court must specify in the order the date and time when, or the period within which, the correction must be published. The court also is required to specify the form, content, extent and manner of publication of the correction. When making a correction order, the court must require the correction to be published in a manner that will have the same audience or readership 'reach' of the defamatory publication, unless the plaintiff otherwise requests.

Correction orders represent a radical new power for courts to dictate the terms of correction of the facts contained in a defamatory publication and to require the publisher to publish it, on risk of being held in contempt of court for failure to do so. This requirement is in addition to a finding of liability for defamation and any award that may be made against a defendant publisher.

The first correction order made under the 2009 Act was made in favour of a plaintiff, Barry Watters, in an action against the *Irish Daily Star Sunday* newspaper. The judge invited the parties to agree the wording of the statement that would be published on foot of the order. In default of agreement, the court would have had the power to determine the contents of the statement to be published. A wording was agreed between the parties and published by the newspaper (see *The Irish Times*, 04.11.2010).

See also

Q11 How is the right to good name and reputation protected under Irish law?

Q51 How are damages assessed in a defamation case?

Q57 What is a declaratory order?

Q57　What is a declaratory order?

A declaratory order is a new form of defamation redress provided for by section 28 of the *Defamation Act, 2009* – in effect, a 'fast-track' procedure that can be invoked where the statement published was false and defamatory.

A declaratory order is sought from the Circuit Court and no damages can be claimed or awarded to the applicant.

A correction order under section 30 of the 2009 Act also may be made alongside a declaratory order if the applicant applies for a correction order. An applicant for a declaratory order also may apply for an injunction order under section 33 of the Act, preventing the respondent publisher from further publishing the defamatory statement in question.

Lawyers acting for applicants for declaratory orders should note that applications should be brought by way of Notice of Motion to the Court in accordance with the procedure specified in the *Circuit Court Rules (Defamation), 2009* (SI 486 of 2009).

A three-part test is set out in section 28(2) of the 2009 Act, which must be satisfied before a declaratory order can be made:

- The statement must have been defamatory of the applicant and the respondent publisher must have no defence to the application.
- The applicant must have requested the respondent publisher to make and publish an apology, correction or retraction of the statement.
- The respondent publisher must have failed or refused to accede to that request or, if they acceded to the request, have failed or refused to give the apology, correction or retraction the same or similar prominence as the original defamatory statement.

Section 28(4) provides that an applicant who makes an application for a declaratory order is not entitled to bring any other proceedings of any nature arising from the defamatory statement in question.

As no damages can be awarded in favour of the successful applicant for a declaratory order, this form of redress is only appropriate where the statement in question is clearly defamatory and the speedy publication of an apology, correction or retraction is the primary objective of the person defamed.

The few applications for declaratory orders that have been brought under the 2009 Act to the date of writing have been vigorously resisted by the respondent newspapers. Despite such vigorous resistance on the part of the *Irish Daily Star Sunday*, an applicant by the name of Watters secured a declaratory order against the newspaper in November 2010, as well as both a correction order under section 30 of the 2009 Act and an order prohibiting further publication of the defamatory statement under section 33 (see *The Irish Times*, 04.11.2010).

It should be noted that the 'fair and reasonable publication' defence provided for by section 26 of the 2009 Act is not available, by virtue of section 26(4), to respondent publishers where an application has been made for a declaratory order. This potentially places a media respondent at a considerable disadvantage in resisting an application for a declaratory order.

See also

Q5   What is the role of the Circuit Court?

Q11   How is the right to good name and reputation protected under Irish law?

Q34   What is the fair and reasonable publication defence?

Q44   Can an apology be construed as an acknowledgment of liability in a defamation action?

Q56   What is a correction order?

Q59   Can an injunction be obtained to prohibit the publication of a defamatory statement?

Q58   What is a verifying affidavit?

Section 8 of the *Defamation Act, 2009* introduced a new procedural requirement in defamation actions. The requirement is for the swearing and filing in court of verifying affidavits, being sworn statements made by the parties to a civil action that any assertions or allegations of fact set out in a pleading served by them in the proceedings are true. Pleadings are formal documents in a court action by which each party to the action sets out the basis of the case they are making, whether as plaintiff or defendant. The objective of the verifying affidavit procedure is to dissuade either party to a defamation action from making false, exaggerated or inaccurate assertions of fact in a pleading.

Section 8(9) entitles both the plaintiff and the defendant to cross-examine the other in relation to the contents of a verifying affidavit, unless the court otherwise directs.

Section 8(5) requires that a verifying affidavit be sworn and filed in court within two months of service on the other party of the pleading to which it relates although, by mutual consent, the parties may agree to a longer period or an extension of the time may be ordered by the court.

Section 8(6) makes it a criminal offence for a person to knowingly swear a verifying affidavit that is false or misleading in any material respect.

Section 8(10) entitles the court to strike out the plaintiff's claim where he fails to comply with the provisions of section 8 or to give judgment in favour of the plaintiff where a defendant fails to comply with the section.

The verifying affidavit requirements of section 8 do not apply to the 'fast-track' proceedings provided for by section 28 of the 2009 Act, whereby a person who has been defamed may seek a declaratory order in the Circuit Court (section 8(13)).

See also

Q5   What is the role of the Circuit Court?
Q28   What is the presumption of falsity?

Q57 What is a declaratory order?

Q59   Can an injunction be obtained to prohibit publication of a defamatory statement?

A court order that compels a person to take or desist from taking a particular action is known as an 'injunction' order.

Section 33 of the Defamation Act, 2009 entitles a court to make an order prohibiting the publication of a defamatory statement – or further publication, where a defamatory statement has already been published.

The power of a court to grant an injunction restraining publication in advance (a 'prior restraint' order) existed at common law before the enactment of the 2009 Act but has been given a statutory basis in defamation law by section 33. Note that:

- The order may be a short-term, emergency measure – an *interim* order.
- Where court proceedings are underway, the order may be made pending a full trial or a further court hearing – an *interlocutory* order.
- The order may be permanent and apply indefinitely into the future – a *permanent* order.

The power of the court to make the order is discretionary; section 33(1) uses "may" when specifying the entitlement of a court to make the order. An order may be made where the statement sought to be prohibited is, in the court's opinion, (i) defamatory and (ii) the defendant has no defence that is reasonably likely to succeed.

Where proceedings for defamation have not already been issued by the applicant in another court (such as the Circuit Court), an application for an order prohibiting publication must be brought before the High Court. The application will be heard in the High Court by a judge only; no jury will be involved.

The common law principles applied to the grant of interlocutory injunctions can be summarised as:

- There must be a serious issue to be tried;
- The court must be satisfied that damages would not provide a sufficient remedy for the plaintiff; and
- The balance of convenience, taking all circumstances into account, must be better served by granting the injunction (see *Campus Oil v Minister for Industry and Energy (No 2) [1983] IR 88*).

Existing case law on 'prior restraint' applications in Ireland indicates that such an order will not be granted unless the proposed publication is defamatory and it is clear that the defendant publisher will not succeed in defending the publication. In *Connolly v RTÉ [1991] 2 IR 446*, it was held that, in applying the balance of convenience test in defamation cases, the court must balance the right to freedom of expression against the plaintiff's right to good name and reputation.

Section 33 appears to go further than existing case law by stating that the order may be made where there is "no defence to the action that is *reasonably likely* to succeed" (emphasis added). This suggests that the judge may engage in an assessment of the merits of any defence that the defendant publisher proposes to make if the publication proceeds, thereby potentially precluding the outcome of the ensuing defamation trial. Such an approach arguably risks excessively encroaching on the exercise of the right to freedom of expression by the media.

The first application for a section 33 order was made in April 2010. In *Meegan v Associated Newspapers (Ireland) Ltd*, the judge declined to make a prohibition order. He followed a rationale in line with the principles established by existing case law as described above and emphasised the discretionary nature of the court's power to make such an order.

Section 33(2) allows the reporting of the fact that a prohibition order has been made but states that such reports must not include the publication of the statement to which the order relates. Reporters should note that, even though the statement which is the subject of a successful application for a prohibition order may be read out in open court, they are not entitled to include that statement in their report of the proceedings. No such restriction on reporting applies if the application is unsuccessful and a prohibition order is not granted. A fair and accurate report of the proceedings will attract absolute privilege under section 17(2)(i) of the 2009 Act.

Where a court makes a declaratory order under section 28 of the 2009 Act, the applicant is entitled to ask the court also to grant a prohibition order in respect of any future publication of the statement or facts to which the declaratory order relates (section 28(6)).

Case law

Cogley v RTÉ [2005] IEHC 180
The plaintiff was the Director of Nursing at a nursing home for elderly patients at Leas Cross in County Dublin. The defendant broadcaster proposed broadcasting a programme that included footage secretly filmed at the nursing home indicating poor standards of care of patients. The plaintiff sought an interlocutory injunction to prohibit the broadcast, on the basis that she believed she would be defamed by it. Her application was refused on the grounds that such an injunction should not be granted if there is any reasonable basis for contending that the defendant may succeed at the trial of the action. Clarke J. held that "the defendant may succeed in defending the action for any one of a number of reasons".

Meegan v Associated Newspapers (Ireland) Ltd, High Court, 19.04.10 (The Irish Times, 20.04.10)
The applicant applied for a section 33 prohibition order restraining publication by the *Irish Mail on Sunday* of certain allegations about his sexual behaviour in Kenya where he worked as a charity worker. The order was denied. The judge was satisfied that there was a basis for contending that the respondent newspaper might succeed in its defence of any defamation proceedings pursued by the plaintiff.

See also

Q6   What is the role of the High Court?
Q10   How is the right to freedom of expression protected under Irish law?
Q30   What is absolute privilege and when does it apply to a publication?

Q60 Can a lodgement in satisfaction of a claim be made in a defamation action?

In a civil claim for damages, a lodgement into court of a sum of money in satisfaction of the plaintiff's claim can be made by the defendant prior to the trial, either with or without an admission of liability by the defendant.

Where a lodgement has been made, the plaintiff may accept the amount of the lodgement in satisfaction of their claim and the matter goes no further. If they do not accept it and the case proceeds to trial, the amount of the lodgement becomes relevant. If the plaintiff is successful and the damages awarded by the court are less than or equal to the amount of the lodgement, the plaintiff is at risk of finding themselves liable to pay a significant portion of the defendant's costs as well as of her / his own costs. Hence, the term 'beating the lodgement'.

Prior to the commencement of the 2009 Act, where the claim was for defamation, a lodgement into court was made only where the defendant admitted liability. Section 29 of the *Defamation Act, 2009* introduced an important new rule that lodgements in defamation claims can be made without any admission of liability by the defendant publisher.

The lodgement procedure allows a defendant (i) to indicate the value they put on the plaintiff's claim for damages should the plaintiff succeed in the claim, and (ii) to exert pressure on the plaintiff, through the ensuing risk of being held liable for a significant portion of both their own and the defendant's costs, to accept the lodgement rather than continuing with the claim.

In High Court defamation trials, the jury is not made aware of the fact that a lodgement has been made and the judge, while aware of the fact of the lodgement, is not made aware of the amount paid into court until liability and damages have been decided by the jury. In Circuit Court cases, which are heard by a judge alone, neither the fact nor the amount of the lodgement is made known to the judge until a determination on liability and damages has been made.

See also

Q5   What is the role of the Circuit Court?
Q6   What is the role of the High Court?
Q9   What are damages and how are they assessed?
Q51   How are damages assessed in a defamation case?

Q61   What is an agreement for indemnity?

An agreement for indemnity under defamation law is an agreement between two parties who each contribute to a publication, whereby one of them indemnifies the other against any financial liabilities (for example, damages and legal costs) that the other may incur as a result of publishing that particular statement or statements.

So, for instance, a writer entering into a publishing contract with a publishing house usually is required to indemnify the publisher in respect of any financial loss or liability the publisher may incur under defamation law (also under the law of confidence, privacy and copyright) as a result of publishing the writer's work. Independent television and radio producers supplying programmes to broadcasters usually are required to provide a similar indemnity to those broadcasters in their commissioning or licensing contracts.

Section 40 of the *Defamation Act, 2009* provides that agreements for indemnity shall be lawful unless, at the time of the publication, the person being indemnified knows that the proposed publication is defamatory and does not have a reasonable belief that any ensuing defamation could be successfully defended. This section seeks to preclude a potentially irresponsible co-publisher, who has been indemnified against losses arising from a proposed publication, from proceeding with that publication where they know it to be defamatory and do not reasonably believe it can be defended.

See also

Q15   What is a publication under defamation law?
Q16   Who is a publisher under defamation law?

Q62   What is an offer of amends?

An offer of amends is a procedure provided for by sections 22 and 23 of the *Defamation Act, 2009*. Its use involves strategic consideration by both the complainant and the publisher against whom a complaint is made.

An offer of amends in respect of an allegedly defamatory publication can be made before defamation proceedings are issued by the complainant or, if proceedings have been issued, at any time up to delivery of the defendant publisher's defence. It must contain the following elements (section 22(5)):

- An offer of a "suitable correction" and "sufficient apology".
- An offer to publish the correction and apology in a manner that is "reasonable and practicable" in the circumstances.
- An offer to pay compensation or damages and costs.

An offer of amends can be made in respect of part only of a published statement or in respect of only a particular defamatory meaning attributable to that statement.

Where the offer is accepted and the manner of its implementation is agreed by both parties, the complainant / plaintiff can apply to the court for an order directing the publisher / defendant to comply with the terms of the agreement reached (section 23(1)(a)). This gives the obligations of the publisher under the agreement the status of an order of court.

Where there is agreement in principle on an offer of amends but disagreement between the parties as to its implementation (for example, disagreement on the terminology and / or manner of publication of the correction and apology), the publisher may apply to court for leave to make a statement of correction and apology in court in terms approved by the court and give an undertaking to the court as to the manner of its publication (section 23(1)(b)).

Where the offer of amends is accepted but there is disagreement between the parties as to the amount of damages or costs to be paid, the publisher may apply to court for a ruling to determine the damages or costs to be paid (section 23(1)(c)).

Where an offer of amends has been made but rejected, the fact of the offer of amends can be relied on by the publisher who made it as a defence in any defamation proceedings brought in respect of the defamatory statement in question. However, this defence will not be successful if the plaintiff proves that the defendant knew, or ought reasonably to have known, at the time of publication that (i) the statement referred to, or was likely to be understood as referring to, the plaintiff and (ii) it was false and defamatory of the plaintiff (section 23(2)). This provision has the effect of discouraging publishers from intentionally or recklessly publishing defamatory statements, and subsequently seeking to protect themselves from liability for defamation by making an offer of amends, relying on that offer as a defence in any ensuing defamation proceedings.

Section 23(5) provides that, if an offer of amends is pleaded as a defence, no other defence may be pleaded – a 'do-or-die' option for a publisher defendant. However, where an offer of amends has been made, there is no obligation on a publisher defendant to plead that offer of amends as a defence (section 23(4)). A publisher who has made an offer of amends that has not been accepted is entitled to make a full defence of the claim on whatever grounds she / he sees fit.

See also

Q44 Can an apology be construed as an acknowledgment of liability in a defamation action?

MEDIA CONTENT REGULATION

Q63   What is the Press Council and what does it do?

The Press Council is an independent, print media regulatory body established by the newspaper industry in January 2008. The Press Council has published a *Code of Practice* with which newspapers and periodicals that are members of the Council are expected to comply. In April 2010, the Minister for Justice, Equality and Law Reform formally recognised the Press Council for the purposes of section 44 of the *Defamation Act, 2009* (SI 163 of 2010). This formal recognition was relevant for the purposes of the fair and reasonable publication defence provided for by section 26 of the Act.

The Press Council is made up of the owners of newspapers, magazines and other print periodicals. A full list of members of the Press Council is available on the Council's website, **www.presscouncil.ie**. The Council has 13 directors – seven representing the public interest, five representing newspaper and periodical owners and one representing journalists. Decisions of the Press Council strictly are, in effect, decisions of the board of directors of the Press Council.

The Press Council appoints a Press Ombudsman, who receives and investigates complaints of breaches of the *Code of Practice*. The Ombudsman focuses initially on resolving the complaint informally between the newspaper or periodical concerned and the complainant. Failing resolution of the complaint through conciliation, he will make a finding in favour of one or other party. He will direct the publication of any finding upholding a complaint in the newspaper or periodical concerned.

If either the complainant or the publication in question does not accept the Ombudsman's decision, they may appeal the decision to the Press Council, which will consider and make a decision on the matter. It is also open to the Ombudsman to refer particular complaints, such as those involving points of significant public interest, directly to the Press Council for determination should he so choose.

The Press Council can, and does, direct that its determinations upholding complaints be published in the newspaper or periodical concerned.

Neither the Ombudsman nor the Press Council can impose financial penalties in respect of breaches of the *Code of Practice* or refusals to abide by their decisions. However, failure to observe the *Code of Practice* and failure to abide by the determinations of the Press Ombudsman and the Press Council are factors that can be taken into consideration by the court in a defamation claim where the defendant publisher is relying on the defence of fair and reasonable publication under section 26 of the 2009 Act. Section 26 thus gives the *Code of Practice* and the findings of the Press Ombudsman and Press Council an unusual form of quasi-enforceability in the courts.

The Press Council publishes a quarterly newsletter and its decisions and those of the Press Ombudsman are published on the Council's website. It is important for newspaper and magazine journalists in particular to monitor the decisions of the Ombudsman and Press Council; familiarity with those decisions could be relevant to making a fair and reasonable publication defence in a defamation action.

The Press Ombudsman will not consider a complaint if legal proceedings have been issued in respect of the publication complained of. However, a complainant to the Press Council is not precluded from bringing legal proceedings arising from that publication subsequent to, or in lieu of, using the Press Council complaints procedure if they so choose.

The Press Council complaints mechanism offers speedy and informal redress for an individual who feels they have been inaccurately portrayed or unfairly treated in a publication by a newspaper or periodical. It offers a relatively low-key mechanism for addressing complaints of invasions of privacy by the print media. Depending on the circumstances, this may be more attractive to a complainant than the potential expense, time and stress of bringing a defamation or privacy action in the courts.

See also

Q34 What is the fair and reasonable publication defence?

Q64   What is the Broadcasting Authority of Ireland and what does it do?

The Broadcasting Authority of Ireland (BAI) is the State regulatory body for broadcasting and has a two-fold function:

- To enter into *contracts* authorising the operation of private sector radio and television broadcasting services.
- To secure *compliance* by both public service and private sector broadcasters with regulatory obligations set out by statute and broadcast codes prepared by the BAI.

The BAI was established on 1 October 2009 under the *Broadcasting Authority Act, 2009*. It is the regulatory authority for both private and public sector broadcasting organisations, and fulfils the roles formerly carried out by the Broadcasting Commission of Ireland (BCI) and the Broadcasting Complaints Commission (BCC), both of which ceased to exist by virtue of the 2009 Act. The BAI's structure and principal objectives are:

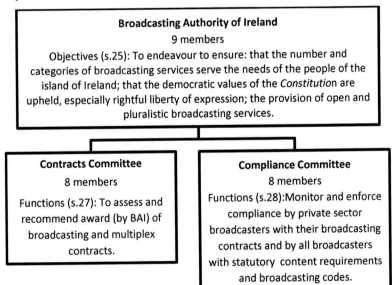

Broadcasting Authority of Ireland
9 members
Objectives (s.25): To endeavour to ensure: that the number and categories of broadcasting services serve the needs of the people of the island of Ireland; that the democratic values of the *Constitution* are upheld, especially rightful liberty of expression; the provision of open and pluralistic broadcasting services.

Contracts Committee
8 members
Functions (s.27): To assess and recommend award (by BAI) of broadcasting and multiplex contracts.

Compliance Committee
8 members
Functions (s.28):Monitor and enforce compliance by private sector broadcasters with their broadcasting contracts and by all broadcasters with statutory content requirements and broadcasting codes.

The 2009 Act specifies the manner of appointment of members of the BAI and each of its statutory committees – the Contracts Committee and the Compliance Committee (section 8). The criteria for membership of the Authority and its statutory committees are set out in section 9 of the 2009 Act with the aim of ensuring that the membership includes people with experience in matters related to broadcasting as well as people with experience of diverse interest areas including the arts, culture, science, technology, law, sport, social, educational and community affairs.

The BAI cannot issue a radio or television broadcasting contract until such time as it has received a licence from the Communications Regulator to allocate a particular frequency range to that contractor / station (section 59).

The Communications Regulator is the Commission for Communications Regulation, a statutory body established by the *Communications Regulation Act, 2002* with responsibility for the regulation of electronic communications (telecommunications, radio communications and broadcasting transmission) and postal services within the State.

TV3, which commenced broadcasting in 1998, is the first and to date only private sector, national terrestrial television service in Ireland. In addition, there are currently 12 other television channels licensed by the BAI. These channels operate on an exclusively commercial basis (community channels on a not-for-profit basis). RTÉ, by comparison, is a public sector broadcaster and is funded partly by an allocation of funds by the State (calculated by reference to the proceeds of television licence fees) and partly on a commercial basis. The daily and hourly advertising time allocation for private sector broadcasters is designated by the BAI (section 42). The BAI also has an input into the approval of the daily and hourly advertising time allocation for RTÉ and TG4 (section 106). A higher advertising minutage is allowed to private sector broadcasters, in consideration of the fact that they do not receive financial support from the State as public sector broadcasters do. TG4 is funded by a combination of public funds, advertising revenue and support by way of supply of some programme material by RTÉ. The proportion of its overall funding received from public funds is greater than in the case of RTÉ, due to its special interest remit as a primarily Irish language station.

On foot of section 154 of the 2009 Act, the BAI has established a Broadcasting Funding Scheme known as Sound and Vision II. Funds in this scheme are allocated by the BAI towards the production costs of selected radio, television or film projects on the broad theme of Irish culture, heritage and experience (excluding news and current affairs productions). The scheme is funded by way of allocation of a sum equivalent to 7% of net annual receipts from the collection of television licences (sections 156 and 157).

The BAI is required by section 42 of the Act to prepare broadcasting codes relating to a range of matters set out in the section relating to programme content standards, advertising and advertising aimed at children (see **Q65**).

The BAI is required by section 43 of the Act to prepare broadcasting rules that address the allocation of broadcast time to advertising and tele-shopping as well as 'access rules' relating to access to broadcasting services by people with visual or hearing impairments.

The BAI is required to impose levies on all broadcasters – public service and private sector – to pay for its operating costs (section 33).

See also

Q65 What regulatory requirements apply to broadcast programme content and advertisements?

Q66 How does the Broadcasting Authority of Ireland secure compliance by broadcasters with regulatory obligations and codes?

www.bai.ie – Broadcasting Authority of Ireland.
www.comreg.ie – Commission for Communications Regulation.

Q65 What regulatory requirements apply to broadcast programme content and advertisements?

Radio and television broadcasters regulated by the Broadcasting Authority of Ireland (BAI) are required to comply with:

- The provisions of sections 39 and 41 of the *Broadcasting Authority Act, 2009*.

- Broadcasting codes prepared by the BAI under section 42 of the 2009 Act.

- Access and advertising / tele-shopping rules made under section 43 of the 2009 Act.

Provisions of sections 39 and 41 of the *Broadcasting Authority Act, 2009*
Section 39 requires broadcasters to ensure that:

- News is reported and presented in an objective and impartial manner and without any expression of the broadcaster's own views (section 39(1)(a)). Note that the Act implicitly acknowledges that it may not be possible to secure balance and fairness in the reporting of news as it breaks. News broadcasting is primarily concerned with straight reportage of events as they unfold. However, it should be borne in mind that news programmes may contain stories that require fair representation of all sides' points of view on a matter of public interest for the purposes of defamation law. Further, news programmes usually comprise a mix of news reportage along with commentary and discussion.

- Current affairs, including matters of public controversy or current public debate, are treated on air in a manner that is "fair to all interests concerned" and presented in an objective and impartial manner without any expression of the broadcaster's own views (section 39(1)(b)). It is from this requirement that the concept of 'balance' in current affairs programming derives. The requirement comes into sharp focus at times of elections and constitutional referenda, although it applies across the spectrum of current affairs programmes and discussions at all times.

- In the case of radio broadcasters, they devote a minimum of 20% of their broadcasting time to news and current affairs programmes. Where programming extends above 12 hours per day, at least two hours of news and current affairs programming must be broadcast in the peak period of 7 a.m. to 7 p.m. (section 39(1)(c)). The BAI is empowered to authorise a derogation from this sometimes controversial requirement in respect of radio stations, where it is satisfied that this would be to the benefit of listeners to that radio service (section 39(3)).

- They do not broadcast material that could reasonably be regarded as causing harm or offence or as being likely to promote or incite to crime or tending to undermine the authority of the State (section 39(1)(d)). This provision reflects the qualification of the right to express convictions and opinions contained in Article 40.6.1° of the *Constitution*.

- The privacy of any individual is not "unreasonably encroached upon" either in broadcast programmes or in the means employed to make those programmes (section 39(1)(e)). This provision implicitly recognises that there may be circumstances where an encroachment of privacy is reasonable and, therefore, not in breach of this statutory provision. There are no hard and fast rules, however, for assessing this criterion of 'reasonableness'. Since this privacy provision relates not only to broadcast programmes but also to the means employed to make those programmes, a broadcaster can be in breach of this provision in a pre-transmission situation.

Section 39(2) contains an explicit provision permitting broadcasters to transmit party political broadcasts, provided that the time allocated for such broadcasts does not result in "unfair preference" being given to any particular party. Stations are not permitted by the BAI to charge a fee for broadcasting a party political broadcast, as this could constitute political advertising, which is prohibited by the Act.

Section 41 is concerned with advertising, and prohibits political advertising or advertising relating to any industrial dispute (section 41(3)). What constitutes 'political advertising' has given rise to occasional controversy in the past – for example, in 2007, the BCI (BAI's predecessor body) directed broadcasters coming under its remit to withdraw a Lenten advertisement by the aid agency Trócaire on the grounds of its apparent breach of an equivalent ban contained in the pre-2009 legislation on advertising towards a political end. The advertisement highlighted the issue of gender inequality in the developing world and referred the public to the organisation's website, which contained a petition against gender inequality that members of the public could sign.

Section 41(4) reiterates a qualified ban on religious advertising that featured in pre-2009 broadcasting legislation. The ban is not an absolute one, but is so narrowly drawn that the usefulness of broadcast media for religious advertising is limited.

Broadcasting codes prepared by the BAI under section 42 of the *Broadcasting Authority Act, 2009*

Section 42 requires the BAI to prepare broadcasting codes that must be observed by broadcasters. The codes must address:

- The matters set out at section 39 and discussed above (excluding the 20% designated news and current affairs programming requirement, which is a scheduling issue).

- The issue of "harmful or offensive material" – in particular, material that portrays violence and sexual conduct (section 42(f)).

- Advertising (including, specifically, advertising directed at children), tele-shopping, sponsorship and other forms of commercial communication (section 42(2)(g) and (h)).

- Certain matters referred to in the *Audio Visual Media Services Directive* (*Directive 2010/13/EU*, which consolidates earlier Directives specified in the 2009 Act), including hate speech, the EU-wide ban on cigarette and tobacco advertising, restrictions on alcohol advertising and the protection of minors (section 42(2)(j)).

Revised broadcasting codes on children's advertising and general advertising were published in 2010 by the BAI. The pre-2009 *Code of Programme Standards* published by the former Broadcasting Commission of Ireland continues to apply to broadcasters, pending revision of that code by the BAI. These codes can be accessed through **www.bai.ie**.

Access and advertising / tele-shopping rules made under section 43 of the 2009 Act

Section 43 requires the BAI to prepare *Broadcasting Rules*. These rules are concerned with:

- The allocation by private sector broadcasters licensed by the BAI of schedule time to advertising and tele-shopping.
- Arrangements for access to broadcasting services for people with visual or hearing impairments.

New *Rules* for the allocation by private sector broadcasters of schedule time to advertising and tele-shopping were published by the BAI in 2010. The *Access Rules* in relation to people with visual or hearing impairments issued by the former Broadcasting Commission of Ireland continue to apply at the time of writing.

See also

Q10   How is the right to freedom of expression protected under Irish law?
Q64   What is the Broadcasting Authority of Ireland and what does it do?
Q66   How does the Broadcasting Authority of Ireland secure compliance with regulatory obligations and codes?
Q67   Is 'hate speech' unlawful?
Q70   How is privacy protected under Irish law?

Q66 How does the Broadcasting Authority of Ireland secure compliance by broadcasters with regulatory obligations and codes?

There are three mechanisms available to the Broadcasting Authority of Ireland (BAI) under the *Broadcasting Act, 2009* to secure compliance with regulatory obligations and codes by broadcasters:

- Consideration by the Compliance Committee of a listener's / viewer's complaint.

- Investigation by the Compliance Committee of a breach of statutory obligations or codes and reference to the Authority.

- Right of reply procedure.

Section 47 of the 2009 Act requires all broadcasters to give "due and adequate consideration" to listener / viewer complaints that are made in good faith and are not of a "frivolous or vexatious nature". Section 47 also requires all broadcasters to set up an internal code of practice for handling listener / viewer complaints and to publish that code on their station's website. Record-keeping is important, as the Compliance Committee is entitled to require the production by broadcasters of records of complaints-handling for up to two years after any complaint is made.

Consideration by the Compliance Committee of a listener's / viewer's complaint

Under section 48 of the 2009 Act, the Compliance Committee may investigate complaints that:

- A broadcaster has breached its obligations under section 39(1) (such as fairness in current affairs programming, but excluding the paragraph concerning the 20% news and current affairs quota); or

- A broadcaster has failed to observe any of the codes provided for by section 42 of the Act (such as a programme standards code or advertising code).

The complaint must be made within 30 days of the broadcast complained of (if more than one broadcast is complained about, the time period is as set out in section 48(2)). The Committee has the option of initially referring the matter to be investigated in accordance with the internal complaints handling procedure of the broadcaster concerned. In certain circumstances set out in the Act, an employee of the broadcaster involved in the making of the programme complained of, or an independent producer who made the programme, may be granted an opportunity in their own right to comment on the complaint (section 48(5)). The Compliance Committee is obliged to give its decision on a complaint in writing and must give reasons for its decision (section 48(7)).

Consideration of complaints made to the Compliance Committee may be carried out in private (section 48(9)). There is provision for the Committee to hold oral hearings on a complaint where it considers this to be appropriate (section 48(16)).

The Compliance Committee has no power to award costs or expenses of any nature (section 48(12)).

The Compliance Committee must publish its findings (unless it deems such publication inappropriate – for example, for privacy reasons). Furthermore, a broadcaster against which a finding has been made, is obliged to broadcast the finding to the same audience reach as the original offending broadcast. The only exception is where the Compliance Committee deems it inappropriate for the broadcaster to do so (sections 48(10) and (11)).

The decisions of the Compliance Committee are published on the BAI website (**www.bai.ie**). It is useful for broadcasters to monitor these decisions so as to become familiar with the manner in which the Committee assesses compliance with the provisions of the section 39(1) obligations of broadcasters and the provisions of the BAI broadcasting codes.

Investigation by the Compliance Committee of a breach of statutory obligations or codes and reference to the Authority

Section 53 gives wide-ranging powers to the Compliance Committee to investigate on its own initiative and to report on a range of apparent breaches of statutory obligation and broadcasting codes or broadcasting rules such as *Access Rules* (see section 53(1)). In this context, a breach means "a serious or repeated failure" to comply with a relevant statutory obligation, code or rule (section 52). Such investigations will be conducted by investigators appointed by the Compliance Committee and broadcasters are obliged to co-operate with the investigators. Failure to co-operate with an investigation can render the broadcaster liable to similar sanctions to those that apply if the broadcaster is found to be in breach of a relevant obligation, code or rule. Broadcasters are given an opportunity to make their own responses to the matter being investigated in a manner similar to that which pertains in respect of a listener / viewer complaint.

The Compliance Committee investigation procedure can lead to the imposition of a fine up to a maximum of €250,000. This new power in respect of regulatory compliance is granted to the BAI by section 54 of the 2009 Act. However, there is quite a complex procedure to be followed before such a fine can be imposed (sections 53, 54 and 55). At the time of writing, no fines have been imposed by the BAI.

Right of reply procedure

The State is obliged to provide a right of reply mechanism in respect of television broadcasts by the EU *Audio Visual Media Services Directive (Directive 2010/13/EU)*. The right of reply provided for by section 49 of the 2009 Act extends to both radio and television broadcasts.

The right of reply procedure is available to any person whose honour or reputation has been impugned by an assertion of incorrect facts or information in a broadcast. This is a new non-judicial remedy for persons aggrieved by the contents of a broadcast. The BAI is obliged to set up a right of reply scheme. At the time of writing, a consultation process on a draft right to reply scheme has concluded but a scheme has yet to be published.

The request for a right of reply must be made initially to the broadcaster. It is only if the broadcaster refuses to grant the right of reply that the refusal can be referred to the BAI's Compliance Committee. The broadcaster is entitled to comment on the matter before the Compliance Committee makes its final decision on whether a right of reply should be granted. The Committee may over-rule the broadcaster's refusal to broadcast a reply and require the broadcaster to grant a right of reply to the complainant. If the broadcaster persists in refusing, the Committee may give the broadcaster a further opportunity to explain its refusal before deciding whether to recommend that the BAI refer the matter to the High Court for a court order securing compliance with the Committee's decision that a right of reply should be granted.

Because the right of reply is relevant where a person's "honour or reputation" is at stake, there are potential defamation implications inherent in granting a right of reply. The provisions of section 49(13) and (14) are important in this regard. These sub-sections provide that the grant of a right of reply does not constitute, in a defamation action, an admission of liability by a broadcaster and is not relevant to the determination of liability (section 39(13)). However, a broadcaster defendant may give evidence in mitigation of damages that a right of reply was granted under section 49 to the plaintiff (section 39(14)).

Where the Compliance Committee has reasonable grounds to believe that a private sector broadcaster licensed by the BAI is not providing a broadcasting service in accordance with its contract (licence), the Committee may investigate the matter (section 50). The Committee has power to recommend to the BAI that it terminate or suspend a broadcasting contract where such a breach is found to have occurred and the Committee believes the seriousness of that breach merits that termination or suspension (section 51).

See also

Q9   What are damages and how are they assessed?
Q44   Can an apology be construed as an acknowledgment of liability in a defamation action?

Q51   How are damages assessed in a defamation case?

Q64   What is the Broadcasting Authority of Ireland and what does it do?

Q65   What regulatory requirements apply to broadcast programme content and advertisements?

Q67   Is 'hate speech' unlawful?

The *Prohibition of Incitement to Hatred Act, 1989* criminalises 'hate speech' in Ireland.

Section 2 of the 1989 Act makes it a criminal offence to distribute, show or play a recording of visual images or sounds that are "threatening, abusive or insulting and are intended or, having regard to all the circumstances, are likely to stir up hatred". The same section makes it a criminal offence to use words, behave or display written material of that nature and also to publish or distribute written material of that nature. Where such acts take place in a private residence and cannot be seen or heard outside that private residence, this can be offered as a defence under section 2. If a public meeting was being held in the private residence when the alleged offence took place, then this defence will not apply.

Section 3 of the 1989 Act makes it a criminal offence for a person to broadcast an item involving "threatening, abusive or insulting images or sounds" if she / he intends by that broadcast to stir up hatred or, having regard to all the circumstances, hatred is likely to be stirred up thereby. The following categories of person are liable to prosecution where such material is broadcast:

- The person providing the broadcasting service concerned;
- Any person by whom the item concerned is produced or directed; and
- Any person whose words or behaviour in the item concerned are threatening or abusive or insulting (see section 3(2)).

A 'saver' provision is provided for broadcasters, producers and directors in circumstances where, in the absence of an intention to stir up hatred, the defendant proves that they did not know or had no reason to suspect that the item concerned would involve the material that gave rise to the prosecution or where, having regard to the circumstances of the broadcast, it was not reasonably practicable to have that material removed (section 3(3)). The defence provided under section 3(3) could be pleaded, for instance, where despite the care taken by a broadcaster, producer or director in the preparation of a broadcast item, a contributor made an outburst that was threatening, abusive or insulting and comprised an offence under section 2.

Where hate speech considerations tend to cause an editorial dilemma – both ethical and legal – for media outlets is in the publication of statements made by members of the public (for example, by way of text messages sent to a radio show) that have racist content or overtones. On the one hand, these statements reflect a racist strand of public opinion in society which – however odious – arguably should be exposed; on the other hand, *verbatim* reporting of such statements can risk stirring up hatred in the minds of some listeners. In such circumstances, communicating the general tenor of such statements rather than reporting them *verbatim* sometimes may resolve this dilemma.

A commercially-released DVD, video or computer game may be banned by the Irish Film Classification Office on the grounds that it would be likely to stir up hatred against a group of persons in the State on account of their race, colour, nationality, religion, ethnic or national origins, membership of the travelling community or sexual orientation (section 7(1)(a), *Video Recordings Act, 1989*).

In respect of the print media, Principle 8 of the *Press Council Code of Practice* is concerned with the subject of 'prejudice'. It states: "Newspapers and periodicals shall not publish material intended or likely to cause grave offence or stir up hatred against an individual or group on the basis of their race, religion, nationality, colour, ethnic origin, membership of the travelling community, gender, sexual orientation, marital status, disability, illness or age".

Section 42 of the Act requires the BAI to prepare broadcasting codes that provide for, among other elements, certain matters referred to in the *Audio Visual Media Services Directive* (*Directive 2010/13/EU* consolidating earlier Directives referred to in the 2009 Act; see section 42(2)(j) of the Act). Article 16, Chapter II of the Directive requires EU Member States to ensure that audio-visual media services provided by media providers under their jurisdiction do not contain any incitement to hatred based on race, sex, religion or nationality.

See also

Q10   How is the right to freedom of expression protected under Irish law?
Q68   Does equality legislation apply to media content?
Q69   How do censorship laws affect the media?

Q68 Does equality legislation apply to media content?

Equality legislation in Ireland (see the *Employment Equality Act, 1998* and the *Equal Status Act, 2000*) prohibits discrimination in a number of spheres, principally in the workplace and in the provision of goods and services, on nine grounds: gender; marital status; family status; age; disability; race; sexual orientation; religious belief; and membership of the traveller community.

Although the legislation does not apply directly to media content, the principles informing the legislation also inform certain regulatory codes affecting the print and broadcast media.

In respect of the print media, Principle 8 of the *Press Council Code of Practice* is concerned with the subject of 'prejudice'. It states: "Newspapers and periodicals shall not publish material intended or likely to cause grave offence or stir up hatred against an individual or group on the basis of their race, religion, nationality, colour, ethnic origin, membership of the travelling community, gender, sexual orientation, marital status, disability, illness or age".

The public service remit for both public service broadcasters in Ireland includes reference to principles of respect for equality. The 2004 *Public Service Charter* for RTÉ, published by the Department of Communications, Marine and Natural Resources, states at paragraph 3: "No editorial or programming bias shall be shown in terms of gender, age, disability, race, sexual orientation, religion or membership of a minority community" (see **www.rte.ie**). Among the principles informing the delivery by TG4 of its service as set out in its 2010 *Public Service Statement* is the following: "Show no editorial or programming bias in terms of gender, age, disability, race, sexual orientation, religion or membership of a minority community" (see **www.tg4.ie**).

Section 42 of the Act requires the BAI to prepare broadcasting codes that provide for, among other elements, certain matters referred to in the *Audio Visual Media Services Directive* (*Directive 2010/13/EU* consolidating earlier Directives referred to in the 2009 Act; see section 42(2)(j) of the Act). Article 16, Chapter II of the Directive requires EU Member States to ensure that audio-visual media services provided by media providers under their jurisdiction do not contain any incitement to hatred based on race, sex, religion or nationality.

A commercially-released DVD, video or computer game may be banned by the Irish Film Classification Office on the grounds that it would be likely to stir up hatred against a group of persons in the State on account of their race, colour, nationality, religion, ethnic or national origins, membership of the travelling community or sexual orientation (section 7(1)(a), *Video Recordings Act, 1989*).

Accordingly, while equality legislation does not affect media content in Ireland, the same social policy objectives that inform equality legislation are expected to be reflected in print and broadcast media content.

See also

Q63   What is the Press Council and what does it do?

Q64   What is the Broadcasting Authority of Ireland and what does it do?

Q65   What regulatory requirements apply to broadcast programme content and advertisements?

Q66   How does the Broadcasting Authority of Ireland secure compliance by broadcasters with regulatory obligations and codes?

Q67   Is 'hate speech' unlawful?

Q69   How do censorship laws affect the media?

Q69   How do censorship laws affect the media?

Ireland's censorship laws allow authorised bodies (described below) to ban certain books, periodicals, films, DVDs / videos and computer games outright. A certification system is in place, by which the commercial release of films and DVDs / videos is permitted, subject to a classification system of the suitability of those films and DVDs for specific categories of audience and viewers.

Censorship laws do not apply to television or radio broadcasters, which are regulated in respect of their content by broadcasting legislation. Accordingly, films shown on television do not require a certificate – although this exclusion is not explicit in the relevant legislation.

Newspapers and magazines are subject to the censorship regime for books and periodicals, although the potential for any genuine newspaper to become subject to any order under the censorship regime is limited, to the point of being negligible. Generally, the regulation of print media content is by way of voluntary adherence to the *Press Council Code of Practice*.

Books and periodicals

The Censorship of Publications Board was first established under the *Censorship of Publications Act, 1929* and re-established by the *Censorship of Publications Act, 1946*. The 1929 and 1946 Acts were further amended by the *Censorship of Publications Act, 1967*. The Board has the power to make prohibition orders banning the sale and distribution of printed books and periodicals. There is no certification or classification system applicable to books and periodicals; they can only be banned outright if the Board sees fit to do so on the grounds set out in the legislation.

A book may be banned on the grounds that (a) it is indecent or obscene or (b) that it advocates the procurement of abortion. A ban on grounds of indecency or obscenity remains in place for 12 years and then automatically expires; a further ban then may be imposed by the Board. A ban on the ground of advocating the procurement of abortion remains in place indefinitely.

A prohibition order banning a book or periodical may be appealed to the Censorship of Publications Appeal Board by the author, editor or publisher of the book or periodical or by five members of the Oireachtas acting jointly.

A list of the books currently banned in Ireland is available through the website of the Department of Justice (**www.justice.ie**). A high proportion of Ireland's most celebrated writers, including James Joyce, Edna O'Brien, John McGahern, Frank O'Connor and Brendan Behan, share the distinction of having had their work banned by the Censorship of Publications Board. In recent years, the banning of books in Ireland is a very rare occurrence.

A periodical, such as a magazine, may be banned for a period of three, six or 12 months depending on its frequency of publication. The grounds for banning a periodical are (a) indecency or obscenity; (b) advocating the procurement of abortion; and (c) the devotion of an unusually large proportion of space to matter relating to crime. The banning of *In Dublin* magazine in August 1999, which carried advertisements for 'massage parlours' and escort services, caused controversy at the time. The most recent banning of a periodical was the banning of a pornographic magazine in 2003.

A book or periodical may be referred by a Customs Officer or a member of the public to the Censorship of Publications Board for examination. The Board also may examine a book or periodical on its own initiative.

Films

The *Censorship of Films Act, 1923* specified that no film may be exhibited in public without a certificate from the Film Censor (section 5). In 2008, following the passing of the *Civil Law (Miscellaneous Provisions) Act, 2008*, the office of the Official Censor was re-named the Irish Film Classification Office (IFCO) and the Film Censor became known as the Director of Film Classification (DFC).

Under section 7 of the 1923 Act, as amended by section 70 of the 2008 Act, IFCO has the power to refuse a certificate or grant a qualified certificate only (for example, over 18s) for the public exhibition of a film if the DFC is of the opinion that the film is (a) likely to cause harm to children; (b) is indecent, obscene or blasphemous; or (c) because its public exhibition would (i) tend to inculcate principles contrary to public morality or (ii) be otherwise subversive of public morality. IFCO is entitled to require that a cut be made to a film as a pre-requisite to the DFC issuing a certificate for its public exhibition.

In practice, the DFC, who is assisted in her / his functions by a Deputy and several Assistant Classifiers, is principally concerned with film classification and issuing certificates for public exhibition based on those classifications. An explanation of the IFCO classification system for films is available on **www.ifco.ie**. Films shown privately, for instance to private film clubs, do not require certification from the DFC.

A right of appeal, which may be exercised by any person, is available to the Classification of Films Appeal Board against a refusal by IFCO of a certificate for public exhibition of a film or against an IFCO classification of a film.

DVDs and videos

Under the *Video Recordings Act, 1989* (as amended by the *Civil Law (Miscellaneous Provisions) Act, 2008*), no video (and the statutory definition of a "video work" applies to DVDs) may be supplied on a commercial basis to the public unless it has been certified as fit for viewing by the Director of Film Classification (DFC) through the Irish Film Classification Office (IFCO). A supply certificate will be subject to a classification given to that video by IFCO. Where IFCO is not prepared to grant any certificate for the supply of a video, the DFC must issue a prohibition certificate prohibiting the supply of the video.

The grounds on which a supply certificate may be denied are that, in the opinion of the DFC the viewing of the film would (a) be likely to cause persons to commit crimes; (b) would be likely to stir up hatred against a group of persons in the State on account of their race, colour, nationality, religion, ethnic or national origins, membership of the travelling community or sexual orientation; (c) would tend, by reason of containing obscene or indecent matter, to deprave or corrupt viewers; or (d) that the video depicts acts of gross violence or cruelty, including acts of torture, against animals or humans (section 7(1)(a) and (b)). A right of appeal is available to any person to the Classification of Films Appeal Board against a prohibition order or the IFCO classification of a video.

The commercial supply or possession for supply of an uncertified video or a video in respect of which a prohibition order is in place is a criminal offence, as is the supply of a video to a person outside the class of people for whom a video has been classified as fit for viewing – for example, the sale or rental of a video to a child where the classification is that it may be sold or rented to viewers over 18 years of age only.

Music videos, unless they are liable to being prohibited under section 7 of the 1989 Act on any of the grounds set out above, are exempt from the certification and classification provisions of the Act by reference to the definition of "exempted work" in section 1 of the 1989 Act.

Computer games

The certification and classification system that applies to films and DVDs / videos under the *Video Recordings Act, 1989* does not apply to computer games, which are covered by the definition of "exempted work" under section 1 of the Act. However, a computer game may be prohibited by the Irish Film Classification Office on any of the grounds set out in section 7 of that Act (see section on DVDs and videos above).

Ireland is a founder member of the Pan-European Game Information (PEGI) ratings system for children's computer games and the Deputy Director of Film Classification is a member of the PEGI Advisory Board. PEGI is a voluntary system of classification supported by the main console manufacturers, including Nintendo, Sony and Microsoft, as well as by developers of computer games across Europe. The objective of PEGI ratings is to enable parents to make informed choices about the suitability of computer games for use by children.

See also

Q63   What is the Press Council and what does it do?
Q64   What is the Broadcasting Authority of Ireland and what does it do?

Q65 What regulatory requirements apply to broadcast programme content and advertisements?

Q66 How does the Broadcasting Authority of Ireland secure compliance by broadcasters with regulatory obligations and codes?

Q67 Is 'hate speech' unlawful?

Q68 Does equality legislation apply to media content?

PRIVACY AND DATA PROTECTION

Q70   How is privacy protected under Irish law?

Privacy is a constitutional right under Irish law. It is not an *explicit* fundamental right under the Constitution but has been recognised by the courts as an *un-enumerated* constitutional right. These are rights deemed to be implicit in the Constitution, which are articulated by the courts on a case-by-case basis.

In *McGee v AG [1973] IESC 2*, the Supreme Court held that a statutory ban on the importation of contraceptives amounted to an unwarranted intrusion on the constitutionally-protected right to marital privacy of the plaintiff, a mother of four who had been advised on health grounds against any further pregnancies.

Ten years later, in *Norris v AG [1983] IESC 3*, the Supreme Court held, by a 3:2 majority judgment, that 19th century legislation criminalising certain homosexual sexual acts did not unlawfully encroach on the constitutional rights of the plaintiff, including his right to privacy. The court acknowledged that Mr Norris (now Senator Norris) had a constitutional right to privacy but held that, in the circumstances of the case, the common good favoured the criminalisation of homosexual behaviour. Mr Norris subsequently obtained a declaration from the European Court of Human Rights that the legislation in question amounted to a denial by the State of his right to respect for his private life under the *European Convention* on Human Rights (Article 8) – see *Norris v Ireland (E.Ct.H.R. 26.10.88, Application no. 10581/83)*. In 1993, legislation was passed in Ireland de-criminalising the offence of buggery (see section 2, *Criminal Law (Sexual Offences) Act, 1993* – however, under section 3 of the Act, buggery of a person under the age of 17 continues to be an offence).

In 1987, two Irish journalists – Geraldine Kennedy and Bruce Arnold – along with Mr Arnold's wife, claimed damages in the High Court against the State after it had been revealed that the State, without lawful justification, had tapped the home telephones of both journalists. This was held to be an unlawful encroachment on their constitutional right to privacy, specifically in their private communications. The State was ordered to pay damages to the plaintiffs – see *Kennedy and Ors v Ireland [1987] 1 IR 587.*

In each of these cases, the courts recognised the existence of a constitutional right to privacy but also that the right was not absolute; that it could be qualified or restricted by reference to the requirements of the common good. This is a critical point to be borne in mind when considering the law of privacy in Ireland.

In *Cogley and Aherne v RTÉ [2005] IEHC 180,* the plaintiffs were respectively the Director of Nursing and the owners of the Leas Cross nursing home in Dublin. RTÉ's *Prime Time* team had filmed surreptitiously in the nursing home and proposed broadcasting extracts of the footage filmed. The plaintiffs sought – and were refused – an injunction prohibiting the broadcast of the programme on the grounds of defamation (Ms Cogley and the Ahernes) and breach of privacy and trespass (the Ahernes). The case required the balancing of the various constitutional rights engaged in the action: the right to freedom of expression, the right to protection of reputation and the right to privacy. The public interest in the matter of the standards of care in the nursing home and the effectiveness of the regulation regime for nursing homes were central to the judge's findings on the issue of privacy and he refused an injunction prohibiting the broadcast.

Any lingering legal doubts as to whether damages were recoverable in an action for unlawful breach of privacy against a private entity (as opposed to the State) were removed by the judgment in *Herrity v Associated Newspapers (Ireland) Ltd [2008] IEHC 249.* In the Herrity case, a series of three articles was published by the newspaper then known as *Ireland on Sunday.* The articles revealed details of a love affair between the plaintiff and a man who, at the time, was her parish priest. The woman's estranged husband had unlawfully intercepted telephone conversations between the plaintiff and her lover. Two of the articles contained transcripts of parts of those telephone conversations. Having considered the prior Irish case law, Judge Dunne summarised the position of the law of privacy in Ireland as follows:

"(1) There is a Constitutional right to privacy.

(2) The right to privacy is not an unqualified right.

(3) The right to privacy may have to be balanced against other competing rights or interests.

(4) The right to privacy may be derived from the nature of the information at issue – that is, matters that are entirely private to an individual and in respect of which it may be validly contended that there is no proper basis for the disclosure either to third parties or to the public generally.

(5) There may be circumstances in which an individual may not be able to maintain that the information concerned must always be kept private, having regard to the competing interests that may be involved, but may make a complaint in relation to the manner in which the information was obtained.

(6) The right to sue for damages for breach of the constitutional right to privacy is not confined to actions against the State or State bodies or institutions".

In applying these findings to the facts of the case, Judge Dunne stated, "There is a hierarchy of constitutional rights and, as a general proposition, I think that cases in which the right to privacy will prevail over the right to freedom of expression may well be far and few between. However, this may not always be the case and there are circumstances where it seems to me the right to privacy could be such that it would prevail over the right to freedom of expression". She held that the State had passed legislation specifically making the unauthorised interception of telephone calls unlawful in order to protect the privacy of an individual's telephone conversations. While she conceded a level of public interest existed in exposing the failure of a parish priest to observe his celibacy vows, and that this could possibly extend to identifying Ms Herrity as his lover, this public interest did not justify the publication of much of the material that appeared in the articles.

In *Hickey v Sunday Newspapers Ltd [2010] IEHC 349*, the plaintiff was the new partner of a man who had been married to a well-known entertainer. The action also was brought in the name of her infant son. Ms Hickey's partner is the father of her child. Ms Hickey, her infant son and her partner had been photographed on the public street, having just come out of the public Registry of Births, Marriages and Deaths. The photographs were published on two separate occasions by the defendant newspaper. The judge hearing the case dismissed the claim. He concluded that Ms Hickey had been photographed on the public street having just performed a public function (the registration of the birth of her son). "This was not a private celebration or event in the plaintiff's own home or at some other location to which a legitimate expectancy of privacy attached", he said. The judge placed emphasis on the fact that the plaintiff herself had given interviews to the media in the past about her relationship with the child's father and the fact of her pregnancy. Another part of the claim brought in defamation was also dismissed. This is the first Irish case that has considered the extent of protection of privacy that a person with a degree of public profile or 'celebrity status' may expect under Irish law.

There has been legal discussion as to the precise legal nature of actions for damages for breach of privacy. The general view is that no common law tort of breach of privacy exists but that a right to claim damages for breach of the constitutional right to privacy exists as a 'constitutional tort'. Whatever its precise legal basis, it is now beyond doubt that a right to claim damages in respect of unlawful invasion of privacy exists under Irish law, both as against the State and against private entities such as newspaper publishers.

The *European Convention on Human Rights*

Section 3(1) of the *European Convention on Human Rights Act, 2003* requires every organ of the State to "perform its functions in a manner compatible with the State's obligations under the *Convention* provisions". Section 2(1) requires that Irish courts, when interpreting or applying the law, shall "in so far as is possible, subject to the rules of law relating to such interpretation and application, do so in a manner compatible with the State's obligations under the *Convention* provisions".

Article 8 of the *Convention* reads: "1. Everyone has the right to respect for his private and family life, his home and his correspondence. 2. There shall be no interference by a public authority with the exercise of this right except such as is in accordance with the law and is necessary in a democratic society in the interests of national security, public safety or the economic well-being of the country, for the prevention of crime, for the protection of health or morals, or for the protection of the rights and freedoms of others".

It can be seen from paragraph 2 of Article 8 that the right to respect for privacy is not absolute; the Article recognises that there are circumstances – related to different aspects of the public interest and the protection of the rights of others (which include the right to freedom of expression) – where that right to privacy may be restricted to a greater or lesser extent.

Section 4 of the 2003 Act requires judges in Irish courts to take "judicial notice" of, among other matters, the decisions of the European Court of Human Rights and to take "due account" of the principles laid down by those decisions, when interpreting and applying *Convention* provisions in Irish courts. Accordingly, the Irish courts have taken increasing cognisance of the decisions of the European Court of Human Rights concerning the interpretation of the Article 8 right.

One of the most significant of these decisions in recent years has been that of *Von Hannover v Germany (E.Ct.H.R. 24.06.2004, Application no. 59320/00)*. The case was brought by Caroline Von Hannover – better known as Princess Caroline of Monaco – who sought a declaration that her right to respect for her privacy under Article 8 of the *Convention* had been infringed by the refusal of the German courts to grant an injunction preventing the re-publication by two German magazine publishers of certain photographs taken of her going about her private life. The court found in favour of Princess Caroline, holding that the decisive factor in finding the balance between the media's right to freedom of expression and the applicant's right to protection of her privacy was the contribution the publication of the photographs made to "a debate of general interest".

The court held that, even though Princess Caroline was well-known to the public, she exercised no official functions and the photographs related exclusively to details of her private life. The court held that the publication of the photographs made no contribution to a debate of general interest. The court also held that the public did not have a legitimate interest in knowing the applicant's whereabouts and what she did in her private life, even when she was in places that were not secluded. The German courts had reasoned that, as a public figure *par excellence*, she could not expect privacy unless she was in secluded places where she could expect to go about her domestic life in private. This rationale was not accepted by the court, which held that, in the circumstances, Princess Caroline was entitled to a "legitimate expectation" of protection of her privacy under German law. This protection had not been provided and Germany was held to be in breach of its Article 8 obligations towards the applicant. This case was considered by the Irish court in the Hickey case referred to above.

The Universal Declaration of Human Rights

The right to privacy is also protected by the *International Covenant on Civil and Political Rights* (ICCPR), which in turn enshrines in an international treaty the rights set out in the United Nations' *Universal Declaration on Human Rights* (see Article 12 referring to privacy). Article 17 of the ICCPR states:

"1. No one shall be subjected to arbitrary or unlawful interference with his privacy, family, home or correspondence, nor to unlawful attacks on his honour and reputation.

2. Everyone has the right to the protection of the law against such interference or attacks."

While Ireland is a signatory to the ICCPR and subscribes to its principles, its provisions have not been incorporated directly into Irish domestic law by legislation.

Legislation

While there is no Irish legislation concerned exclusively with the law of privacy, a number of statutory provisions deal with aspects of personal privacy. A Privacy Bill that was published and introduced in the Seanad in 2006 attracted extensive criticism of its provisions from the media and some lawyers, who argued that its provisions would be unduly restrictive of the right to freedom of expression. At time of writing, that Bill has not been enacted.

See also

Q1   What are the sources of Irish law?
Q10   How is the right to freedom of expression protected under Irish law?
Q71   What legislation provides for the protection of privacy under Irish law?

     www.bailii.org – database of UK and Irish case law.
     www.echr.coe.int – see Hudoc database of European Court of Human Rights case law.

Q71 What legislation provides for the protection of privacy under Irish law?

The right to privacy is a constitutional right in Ireland, which the courts and other organs of the State are constitutionally obliged to protect and vindicate. The right to privacy must be observed and respected by private individuals and entities, as well as by State authorities. The courts will award damages against a State authority, individual or entity that unlawfully breaches a plaintiff's privacy.

There is no specific privacy legislation under Irish law. A Privacy Bill was introduced to the Seanad in 2006 but has not proceeded further in the legislative process to date. The Bill, among other proposals, contained a provision that would have created a statutory tort (civil wrong) of 'violation of privacy'. When initially published, the Bill attracted extensive criticism from media organisations and some lawyers who believed that its provisions unduly restricted the right to freedom of expression.

Several items of legislation contain reference to the protection of privacy. Those most relevant to the media are summarised below.

Section 39(1)(e) of the *Broadcasting Act, 2009*
"Every broadcaster shall ensure that ...

(e) in programmes broadcast by the broadcaster, and in the means employed to make such programmes, the privacy of any individual is not unreasonably encroached upon."

This statutory requirement applies, not only to the broadcast of programmes, but also to the means employed to make such programmes. Thus it is possible for a programme producer to be held accountable for a breach of privacy that occurs during the production process. There is no indication in the Act of what will or will not be regarded as a 'reasonable', as opposed to 'unreasonable', encroachment on privacy. It is suggested that this can be assessed by reference to the extent to which the common good or public interest will be served, despite that encroachment on privacy.

The Broadcasting Authority of Ireland (BAI) is required, under section 42 of the 2009 Act, to prepare broadcasting codes that address, among other matters, the privacy requirements reflected in section 39(1)(e). At the time of writing, no broadcasting code dealing with privacy has been prepared by the BAI. The corresponding code for broadcasters in the UK was prepared by Ofcom and is available on the Stakeholders / Broadcasting section of its website (**www.ofcom.org.uk** – see Section 8, which concerns privacy). The *RTÉ Programme Standards Guidelines* also consider the issue of privacy (see **www.rte.ie**). These codes do not have the status of law but they contain useful guidance for media producers and outline the relevant considerations when balancing freedom of expression and public interest against the right to protection of privacy. A breach of section 39(1) or breach of a broadcasting code can give rise to a complaint and / or BAI investigation.

Section 10 of the *Non-Fatal Offences Against the Person Act, 1997*

Section 10 (1) creates the criminal offence of harassment in the following terms:

> "Any person who, without lawful authority or reasonable excuse, by any means including by use of the telephone, harasses another by persistently following, watching, pestering, besetting or communicating with him or her, shall be guilty of an offence".

Sub-section 2 sets out more particularly the behaviour that will be regarded as harassment:

> "For the purposes of this section a person harasses another where –
>
> (a) he or she, by his or her acts intentionally or recklessly, seriously interferes with the other's peace and privacy or causes alarm, distress or harm to the other, and
>
> (b) his or her acts are such that a reasonable person would realise that the acts would seriously interfere with the other's peace and privacy or cause alarm, distress or harm to the other".

Section 10 allows the court to make an order prohibiting an individual from approaching or communicating with the person who has made the complaint of harassment. The offence of harassment and / or a breach of an order made under section 10 attract a term of imprisonment and / or a fine.

Note that the offence is committed where there is no 'lawful authority' or 'reasonable excuse' for the harassment. This suggests that, if there is a genuine public interest basis for the behaviour in question, it may not be found to constitute the offence of harassment, depending on the circumstances.

Data Protection Acts, 1988 - 2003

The regime established by the *Data Protection Act, 1988* and the *Data Protection (Amendment) Act, 2003* is concerned with the collection and use of personal data by individuals and organisations. One provision of data protection legislation has particular relevance for journalists, as well as for artists, writers and publishers.

Section 22A of the *Data Protection Act, 1988*, as inserted by section 21 of the *Data Protection (Amendment) Act, 2003*, exempts those processing personal data – which includes information such as names, addresses, telephone numbers – from obligations (including non-disclosure obligations) imposed by data protection legislation where that information is processed only for journalistic, artistic or literary purposes.

First, the processing of the data must be only with a view to the publication of any journalistic, literary or artistic material; second, the person or organisation holding the data must reasonably believe that, having regard in particular to the special importance of the public interest in freedom of expression, such publication would be in the public interest; and finally, the person holding the data must reasonably believe that compliance with relevant data protection rules (including non-authorised disclosure) would be incompatible with journalistic, artistic or literary purposes.

An individual who believes that their personal data has been used in a manner inconsistent with this journalistic exemption from data protection rules may make a complaint to the Data Protection Commissioner (see **www.dataprotection.ie**).

Section 62 of the *Garda Síochána Act, 2005*

This section makes it a criminal offence for a serving or former Garda, or any other person working with or for An Garda Síochána, to disclose information obtained through their work, the disclosure of which the Garda or other person knows is likely to have a harmful effect. This includes information the disclosure of which "results in the publication of personal information and constitutes an unwarranted and serious infringement of a person's right to privacy" (see section 62(1)(h)).

The *European Convention on Human Rights Act, 2003*

The *European Convention on Human Rights* was incorporated into Irish domestic law by the *European Convention on Human Rights Act, 2003*. The Act requires organs of the State (including the legislature and the judiciary) to perform their functions in a manner compatible with the *Convention* (section 3). The courts are required to interpret Irish law in a manner compatible with the State's obligations under the *Convention* (section 2) and to take account of decisions of the European Court of Human Rights when interpreting and applying *Convention* provisions in Irish courts (section 4).

There has been extensive case law in the European Court of Human Rights considering the application of Article 8 in a variety of circumstances. In the case of *Von Hannover v Germany* (see **Q70**), the failure by the German courts to prohibit the publication of certain photographs of Princess Caroline of Monaco was found to amount to a failure by the German State to provide for the protection of the Princess' right to privacy as provided for under Article 8 of the *Convention*. This case was considered by the Irish High Court in the case of *Hickey v Sunday Newspapers Ltd [2010] IEHC 349* (see **Q70**).

See also

Q65   What regulatory requirements apply to broadcast programme content and advertisements?

Q66   How does the Broadcasting Authority of Ireland secure compliance by broadcasters with regulatory obligations and codes?

Q70   How is privacy protected under Irish law?

Q72   Are image rights protected under Irish law?

Q81   Do celebrities and politicians have the same rights of privacy as private citizens?

Q72   Are image rights protected under Irish law?

There is no statutory protection for image rights under either Irish or English law. The Irish *Privacy Bill, 2006* contains a provision that includes the unauthorised use of an individual's name, likeness or voice for advertising purposes or for financial gain in the proposed tort (civil wrong) of violation of privacy. At the date of writing, that Bill has not been enacted. In the United States, legal protection exists for 'publicity rights'.

There is very little Irish case law to date on the question of protection of image rights. Existing common law (including case law from England, which can be referred to before Irish courts) and constitutional law in Ireland suggests that there exists a legal basis on which an individual could seek an award of damages from the courts in respect of the unauthorised use of their image in certain circumstances, such as photographs taken on an essentially private occasion and photographs used in a commercial context where a commercial value can be put on the individual's image. The law on this point is not certain, pending further development either in the courts or by legislation.

The tort of 'passing off'

'Passing off' is a long-established tort under common law. Traditionally, it has been concerned with the promotion by a manufacturer or trader of their goods or services in a manner that appropriates or exploits the goodwill attached to the goods or services of another manufacturer or trader. When this is done to the extent that a consumer is likely to be misled or confused by the presentation of the product that is being 'passed off' as the product of another, an action may be brought for an award of damages by the person or business whose commercial goodwill (which includes, for example, brand recognition and customer loyalty) has been appropriated without permission. The law recognises that commercial goodwill has a value in the same way that other forms of property have a value.

In the case of *Irvine v Talksport Ltd [2002] EWHC 367 (Ch) – [2003] EWCA Civ 423* (appeal hearing on the issue of damages only), an altered image of racing driver Eddie Irvine was used without his permission for the promotion of a radio station, Talksport. The High Court in England held that the unauthorised use of Mr Irvine's image amounted to passing off by way of false endorsement; Mr Irvine's image was used in such a manner that he appeared to be endorsing Talksport. The Court of Appeal increased the damages awarded from £2,000 to £25,000, on the basis that £25,000 was the value of the endorsement fees Mr Irvine could command for comparable endorsements in the advertising market.

The Irvine case demonstrates that the courts in England are prepared to recognise that a commercial value can attach to a celebrity figure's image. Furthermore, the courts in England regard the appropriation of that image without consent as the unlawful appropriation of a form of property right. This case is one that, no doubt, would be referred to by a plaintiff were a similar case to come before the Irish courts.

The tort of breach of confidentiality
The common law of confidentiality has been invoked in order to protect image rights in the UK courts. Two English cases in particular illustrate this point.

In *Douglas and Others v Hello! Ltd [2005] EWCA Civ 595*, actors Michael Douglas and Catherine Zeta-Jones were awarded £3,750 each for mental distress and a combined sum of £7,000 for additional expenses and disruption on foot of a claim for breach of privacy and confidentiality. Photographs of their private wedding reception had been taken and published without their authorisation in *Hello!* magazine. The award was upheld by the English Court of Appeal. The case, in which the proprietor of *OK!* magazine was also a plaintiff, substantially involved legal issues concerning alleged wrongful interference by *Hello!* magazine with the contractual relationship between Douglas and Zeta-Jones and *OK!* magazine in circumstances where *OK!* had contracted with Douglas and Zeta-Jones for the exclusive right to take and publish photographs of the wedding. The case is relevant, from the point of view of image rights, in that the court held that the wedding was a private occasion and, as such, unauthorised photographs of the event were protected by the law of confidentiality. While the sum awarded by way of damages was small, the fact that damages were awarded for breach of confidentiality on foot of a claim for breach of privacy and confidentiality was significant at the time.

In *Campbell v MGN Ltd [2004] UKHL 22*, the House of Lords by a 3:2 majority re-instated a High Court award – of £3,500 in total – in favour of super-model Naomi Campbell for breach of privacy by way of breach of an obligation on the *Daily Mirror* newspaper to keep certain information about her private life confidential; that information included certain details about her attendance at Narcotics Anonymous meetings and a photograph taken of her in the public street leaving a Narcotics Anonymous meeting.

Privacy law in the UK has evolved by way of the law of confidentiality and, latterly, by reference to Article 8 (protection of privacy) of the *European Convention on Human Rights*, which was incorporated into UK domestic law by the *Human Rights Act, 1988*. Privacy is not a constitutionally-protected right under UK law.

The constitutional right to privacy under Irish law
In Ireland, privacy is a constitutionally-protected right and an unlawful breach of privacy may give rise to a right to claim for damages for a breach of constitutional duty without the courts needing to rely on the tort of breach of confidentiality.

In 2008, the High Court, on appeal from a decision of the Circuit Court, awarded €11,000 in damages to a GAA player named Sinnott, who sued for invasion of privacy and infliction of emotional harm arising from the publication of a photograph that showed his private parts exposed. The photograph was taken during a GAA match and was published by the *Carlow Nationalist*. A newspaper report of the outcome of this claim was published in *The Irish Times* of 31 July 2008.

The European Court of Human Rights decision in *Von Hannover v Germany (E.Ct.H.R. 24.06.2004, Application no. 59320/00)* was taken into consideration by the High Court in a significant privacy case involving unauthorised use of the plaintiff's image, *Hickey v Sunday Newspapers Ltd [2010] IEHC 349*. (See **Q70** for a more extensive discussion of both these cases; also **Q81**.)

The Von Hannover case concerned the publication of unauthorised photographs of Princess Caroline of Monaco going about her private life. Princess Caroline maintained that the failure of the German courts to prohibit the further publication of the photographs was in breach of her right to respect for her privacy under Article 8 of the *European Convention on Human Rights*. In the Hickey case, the High Court held that the publication of photographs taken of the plaintiff in the public street without her consent and published by the defendant newspaper did not amount, in the circumstances of the case, to a breach of her privacy. In his judgment, the judge observed, "That is not to say, however, that there will never be occasions where a person photographed in a public place can successfully invoke privacy rights".

Data protection legislation

A limited measure of image rights protection can be availed of, depending on the circumstances, under section 6A of the *Data Protection Act, 1988* (as inserted by section 8 of the *Data Protection (Amendment) Act, 2003*). This section entitles a data subject (a photograph can comprise 'personal data' for the purpose of Data Protection legislation) to object to the 'processing' (which can include disclosure by way of publication) of personal data about them, even when that processing may be for a legitimate specified reason or in the public interest, on the grounds that such processing would be likely to cause substantial and unwarranted damage or distress to the data subject or another person. One of the factors relevant to the application of this section is the data subject's right to privacy with respect to the processing of the data (section 6A(2)(b)). It is a matter for the Data Protection Commissioner to adjudicate on any complaint that a request to a data controller under this section has not been complied with and whether that refusal was justified.

Data protection legislation is considered in more detail in **Q77** and **Q78**.

Copyright

A measure of protection of image rights can be availed of under the law of copyright. Photographs are copyright works. If photographs are published without the consent of the copyright-holder, a claim for breach of copyright potentially can be made for the unauthorised publication of those copyright photographs.

In 2009, the singer Madonna settled a claim for damages for invasion of privacy and breach of copyright arising from publication by the *Mail on Sunday* of photographs of her wedding, which had been a strictly private affair. No photographs of the event had been sold or made available to the media. The photographs had been kept in an album in the singer's home and secretly copied by an interior designer working at the house, who subsequently sold them to the newspaper. While the wedding took place in Scotland in 2000, the photographs were not published until October 2008 (three days after Madonna and her then husband, Guy Ritchie, announced their intention to divorce). As part of the settlement, the newspaper apologised for invading the plaintiff's privacy and breaching her copyright (*The Guardian*, 6.10.2009).

The *Press Council Code of Practice*

The *Press Council Code of Practice* includes the following Principle: "3.2 Publications shall not obtain information, photographs or other material through misrepresentation or subterfuge, unless justified by the public interest". While the *Code* does not have the force of law, an alleged breach of the *Code* may be referred by way of complaint to the Press Ombudsman.

Practical precautions

Taking the legal principles and provisions outlined above into account, a general guideline for advertisers and publishers is to obtain prior consent to the use of an individual's image for use in commercial advertisements, especially the use of the image of a celebrity figure whose image is likely to have a market-value. Any other use of an individual's image without consent must be capable of being justified, either by reference to the public circumstances in which the image was photographed or filmed, or the public interest. This usually will be the case in respect of news photographs or 'general vision' shots used in television programmes. However, the observation of Judge Kearns in the Hickey case concerning the taking of photographs in public places (above) should be borne in mind.

There are certain locations where members of the public could reasonably be deemed to expect the presence of television cameras and press photographers, such as at public street parades and high-profile sports events. The context in which such footage or photographs is used, however, needs to be considered on a case-by-case basis to ensure that privacy of any individual is not encroached upon unreasonably. Where filming or photography takes place in locations where cameras might not necessarily be expected, some form of notification should be given to members of the public attending at that location that filming or photography will take place.

Case law

Irvine v Talksport Ltd [2002] EWHC 367 (Ch) – [2003] EWCA Civ 423
(appeal hearing on the issue of damages only)
A UK radio station was re-branding as a sports radio station. A promotional pack was prepared and distributed by the radio station to potential advertisers. The pack included a leaflet, on the front of which was a photograph of racing driver Eddie Irvine. The photograph originally had been one of Mr Irvine talking on his mobile phone but the image had been altered for the purposes of the promotion so that Mr Irvine was shown holding a radio with the Talksport logo on it to his ear. The High Court in England held that the unauthorised use of Mr Irvine's image amounted to passing off by way of false endorsement; Mr Irvine's image was used in such a manner that he appeared to be endorsing Talksport. The Court of Appeal increased the damages awarded from £2,000 to £25,000, on the basis that this was the value of the endorsement fees Mr Irvine could command for comparable endorsements in the advertising market.

Douglas and Others v Hello! Ltd [2005] EWCA Civ 595
Actors Michael Douglas and Catherine Zeta-Jones were awarded £3,750 each for mental distress and a combined sum of £7,000 for additional

expenses and disruption on foot of a claim for damages for breach of privacy and confidentiality. The award was upheld by the English Court of Appeal. Douglas and Zeta-Jones married at the Plaza Hotel, New York in November 2000. They contracted with *OK!* magazine for the right of *OK!* to take photographs of the event and to publish those images. An uninvited photographer managed to gain entry to the wedding reception. He took photographs and sold them to *Hello!* magazine, which rushed to publish a special edition ahead of the authorised photographs being published by *OK!* magazine. As a result, *OK!* was constrained to bring forward its own publication date. The proprietor of *OK!* magazine was also a plaintiff in the case, which substantially involved legal issues concerning alleged wrongful interference by *Hello!* with the commercial contract made between Douglas and Zeta-Jones and *OK!*. From the point of view of image rights protection, it was held that the wedding was a private occasion and unauthorised photographs of the event were protected under the law of confidentiality.

Campbell v MGN Ltd [2004] UKHL 22

The *Daily Mirror*, in February 2001, had published articles stating that, contrary to her public assertions that she did not abuse drugs, super-model Naomi Campbell was a drug addict and attending meetings of Narcotics Anonymous (NA). One of the articles gave detailed information about her attendance at NA meetings and was accompanied by a photograph of her leaving an NA meeting in London. While the publication of the information that Ms Campbell had lied about her drug addiction was held to be lawful and in the public interest, the publication of certain details about her attendance on the NA programme and, in particular, the publication of the photograph of her in the public street leaving an NA meeting, taken without her authorisation, was held to amount to the unauthorised publication of confidential information. The House of Lords by a 3:2 majority re-instated a High Court award – of £3,500 in total – made in favour of Ms Campbell for breach of privacy by way of breach of an obligation on the newspaper to keep certain information about her private life confidential.

See also

www.bailii.org – database of UK and Irish case law.
www.echr.coe.int – see Hudoc database of European Court of Human Rights case law.
www.dataprotection.ie
www.presscouncil.ie

Q73 Can it be an invasion of privacy to 'doorstep' someone?

'Door-stepping' involves a journalist attempting to film, record or otherwise secure an interview or response to questions from an individual without prior arrangement, consent or warning. Door-stepping can take place at a private premises or in a public location. Door-stepping can also be conducted by telephone, where a telephone conversation with an individual is broadcast or published without their prior consent.

Depending on the circumstances, door-stepping an individual can amount to an invasion of her / his privacy, a constitutionally-protected right any unlawful breach of which can give rise to a claim for damages. If the door-stepping takes place at the family home or workplace of the individual, the privacy of their family members or work colleagues also may be unlawfully violated. In practice, privacy claims arising from door-stepping incidents have not – as yet – been brought in the Irish courts. Regulatory complaints of invasion of privacy by way of door-stepping by telephone have been upheld by the Broadcasting Complaints Commission (whose role is now fulfilled by the Compliance Committee of the Broadcasting Authority of Ireland (BAI)).

Questioning by journalists of public figures, such as politicians, while those individuals go about their official business is generally acceptable. Questioning such public figures as they go about essentially private or domestic business will not necessarily be justifiable.

Persistent appearances by a journalist at the home or workplace of an individual, without lawful justification – such as a 'public interest' justification – in a manner that seriously interferes with the individual's peace or privacy or causes alarm, distress or harm potentially could lead to a criminal charge of harassment under section 10 of the *Non-Fatal Offences Against the Person Act, 1997.*

Section 39(1)(e) of the *Broadcasting Act, 2009* requires broadcasters, in both the making and broadcasting of programmes, not to "unreasonably encroach" on the privacy of any individual. Breach of this statutory obligation can lead to a complaint being made to the Compliance Committee of the BAI or to an investigation by the BAI.

The *Press Council Code of Practice* (Principle 5) imposes a non-statutory obligation on Press Council members (comprising newspaper and magazines publishers) to respect privacy (see **www.presscouncil.ie**). The Principle comprehensively sets out the considerations that apply in counter-balancing privacy, freedom of expression and the public interest. Two parts are particularly relevant to the discussion of door-stepping:

"5.1 Privacy is a human right, protected as a personal right in the Irish *Constitution* and the *European Convention on Human Rights*, which is incorporated into Irish law. The private and family life, home and correspondence of everyone must be respected.

5.4 Public persons are entitled to privacy. However, where a person holds public office, deals with public affairs, follows a public career, or has sought or obtained publicity for his activities, publication of relevant details of his private life and circumstances may be justifiable where the information revealed relates to the validity of the person's conduct, the credibility of his public statements, the value of his publicly-expressed views or is otherwise in the public interest."

The decision by a print journalist as to whether to use door-stepping in a journalistic investigation can usefully be assessed by reference to Principle 5 in combination with the consideration of Principle 3, which is concerned with fairness and honesty:

"3.1 Newspapers and periodicals shall strive at all times for fairness and honesty in the procuring and publishing of news and information.

3.2 Publications shall not obtain information, photographs or other material through misrepresentation or subterfuge, unless justified by the public interest.

3.3 Journalists and photographers must not obtain, or seek to obtain, information and photographs through harassment, unless their actions are justified in the public interest."

Note that these Principles do not have the force of law. They comprise industry guidelines for print journalists and editors and provide a useful summary of the considerations that need to be taken into account when contemplating a door-step interview.

For all the categories of violation of privacy outlined above – statutory, regulatory and under constitutional law – an encroachment on privacy may be justifiable by reference to the public interest. There is no statutory guidance as to what circumstances will amount to a public interest justification for an invasion of privacy. Relevant case law indicates that a compelling argument grounded in consideration of the 'common good' or the 'public interest' can tip the balance in favour of freedom of expression when both this right and the right to protection of privacy are at issue in a court case. Journalists, broadcasters and publishers, therefore, need to consider the basis on which the common good or public interest will be served by door-stepping an individual, prior to engaging in such tactics to secure an interview.

The BAI is charged, by section 42 of the *Broadcasting Authority Act, 2009*, with preparing codes relating to certain statutory obligations of broadcasters, including obligations concerning privacy. At the date of writing, the BAI has not published such a code. The current *Code of Programme Standards* carried over from the pre-2009 Broadcasting Commission of Ireland does not specifically address privacy issues.

Two existing documents that provide practical guidance to broadcast media producers in relation to door-stepping are the *RTÉ Programme Standards Guidelines* (see **www.rte.ie**) and the UK *Ofcom Broadcasting Code 2009* (section 8) and accompanying guidelines, which can be found on the Stakeholders / Broadcasting sections of **www.ofcom.org.uk**.

By reference to case law and to the guidelines referred to above, the following factors need to be considered by a journalist or programme-maker proposing to door-step an interviewee:

- Is there an overriding public interest that justifies the inherent invasion of privacy involved in door-stepping the interviewee?

- Have reasonable opportunities been given to the interviewee prior to door-stepping them to respond to the queries that the journalist, in the public interest, seeks to raise?

- Have those reasonable opportunities been unreasonably ignored or refused?

- Do the circumstances justify door-stepping the interviewee, even where no prior opportunities have been offered to them to respond? Such circumstances may include the potential frustration of an investigation if the interviewee has prior notice of it or the likely flight of the interviewee from the jurisdiction if they become aware of the investigation.

'Public interest' v 'interesting to the public'

While certain journalistic investigations may be clearly in the public interest as well as being interesting to the public, there can be occasions where the two concepts diverge. On the one hand, the Supreme Court has asserted that the right to freedom of expression "extends the same protection to worthless, prurient and meretricious publication as it does to worthy, serious and socially valuable works" (Judge Fennelly in *Mahon v Post Publications [2007] IESC 15*). On the other hand, recent case law, such as *Herrity v Associated Newspapers (Ireland) Ltd [2008] IEHC 249*, makes clear that, in certain circumstances, the right to freedom of expression will not outweigh the right to protection of privacy.

The distinction between what is of public interest and what is merely interesting to the public can be difficult to discern when reporting on the activities of celebrity figures. Many celebrities actively court the attention of the media and their activities may form such an integral part of public discourse that those activities may be regarded as matters of public interest. The judgment of the High Court in *Hickey v Sunday Newspapers Ltd [2010] IEHC 349* (see **Q70** and **Q81**) indicates that the extent to which someone deliberately puts their private affairs into the public domain will be relevant to the extent of protection an Irish court subsequently will extend to those private affairs if they are discussed in the media.

See also

Q10   How is the right to freedom of expression protected under Irish law?

Q32   Is consent a defence to a defamation action?

Q34   What is the fair and reasonable publication defence?

Q63   What is the Press Council and what does it do?

Q65   What regulatory requirements apply to broadcast programme content and advertisements?

Q66   How does the Broadcasting Authority of Ireland secure compliance by broadcasters with regulatory obligations and codes?

Q71   What legislation provides for the protection of privacy under Irish law?

Q74   Is consent required to broadcast or otherwise publish a person's voice or image?

Q81   Do celebrities and politicians have the same rights of privacy as private citizens?

www.bai.ie – website of Broadcasting Authority of Ireland.
www.bailii.org – database of UK and Irish case law.

Q74 Is consent required to broadcast or otherwise publish a person's voice or image?

Privacy is a personal right guaranteed by the Irish *Constitution* as an un-enumerated constitutional right. Respect for privacy is also a personal right protected by the *European Convention on Human Rights* (incorporated into Irish domestic law in 2003) and a right referred to in Article 12 of the UN *Declaration on Human Rights,* as reflected in Article 17 of the *International Covenant on Civil and Political Rights,* to which Ireland is a signatory.

Depending on the circumstances, the broadcast or publication of a person's voice or image without consent can amount to an unlawful invasion of her / his privacy, giving rise to a claim for damages. Whether this encroachment is lawful depends on the extent of the reasonable expectation of privacy which that person enjoys in the circumstances and the extent of the public interest served by that encroachment.

The expectation of privacy of a person in the public street inevitably will be less than their legitimate expectation of privacy in their home or at a private location. "One intuitively feels that a right of privacy is less easily established in public places where a person, in the words of TS Eliot, has had time 'to prepare a face to meet the faces that you meet'" (Mr Justice Kearns in *Hickey v Sunday Newspapers Ltd [2010] IEHC 349* – see **Q70** and **Q81**). In the same judgment, the judge commented on the decision in *Von Hannover v Germany (E.Ct.H.R., 24.06.2004, Application no. 59320/00* – see **Q70**): "The case is not an authority for the proposition that every occasion on which an unwanted photograph is taken or published of a private person in a public place constitutes a breach of privacy ... all the circumstances of the individual case have to be taken into account".

Bear in mind that many places to which the public has access – such as shopping centres, airports or hospitals – are, in fact, private premises. Consent from the proprietors should be obtained prior to filming or photographing in such locations. Depending on the circumstances, members of the public attending at such places will have a greater or lesser expectation of privacy. A patient attending at the accident and emergency room of a hospital arguably has a greater entitlement to expect respect for their privacy than a person attending a football match in a sports stadium.

'General vision' footage filmed in a public street needs to be filmed and used with care. Deliberately filming someone carrying out what is essentially a private act, albeit that they are doing so in a public location, could amount to a violation of their privacy. The law in this area is very uncertain. Furthermore, many parents are very sensitive about how images of their children are used. Common-sense guidelines include:

- Keeping general vision shots very 'general'.
- Being aware of parental sensitivities when filming children in public places.
- Making sure the broadcast or publication of general vision footage or images is justifiable by reference to some aspect of the public interest.

Where an identifiable individual makes a contribution to, for example, a radio or television programme as an interviewee, their consent should be obtained to the recording and broadcast of that interview. Consent may be implied – for example, where there is voluntary participation by a person in a 'vox pop' interview or a news programme. In other circumstances, obtaining consent in writing may be more appropriate to put the matter of consent beyond doubt.

Surreptitious recording / filming, as well as broadcasting or publishing that recording, can amount to an infringement of privacy unless there is some clear justification for that recording referable to the public interest. The same principles apply to surreptitious recording as apply to 'door-stepping' interviewees (see **Q73**).

In *Cogley and Aherne v RTÉ [2005] IEHC 180* (see **Q70**), surreptitious filming in a private nursing home was held not to be a violation of privacy of the owners of the nursing home such as would justify prohibiting the broadcast of the programme that featured the resulting footage. The court held that the proposed programme raised important questions in the public interest, being the care standards in the home and the adequacy of the regulatory regime for private nursing homes. As regards the privacy of the patients in the home, the images of the patients filmed had been blurred where consent had not been obtained.

'Candid camera' programmes, by their very nature, involve filming individuals without their consent. Such material should not be broadcast or otherwise published (for example, online) without the consent of the subjects filmed.

Section 39(1)(e) of the *Broadcasting Authority Act, 2009* requires every broadcaster to ensure that they do not "unreasonably encroach" on the privacy of any individual in either the making or broadcasting of a programme. A useful database of decisions by the Broadcasting Complaints Commission (the BCC, the role of which is now fulfilled by the Complaints Committee of the Broadcasting Authority of Ireland), including decisions on complaints of breaches of the pre-2009 equivalent provision to section 39(1)(e), is available on **www.bcc.ie**.

A number of complaints about radio stations 'cold-calling' interviewees and putting them on air without their consent have been upheld in the past by the BCC. Putting interviewees directly on air without prior consent can amount to an unreasonable encroachment on their privacy, contrary to section 39(1)(e). A clear public interest justification for putting a caller live on air without prior consent needs to be identified before doing so.

The *Press Council Code of Practice*, Principles 3 and 5, are concerned with 'fairness and accuracy' and 'privacy' respectively. Principle 3.2 is particularly relevant to the issue of consent: "Publications shall not obtain information, photographs or other material through misrepresentation or subterfuge, unless justified in the public interest".

The principles outlined above may seem extraordinary to a generation reared in the era of self-publication and video uploads to websites such as YouTube and Facebook. There is a generational attitude towards privacy that is not concomitant with the prevailing law on privacy in Ireland. Nonetheless, for those working in the media – of whatever generation – familiarity with the law on privacy and surreptitious filming and recording is important. Put simply, just because video footage and sound recordings are available on an Internet site does not meant that their publication online complies with the law of privacy.

See also

Q75 Is it illegal to record a conversation without consent?

Despite the absence of a specific statutory prohibition on the surreptitious recording of a conversation, the surreptitious recording of a conversation without the consent of one or more participants in that conversation generally will be unlawful, unless the recording is justifiable by reference to the circumstances in which it takes place.

Common law / constitutional law

The courts will protect the constitutional right to privacy by way of making an award of damages in favour of a plaintiff whose privacy has been unlawfully breached. In two cases, surreptitious recording of private telephone conversations resulted in an award of damages. In *Kennedy and Others v Ireland [1987] 1 IR 587* (see **Q70**), the State was ordered to pay damages to two journalists whose telephone lines were unlawfully tapped by the State. In *Herrity v Associated Newspapers (Ireland) Ltd [2008] IEHC 249* (see **Q70**), a woman whose private telephone conversations with her lover were unlawfully intercepted and recorded by her estranged husband won an award against the newspaper that published part of the contents of those conversations. By reference to the general principles of privacy law, a persuasive public interest justification is required for the surreptitious recording of a conversation or the publication of the contents of that recording to be lawful.

Data protection legislation

Making a recording of a person's voice comprises the collection of personal data for the purpose of data protection legislation. That data must be processed (which includes collection / recording of the data) in accordance with the rules of data protection (see **Q77**). Accordingly, when a service such as a customer helpline records calls to the helpline, the caller must be told that the call will be recorded and also advised of the specific purpose for which the recording is being made and will be used (for example, training and quality control).

An important exemption from data protection requirements for 'processing' personal data is set out in section 22A of the *Data Protection Act, 1988* (as inserted by section 21 of the *Data Protection (Amendment) Act, 2003*) and applies where processing of personal data is carried out with a view to publishing that data for journalistic, artistic or literary purposes. Under the section – as in other areas of law – there must be a public interest justification for making and / or publishing a surreptitious recording of someone's voice.

Broadcasting legislation

Section 39(1)(e) of the *Broadcasting Authority Act, 2009* requires every broadcaster to ensure that "in programmes broadcast by the broadcaster, and in the means employed to make such programmes, the privacy of any individual is not unreasonably encroached upon". The reasonableness or otherwise of the means employed to make programmes, such as the surreptitious recording of telephone or other conversations, must be assessed by reference to the circumstances of each case and, in particular, by reference to the public interest served by the encroachment on the privacy of an individual inherent in making surreptitious recordings of conversations.

Telecommunications legislation

Section 98 of the *Postal and Telecommunications Services Act, 1983* makes it a criminal offence to "intercept or to authorise, permit or facilitate the interception of a telecommunications communication" (which includes a telephone conversation) and equally makes it a criminal offence to disclose the contents of an intercepted communication. Section 98(6) of the Act (as inserted by section 13(3) of the *Interception of Postal Packets and Telecommunications Messages (Regulation) Act, 1993*) includes listening to or recording a telecommunications message in the definition of "interception" but excludes from that definition listening to or recording that takes place where the recording is made with the consent of either the person on whose behalf the communication is made or the person intended to receive it.

Section 98 was relevant in the Herrity case (above) in that the interception was not authorised by either the person making the phone calls or the person receiving them; Ms Herrity's telephone line was held in her own name, not that of her estranged husband.

The Privacy Bill

The *Privacy Bill, 2006* contains a provision rendering it an actionable (meaning damages can be claimed) violation of privacy to "subject an individual to surveillance" (section 3(2)(a)). Included in the definition of 'surveillance' in the Bill is "the recording by any means of a conversation between two or more individuals without the knowledge of one or more of those individuals by any person including one of those individuals" (section 1). The Bill has not been enacted to date.

The Press Council

While not having legal force, the *Press Council Code of Practice* and the decisions of the Press Ombudsman and Press Council on the application of that *Code* provide useful guidance on the adjudication of complaints of invasion of privacy by the print media.

Principle 5 of the *Code* concerns privacy and Principle 5.2 is particularly relevant: "Readers are entitled to have news and comment presented with respect for the privacy and sensibilities of individuals. However, the right to privacy should not prevent publication of matters of public record or in the public interest".

Principle 3 concerning fairness and honesty is also relevant, in particular Principle 3.2, which states: "Publications shall not obtain information, photographs or other material through misrepresentation or subterfuge, unless justified by the public interest". Surreptitious recording of a telephone or other conversation can be regarded as 'material obtained through misrepresentation or subterfuge', depending on the circumstances in which the recording is made.

See also

Q63   What is the Press Council and what does it do?
Q65   What regulatory requirements apply to broadcast programme content and advertisements?

Q66   How does the Broadcasting Authority of Ireland secure compliance by broadcasters with regulatory obligations and codes?

Q70   How is privacy protected under Irish law?

Q71   What legislation provides for the protection of privacy under Irish law?

Q74   Is consent required to broadcast or otherwise publish a person's voice or image?

Q77   What are the fundamental requirements of data protection legislation?

www.presscouncil.ie

Q76   What remedies are available to a person whose privacy has been breached?

Privacy is a constitutional right of the citizen protected by the Irish *Constitution*. It is also a personal right of the individual set out in the *European Convention on Human Rights* (Article 8), which the State is obliged by the provisions of the *European Convention on Human Rights Act, 2003* to protect.

Action for damages
It is well-established by case law that there exists a legal right to claim damages against either the State or a private individual or entity where there has been an unlawful encroachment by the defendant on the plaintiff's constitutional right to privacy.

Pre-publication injunctions
The courts in Ireland will be slow to make a 'prior restraint' order prohibiting a publication where there is any reasonable basis for concluding that the defendant publisher may successfully defend the publication at the trial of the action. The current principal Irish case concerning a 'prior-restraint' application on privacy grounds is *Cogley and Aherne v RTÉ [2005] IEHC 180* (see **Q70**).

In declining an injunction application prohibiting the proposed broadcast by RTÉ of a television programme that incorporated footage secretly filmed in a private nursing home, the judge said: "It should be noted that one of the underlying reasons for the reluctance of the courts in this jurisdiction to grant injunctions at an interlocutory stage in relation to defamation stems from the fact that if the traditional basis for the grant of an interlocutory injunction (i.e. that the plaintiff had established a fair issue to be tried) was sufficient for the grant of an injunction in defamation proceedings public debate on very many issues would be largely stifled ... In that regard it is important to note that both the constitution itself and the law generally recognises the need for a vigorous and informed public debate on issues of importance ... Similar considerations also apply to a situation where a party may contend that there has been a breach of his right to privacy but where there are competing and significant public interest values at stake".

The public interest therefore is a core consideration for the court where an application for a 'prior restraint' order is sought in respect of a publication, whether the application is grounded in privacy law or in defamation law.

Non-judicial complaints mechanisms

Section 39(1)(e) of the *Broadcasting Act, 2009* requires broadcasters to ensure that, in the production and broadcast of their programmes, there is no unreasonable encroachment on the privacy of any individual. A complaint that this statutory requirement has been breached can be made to the Compliance Committee of the Broadcasting Authority of Ireland (BAI). Where a complaint is upheld, the finding must be broadcast by the broadcaster concerned – unless the Compliance Committee deems it inappropriate to do so (which may be, for example, in the interests of protecting the complainant's privacy).

Alleged failure by a newspaper or magazine to observe the *Press Council Code of Practice* can be complained to the Press Ombudsman. Principle 5 of the *Code of Practice* concerns respect for privacy. The Press Ombudsman and the Press Council will direct the publication of any of their decisions upholding a complaint by the newspaper or magazine concerned. The complainant may request that they remain anonymous in any published decision.

The Compliance Committee of the BAI and the Press Council offer relatively low-key mechanisms for addressing complaints that a broadcast and print media outlet (respectively) has encroached on the privacy of an individual in an unwarranted manner.

Complaint to the Data Protection Commissioner

Personal information about individuals – such as their name, address, telephone number or photographic image – all can comprise personal data. The collection, use and disclosure of that personal data must be carried out in accordance with data protection legislation.

An important exemption from data protection requirements for 'processing' personal data is set out in section 22A of the *Data Protection Act, 1988* (as inserted by section 21 of the *Data Protection (Amendment) Act, 2003*). Section 22A applies where processing of personal data is carried out with a view to publishing that data for journalistic, artistic or literary purposes. Under the section – as in other areas of law – there must be a public interest justification for publishing personal data about an individual.

Where an individual believes that the journalistic use of their personal data did not properly fall within the section 22A journalistic use exemption, they are entitled to make a complaint to the Data Protection Commissioner (see **Q78**).

On a purely legal point, it should be noted by lawyers that section 7 of the *Data Protection Act, 1988* confirms that, for the purposes of the law of torts, a data controller and a data processor owe a duty of care to a data subject in the collection of or dealing with personal data.

While there is a right to claim damages for invasion of privacy, the outcome of such claims is decided on a case-by-case basis and the success of such claims cannot be assured, particularly where an extensive body of precedent case law has not yet evolved through the courts. The further public exposure that a claim through the courts can attract, as well as the expense involved in bringing a privacy claim, can be a disincentive for plaintiffs to pursue civil actions for damages. In such instances, the regulatory complaints mechanisms outlined above may provide a more satisfactory avenue of redress.

See also

Q32   Is consent a defence to a defamation action?
Q34   What is the fair and reasonable publication defence?
Q59   Can an injunction be obtained to prohibit publication of a defamatory statement?
Q63   What is the Press Council and what does it do?
Q65   What regulatory requirements apply to broadcast programme content and advertisements?

Q66   How does the Broadcasting Authority of Ireland secure compliance by broadcasters with regulatory obligations and codes?

Q70   How is privacy protected under Irish law?

Q71   What legislation provides for the protection of privacy under Irish law?

Q77   What are the fundamental requirements of data protection legislation?

Q78   How is data protection law enforced?

www.bai.ie – website of the Broadcasting Authority of Ireland.
www.bailii.org – database of Irish and UK case law.
www.dataprotection.ie
www.presscouncil.ie

Q77   What are the fundamental requirements of data protection legislation?

Motivated by a combined concern at the manner in which population statistics had been used by the Nazi regime in Germany and the emergence of technology that could store and process significant amounts of data, measures emerged from various European bodies from the late 1970s onwards to regulate the manner in which personal information about individuals was collected, stored and used.

The EU *Data Protection Directive* (*Directive 95/46/EC*) incorporated the principles of data protection contained in two earlier international instruments:

- The OECD *Guidelines Governing the Protection of Privacy and Trans-Border Flows of Personal Data, 1980.*
- The Council of Europe's *Strasbourg Convention for the Protection of Individuals with regard to Automatic Processing of Personal Data, 1981.*

The *Data Protection Directive* extended the principles of data protection to personal data kept on manual files, as well as automated filing systems. It also provided for more specific protections and exemptions concerning the use of personal data beyond those specified in the *Strasbourg Convention.*

The *Data Protection Act, 1988* was enacted following Ireland's ratification of the 1981 *Strasbourg Convention* and established the office of the Data Protection Commissioner (DPC).

The enactment of the *Data Protection (Amendment) Act, 2003* brought Irish data protection law into line with the requirements of the *Data Protection Directive.*

The *Electronic Privacy Directive* (*Directive 2002/58/EC*) provided for the privacy and security of personal data for users of publicly-available electronic communications services, such as telephone communications systems, email, text and Internet services. The *Electronic Privacy Directive* was incorporated into domestic law by the *Electronic Privacy Regulations, 2003* (SI 535 of 2003, as amended by SI 526 of 2008).

Personal data is information about a living person from which that person is identified or can be identified by reference to that data or by reference to that data and other information held or which is likely to come into the possession of the person holding and controlling that information. In practice, any information that fully or partially identifies a person can comprise 'personal data'.

A data controller is a person or entity that holds and controls the use of personal data. A data controller is in a position to decide how personal data held by her / him / it will be used. Certain categories of data controller – such as banks and financial institutions – are obliged to register as data controllers with the Data Protection Commissioner (see **www.dataprotection.ie**).

A data processor is a person or entity that processes data on behalf of a data controller (but the term does not include an employee of a data controller who processes personal data on behalf of their employer in the course of their employment).

The term 'data processing' covers any use of data, including collecting, recording, storing, consulting, transmitting and making data available. The publication of personal data is therefore an act of 'data processing'.

In business, data controllers frequently outsource the processing of personal data to data processors in other jurisdictions. The 1988 Act (as amended – section 11) prohibits the transfer of personal data to processors outside the European Economic Area (EEA – being the EU member states plus Norway, Liechtenstein and Iceland) unless "an adequate level of protection" will apply to the data in the jurisdiction to which it is exported. This provision applies, for example, to the transfer of customer information by an Irish company to an overseas contractor supplying customer support services on behalf of the Irish company.

The DPC can supply information about other jurisdictions where she / he is satisfied adequate protection will apply under the law of those jurisdictions to personal data exported from Ireland. The US Federal

Trade Commission, in liaison with the EU Commission, has established a 'safe harbor' regime whereby it maintains a list of data processors in the US that have self-certified that they observe standards of data protection equivalent to that which applies in the EU. Transfer to other jurisdictions, where the extent of adequate protection available to exported data is not assured, may require the inclusion of EU standard contract terms in the contracts entered into by Irish data-exporters with overseas processors. These standard terms secure, through contracts with overseas data processors, a level of protection that is adequate by reference to EU data protection law.

Any person or entity that collects and uses personal data about an individual (a 'data subject') is obliged to comply with data protection legislation. Personal data can include data such as names, addresses, telephone numbers, voice or image recordings and email addresses.

Certain personal data can be 'sensitive personal data', which term refers to information about a data subject's racial or ethnic origin, religious beliefs, political opinions, health and sexuality or criminal record (the list is not exhaustive) (section 1(1) of the 1988 Act, as amended). Additional protection applies to the collection and use of sensitive personal data.

The DPC's website identifies eight fundamental rules of data protection derived from the provisions of the combined *Data Protection Acts, 1988 to 2003* (**www.dataprotection.ie**). The principles informing these rules are described below:

1. Personal data must be obtained and processed fairly. A data subject is entitled to be informed of the fact that data is being collected about them, by whom it is being collected, the purposes for which it is being collected and to whom it will be disclosed.

2. Personal data may only be kept and used for specified, clearly stated and lawful purposes. This requirement precludes the use of personal data for uses other than or beyond those uses for which it was collected; the proposed uses must be clearly stated to the data subject and those uses must be lawful.

3. Personal data must only be processed (which term includes publishing the data) in a manner that is consistent with the stated purposes for which it was collected.

4. Personal data must be kept safe and secure by the person or entity holding it, whether in electronic, manual or other form. This requirement affects email and computer access security measures along with the disposal of written paper records and information held in other formats.

5. Personal data must be kept accurate, complete and up-to-date by the person or entity holding it. Decisions about data subjects (for example, the granting of loans or credit facilities by financial institutions) should not be made on the basis of information that is out-of-date.

6. The extent of personal data collected must be adequate for and relevant to the stated purpose for which it is collected. The data collected must not exceed what is necessary for those stated purposes.

7. Personal data should not be retained for longer than is necessary for the stated purposes for which it is collected. The duration for which the data can lawfully be retained will vary from case to case depending on the purposes for which it was collected.

8. A data subject is entitled to know what information is held about them by a data controller and has a right to be given a copy of that data on request. A data subject is also entitled to require the correction of any inaccurate information held about her / him by a data controller.

Radio stations or magazines that hold competitions for listeners or readers must collect no more personal information about competition entrants than is necessary for the purposes of the competition – unless alternative or additional purposes are notified to the entrants prior to entering the competition. The competition organiser is not at liberty to use that personal data for any other purpose, unless that additional use is specified to the entrant prior to submitting their entry to the competition. Increasingly, companies organise promotional competitions through online social media such as Facebook. Data protection legislation applies to personal data supplied to companies established in Ireland that collect data from Internet users.

Callers and texters to radio stations provide their names and telephone numbers to those stations. It can be reasonably implied that a caller or texter knows the purpose for which they are providing this information – being interaction with the radio show in question. However, that information ought not be made available to third parties or used for other purposes by the radio station without first obtaining the caller's or texter's consent.

Journalists investigating stories for news, current affairs or other journalistic purposes collect personal data about individuals. An important exemption from data protection requirements for processing personal data is set out in section 22A of the *Data Protection Act, 1988* (as inserted by section 21 of the *Data Protection (Amendment) Act, 2003*). The exemption applies where the processing of personal data is carried out with a view to publishing that data for journalistic, artistic or literary purposes. Under the section, there needs to be a public interest justification for publishing personal data about an individual.

With the rapid advances made in Internet technology, it is not only institutions or corporations that can accumulate and process vast amounts of personal data. It is now possible for individuals to obtain and process large amounts of personal data about other people on private computers, particularly through social networking sites and from other Internet sources. Compliance with data protection by non-institutional and non-corporate data controllers is, therefore, difficult to monitor.

See also

Q76   What remedies are available to a person whose privacy has been breached?

Q78   How is data protection law enforced?

Q79   What is the purpose of on-line privacy statements?

Q78   How is data protection law enforced?

The office of the Data Protection Commissioner (DPC) was established by the *Data Protection Act, 1988*, which was amended by the *Data Protection (Amendment) Act, 2003*. The DPC's role is to protect privacy, both by promoting awareness of and compliance with data protection legislation.

Promoting compliance

The DPC has been innovative and pro-active in promoting awareness of data protection issues in Ireland. See, for example, the selection of entries to the 2009 short film competition promoted by the DPC on YouTube on the theme, 'Private Eye, Public Eye', as well as the extensive information available on **www.dataprotection.ie**.

The DPC also has power under section 13 to approve codes of data protection practice developed by trade associations and other bodies. Data protection codes for An Garda Síochána, the insurance sector and the Personal Injuries Assessment Board have been approved by the DPC.

Securing compliance

The DPC seeks to secure compliance with data protection legislation through a number of mechanisms, including:

- Complaints and investigations.
- Information notices.
- Enforcement notices.
- Prohibition notices.

Complaints and investigations

Section 10 of the 1988 Act (as amended) entitles the DPC to investigate, on his own initiative or on foot of a complaint received from a data subject, purported breaches or suspected non-compliance with data protection legislation.

Where a complaint is received, the DPC will investigate it and try to negotiate a resolution of the complaint between the complainant and the data controller concerned. Failing a negotiated resolution, the DPC will make a decision on the complaint and notify the complainant in writing of his decision. A complainant is entitled to appeal this decision to the Circuit Court.

The DPC has a general power under section 10 to carry out such investigations as he deems appropriate to secure compliance with data protection legislation. This generally takes place by way of a privacy audit of a data controller, which can result in recommendations by the DPC for improving standards of compliance by the audited organisation or business.

Information notices
Section 12 of the 1988 Act (as amended) empowers the DPC to issue an information notice to a person requiring the production of information to enable the DPC to perform her / his functions. This can include information required by the DPC to assess the extent or otherwise of compliance by the data controller with data protection legislation. Failure or refusal, without reasonable excuse, to comply with an information notice or knowingly giving false or misleading information to the DPC on foot of an information notice is a criminal offence.

Enforcement notices
Section 10 of the 1988 Act (as amended) empowers the DPC to issue an enforcement notice requiring a person to take specified steps to remedy a failure to comply with data protection legislation or to comply with the legislation. An enforcement notice can be appealed by the person notified to the Circuit Court. In the absence of an appeal, that person must comply with the notice within the period specified in the notice. The enforcement notice may require the person to take specific steps to comply with data protection legislation, including the blocking, rectification, erasure or destruction of all or any of the data that is the subject of the notice. Failure or refusal, without reasonable excuse, to comply with an enforcement notice is a criminal offence.

Prohibition notices

Under section 11 of the 1988 Act (as amended), the DPC may issue a prohibition notice prohibiting, either permanently or pending the taking of specified data protection measures, the transfer of personal data from Ireland to a state outside the European Economic Area. This can arise where an Irish-based company proposes to transfer personal data outside the State to be processed by a contractor company overseas – for example, customer support services for computer manufacturers or mobile phone companies.

The DPC supplies information about other jurisdictions where she / he is satisfied adequate protection will apply under the law of those jurisdictions to personal data exported from Ireland. The US Federal Trade Commission, in liaison with the EU Commission, has established a 'safe harbor' regime whereby it maintains a list of data processors in the US that have self-certified that they observe standards of data protection equivalent to that which applies in the EU. Transfer to other jurisdictions, where the extent of adequate protection available to exported data is not assured, may require the inclusion of EU standard contract terms in the contracts entered into by Irish data-exporters with overseas processors. These standard terms secure, through contracts with overseas data processors, a level of protection that is adequate by reference to EU data protection law.

Failure to comply with a prohibition notice without reasonable excuse is a criminal offence.

Authorised officers

Section 24 of the 1988 Act gives the DPC power to appoint authorised officers to enter a data controller's or data processor's premises. Authorised officers have a wide range of powers, including the power to require the disclosure to an officer of data or other information necessary to enable the DPC to carry out his functions, as well as the power to inspect and make copies of any such material disclosed. Obstructing an authorised officer, refusing without reasonable excuse to give an authorised officer information or to knowingly give an authorised officer misleading or false information is a criminal offence.

Prosecutions by the DPC

Under section 30 of the 1988 Act, the DPC has the power to prosecute offences under the Act. Penalties are by way of fine, which can range from €3,000 to €100,000.

See also

Q77   What are the fundamental requirements of data protection legislation?

Q79   What is the purpose of online privacy statements?

Every time an individual submits personal information to a website, social networking page, on-line forum or an online trader, they provide personal data about themselves.

The rules of data protection apply to the collection and use of such personal data. Accordingly, the person or business controlling a website to which personal data is submitted is a data controller and must comply with data protection legislation. The website proprietor / data controller, therefore, must notify the person submitting personal data of the website proprietor's identity, the purpose for which the data is being collected, and the manner in which it will be used, including how and to whom it will be disclosed.

The purpose of a privacy statement is to provide this information to a third-party visitor or user of a website so that they are aware of the identity of the data controller and the purposes for which they are submitting their personal data to that data controller.

It is not legally possible to 'opt out' of data protection law requirements by simply advising website users that data protection rules will not apply to information submitted *via* that website.

Even the collection of information by 'cookies' that track the access to a particular website from a personal computer require the inclusion of a privacy statement on a website using cookies. The privacy statement must inform the user of the fact that cookies are used by the website, and must state who owns or controls the site and the manner in which the tracking information obtained through the placement of cookies will be used.

Many websites are owned or controlled by individuals or businesses outside the European Economic Area. Accordingly, EU (or equivalent) data protection law may not apply to websites controlled by those individuals or businesses. This can render expectations of compliance with EU-equivalent data protection standards unrealistic. Accordingly, care always must be taken when submitting personal data online. Internet users must satisfy themselves that the privacy of any personal information they submit online will be protected.

See also

Q77 What are the fundamental requirements of data protection legislation?

Q78 How is data protection law enforced?

Q80   What is the difference between the law of privacy and the law of confidentiality?

The law of confidentiality has evolved over many decades at common law. It is primarily concerned with protecting confidential information from disclosure to a wider group of people or the public generally. The tort (civil wrong) of breach of confidentiality is long-established and gives the person who suffers damage as a result of the wrongful disclosure of confidential information a remedy by way of a claim for damages.

In Ireland, the legal protection for personal privacy is rooted firmly in the *Constitution*, which implicitly guarantees the right to protection of personal privacy. Individuals whose constitutional right to privacy has been unlawfully violated are entitled to claim damages for breach of that right in the courts – see *Herrity v Associated Newspapers (Ireland) Ltd [2008] IEHC 249* (see **Q70**). The right to respect for privacy set out in the *European Convention on Human Rights* (Article 8) was incorporated directly into Irish law by the *European Convention on Human Rights Act, 2003*. Article 8 of the *Convention* provides another leg on which to support the protection of privacy under Irish law. However, the primary source of legal protection for privacy in Ireland is the *Constitution* itself.

In the UK, by contrast, the legal protection afforded to privacy has evolved primarily from the common law of confidentiality and, latterly, by the UK's obligations under the *European Convention on Human Rights* to provide protection for the right to respect for privacy. The *Convention* was incorporated into domestic UK law by the *Human Rights Act, 1998*.

The law of confidentiality was relied on to a significant extent by the UK courts in *Campbell v MGN Ltd [2004] UKHL 22* (see **Q72**), in which supermodel Naomi Campbell secured a modest amount by way of damages in respect of an unlawful violation of her privacy by a newspaper. Four years later, in *Mosley v Newsgroup Newspapers [2008] EWHC 1777 (QB)*, significant reliance was placed on the UK's obligations under the *European Convention on Human Rights* when the High Court in London awarded Max Mosley, President of the motor-racing body, the

Fédération Internationale de l'Automobile, damages of £60,000 against the *News of the World* for violation of privacy. An article and images of the claimant engaging in a sado-masochistic 'sex party', which the newspaper described as "a Nazi orgy", had been published by the newspaper. The court held that the event, while unconventional, had not been a Nazi orgy and the public interest argument justifying the publication by the newspaper, on the grounds that it had been, was rejected.

However, the law of confidentiality in Ireland continues to offer an avenue of redress for a person or business where confidential information – commercial, industrial or personal – is disclosed without consent. Furthermore, the law of confidentiality has been relied upon in attempts to prevent publication of material, where the applicant has asserted that the information about to be published was subject to an obligation to maintain confidentiality.

An unsuccessful attempt was made by the British government to invoke the law of confidentiality in the Irish courts to prevent the publication of *One Girl's War,* the memoirs of Jean Wright, a former M15 agent. The defendant publisher's right to freedom of expression guaranteed by Article 40.6.1º(i) of the *Constitution* prevailed, as there was no public interest in Ireland that would be affected by the publication of the book. It was held further that no absolute confidentiality attached to information communicated between a government and an individual (*AG for England and Wales v Brandon Book Publishers Ltd [1986] IR 597*).

In a significant judgment in 1998, the Supreme Court upheld a refusal by a High Court judge to grant an injunction preventing the use (including broadcast) by RTÉ of confidential information about certain customers of National Irish Bank (NIB). Information about customers who had moved funds off-shore to evade income tax, and who were facilitated in that process by NIB, came into the hands of RTÉ. The Supreme Court held by a 3:2 majority judgment that the public interest served by exposing wrong-doing – in this case, tax evasion – outweighed the right of the bank and its customers to the maintenance of confidentiality. The majority judgment of the Supreme Court also observed, however, that the publication of false information that a particular bank customer had evaded tax would be a serious libel (*National Irish Bank v RTÉ [1998] IESC 2*).

The right of journalists to maintain the confidentiality of sources, while frequently upheld by the courts in the interests of freedom of expression for the media, is not an automatically-protected right. As in other areas of law concerned with the protection of confidentiality and privacy, the public interest served by the disclosure (or non-disclosure) of a confidential source is the central consideration for a court when an order for such disclosure is sought.

In *Mahon v Keena [2009] IESC 64*, a High Court order requiring journalist Colm Keena and his editor at *The Irish Times*, Geraldine Kennedy, to answer questions before the Mahon Tribunal about the source of confidential information was overturned by the Supreme Court. The contents of leaked confidential Tribunal correspondence had led to the publication of an article in September 2006 about payments made to Bertie Ahern, then Taoiseach. The fact that the correspondence in question had been destroyed by Ms Kennedy – an act described as "reprehensible" by both the High Court and the Supreme Court – carried great weight before the divisional High Court, which originally ordered the journalists to answer the Tribunal's questions about the source of the leaked correspondence. Despite its disapproval of the actions of Ms Kennedy, the Supreme Court held that, when balancing the public interest that would be served by upholding the High Court order against the public interest served by upholding the journalists' right to freedom of expression, no over-riding requirement in the public interest could be established, in the circumstances, that would justify requiring the journalists to answer the Tribunal's questions.

The competing public interest and freedom of expression arguments made by both sides in the case are usefully summarised in *The Irish Times*' reports of the appeal hearing, published on 9 and 10 December 2008. Despite the judgment in their favour, costs in the case were subsequently awarded against Mr Keena and Ms Kennedy. *The Irish Times* has brought a case against the State before the European Court of Human Rights arising from the costs decision, primarily on the grounds that it is in breach of the journalists' Article 6 right to a fair trial and to their Article 10 right to freedom of expression.

It can be seen, therefore, that, in Ireland, the law of confidentiality can be relevant to the media but the law protecting personal privacy is grounded in the *Constitution*, supplemented by the protection of privacy provided for by the *European Convention on Human Rights*.

See also

Q1 What are the sources of Irish law?

Q70 How is privacy protected under Irish law?

Q72 Are image rights protected under Irish law?

Q76 What remedies are available to a person whose privacy has been breached?

Q81 Do celebrities and politicians have the same rights of privacy as private citizens?

Q81   Do celebrities and politicians have the same rights of privacy as private citizens?

The right to privacy guaranteed by the *Constitution* and provided by the *European Convention on Human Rights* applies for the benefit of all individuals, regardless of their status or function in society. A person's status or function in society may be a relevant factor, however, in determining how the principles of the law of privacy are applied to the protection of their privacy.

The *Press Council Code of Practice*, while not having the force of law, usefully and concisely expresses the broad principle that the public interest served by the disclosure of otherwise private information about an individual, such as a politician, may render that disclosure justifiable: "5.4 Public persons are entitled to privacy. However, where a person holds public office, deals with public affairs, follows a public career, or has sought or obtained publicity for his activities, publication of relevant details of his private life and circumstances may be justifiable where the information revealed relates to the validity of the person's conduct, the credibility of his public statements, the value of his publicly expressed views or is otherwise in the public interest".

There are two European Court of Human Rights cases in particular that provide an interesting contrast of how the disclosure of private information will be regarded by that court in different circumstances involving public figures.

In *Von Hannover v Germany (E.Ct.H.R. 24.06.2004, Application no. 59320/00)* (see **Q72**), the court found that the failure of the German courts to prohibit the further publication of certain photographs of Princess Caroline of Monaco going about her private life constituted a failure by the German state to observe its obligation under Article 8 of the *European Convention on Human Rights* to provide for the protection of her privacy.

Princess Caroline of Monaco is a person well-known to the general public. The German courts had found that, by virtue of her status as a public figure *par excellence*, she could not expect protection from media attention when she was in public places. However, the European Court of Human Rights rejected this conclusion and held that she had a legitimate expectation of protection of her privacy, even when she was in "places that cannot always be described as secluded". The Court held that the public interest served by articles accompanied by photographs of her going about her private life in public places did not "contribute to any debate of general interest to society". The court took into account that the publication of the articles and photographs in question aimed to satisfy public curiosity rather than contributing to a debate of general interest, having noted in particular that Princess Caroline performed no function on behalf of the state of Monaco or any of its institutions. It also took into account the context in which the photographs were taken, without Princess Caroline's knowledge or consent, and the level of harassment frequently endured by public figures in their daily lives.

The judgment stated: "The Court considers that a fundamental distinction needs to be made between reporting facts – even controversial ones – capable of contributing to a debate in a democratic society relating to politicians in the exercise of their functions, for example, and reporting details of the private life of an individual who, moreover, as in this case, does not exercise official functions."

By contrast, in *Éditions Plon v France (E.Ct.H.R. 18.05.04, Application no. 58148/00)*, the court found that the prohibition by the French courts of the further publication of a book that revealed private details of the medical condition of the deceased former President François Mitterrand was in breach of the right of the publisher to freedom of expression (Article 10 of the *Convention*).

President Mitterrand of France died of cancer in January 1996. He had known of his condition since shortly after his election to the presidency in 1981 but deliberately concealed it from the public until 1992. He continued to serve as President until 1995.

The book, which had been co-authored by Mitterand's doctor, disclosed medical information about the former President in breach of a legal obligation to keep such information confidential. The public interest served by the publication, however, tipped the balance in favour of the applicant, despite this breach of confidentiality. The permanent injunction against further publication of the book (of which 40,000 copies already had been sold) was found to be in breach of the publisher's Article 10 right to freedom of expression: "The Court considers that the book was published in the context of a wide-ranging debate in France on a matter of public interest, in particular the public's right to be informed about any serious illnesses suffered by the head of State, and the question whether a person who knew that he was seriously ill was fit to hold the highest national office. Furthermore, the secrecy which President Mitterrand imposed, according to the book, with regard to his condition and its development, from the moment he became ill and at least until the point when the public was informed (more than 10 years afterwards), raised the public interest issue of the transparency of political life" (see paragraph 44 of the judgement).

The Irish courts are obliged by section 4 of the *European Convention of Human Rights Act, 2003* to take "judicial notice" of decisions of the European Court of Human Rights when considering a case that involves the interpretation and application of a *Convention* provision such as the right to respect for privacy set out in Article 8.

Under English common law, in *Campbell v MGN Ltd [2004] UKHL 22* and *Douglas and Zeta-Jones v Hello! Ltd [2005] EWCA Civ 595*, the extent of the protection of personal privacy of high-profile celebrity figures was considered (see **Q72**). In *Ash v McKennitt [2006] EWCA Civ 1714*, the English Court of Appeal upheld an injunction prohibiting the publication in a book of certain details of the private life of the applicant, Loreena McKennitt, by a former friend and confidante, Niema Ash. Ms McKennitt is a well-known Canadian singer and musician.

Ms Ash argued her own right to freedom of expression to write about the shared experience of her life in the company of Ms McKennitt. It was held that the particular information revealed about Ms McKennitt in the book comprised confidential information primarily about Ms McKennitt's life, not Ms Ash's life, which information had come into Ms Ash's knowledge in the context of a relationship that carried an expectation of confidentiality. Furthermore, the Court of Appeal took the view that, even though Ms McKennitt had put selected elements of her personal story into the public domain, in the circumstances, she was entitled to exercise a degree of control over what elements of her private life she made public.

Recent years have seen a significant increase in the UK in the number of injunctions granted in favour of celebrity figures seeking to prevent publication of aspects of their private lives.

In Ireland, the protection of privacy is rooted in constitutional law rather than the law of confidentiality. The judgment in *Hickey v Sunday Newspapers Ltd [2010] IEHC 349* (see **Q70**) provided a useful indication of how the Irish courts will approach the issue of the protection of the privacy of individuals who have a level of 'celebrity' status. That case was concerned with the publication of a photograph taken in the public street shortly after the plaintiff had been engaged in carrying out business in a public office, being the registration of the birth of her child. The court attached weight to the fact that the plaintiff herself had put the facts of her relationship with the child's father (the former husband of a well-known entertainer and having a degree of 'celebrity' status himself) and of her pregnancy into the public domain by way of a magazine article and a newspaper interview respectively.

See also

www.bailii.org – database of UK and Irish case law.
www.echr.coe.int – see Hudoc database of European Court of Human Rights case law.

COPYRIGHT

Q82   What is intellectual property?

The concept of property is based on ownership. The owner of a piece of property is entitled to use, give away, sell, rent, licence or otherwise deal with that property on such lawful terms as she / he sees fit for the purposes of financial gain – or for non-profit purposes, if they so wish. Despite the negative connotations of the word in everyday language, the legal term for the use of a piece of property by the owner for gain or benefit is 'exploitation'. The right to exploit a piece of property arises by virtue of the ownership right held by the owner.

Property can be divided into two categories: tangible property and intangible property. Tangible property (from the Latin verb *tangere*, meaning 'to touch') has physical substance. Intangible property is a property right in assets that cannot be touched, such as trade know-how, the goodwill in a business, trade marks and copyright.

Intellectual property (IP) is a form of intangible property. It is the property right that exists in the expression of ideas, creativity and thinking. Given that no-one can be certain what mental processes are underway, or have occurred, in the mind of any person, intellectual property rights (IPR) do not exist in thoughts or creative ideas that are merely in someone's mind; IPR only comes into being when those thoughts or creative ideas are given physical expression – for example, in the writing of a poem, the recording of a melody, the making of a drawing or logo, the drawing of plans for a piece of machinery, the specification in a document of the chemical formula and manufacturing process for a pharmaceutical drug.

In IP law, it is not the physical piece of paper or micro-chip on which the original thought or idea has been expressed that has value; it is the idea expressed on that piece of paper or in that digital format that has value and in which the IPR in question exists.

See also

Q83   How are intellectual property rights protected by legislation?

Q83 How are intellectual property rights protected by legislation?

Although other forms of intellectual property (IP) can be protected under common law, specific statutory protection is available for:

- Copyright.
- Patents.
- Trade Marks.
- Designs.

Copyright

Copyright is concerned with the intellectual property rights (IPR) in works such as literary, dramatic, musical and artistic works, films, sound recordings, broadcasts and computer programmes.

The principal legislation protecting copyright in Ireland is the *Copyright and Related Rights Act, 2000* (as amended by the *Copyright and Related Rights (Amendment) Acts of 2004 and 2007*).

There is no register of copyrights in Ireland. Copyright is deemed at law to arise by virtue of the creation of the work in question and no registration is necessary for copyright to subsist in a work.

Patents

Patent law is concerned with protecting the right of ownership in the idea for an invention that has an industrial application. The person who creates an invention can register a patent for it. The invention does not need to have been built or constructed to be registered as a patent; the idea merely needs to have been given some form of physical expression (for example, in a drawing or a set of plans). An example of a patentable invention is the formula for a new pharmaceutical drug.

Registration can be made in a national and / or international patent registry. Registration is proof of ownership of the original idea for an invention and entitles the patent-holder to seek the protection of the law within the territory of registration should anyone manufacture or use the idea for that invention without consent.

Patents do not last indefinitely. The duration of protection offered by registration of a patent in Ireland (in common with most jurisdictions) is limited to a maximum of 20 years. The initial registration has a three year duration and renewal up to the maximum of 20 years can be made on payment of annual renewal fees. Ireland also offers a form of 'short-term' registration, which can be made for a maximum of 10 years.

The principal Act governing the registration of patents in Ireland is the *Patents Act, 1992*, as amended by the *Patents (Amendment) Act, 2006*.

Trade Marks

Trade mark protection law is concerned with the right of ownership in the distinctive means used by an individual, business or organisation to represent the identity of their product or service and by which that product or service is distinguished from the products or services of other individuals, businesses or organisations. Usually, this will be by way of a particular name and / or logo.

Registration of a trade mark gives the trade mark-holder a statutory right to take legal action to prevent the unauthorised use of their registered trade mark and also to licence the use of the trade mark by third parties. The initial period of protection granted by trade mark registration is 10 years, but registration may be renewed indefinitely for further periods of 10 years on payment of the applicable renewal fees.

The registrant of a trade mark must choose the categories of product or service in which she / he wishes to register the trade mark and also the territories in which she / he might usefully register it. This latter consideration will depend on the territorial extent of the market for, or reach of, the registrant's product or service.

Individuals, such as sports stars and other celebrities, who earn their living (or a part of their living) from exploitation of their public image, often seek to register their names or initials / logo as trademarks. Illustrations of this can be found by accessing the CTM (community trade mark) database of the EU trademark registration agency, the

Organisation for the Harmonisation of the Internal Market (OHIM), on which trademarks are registered for individuals such David Beckham, Roger Federer and Tiger Woods.

The principal legislation providing for the registration and protection of trade marks in Ireland is the *Trade Marks Act, 1996*.

Designs

Design protection law is concerned with the distinct appearance of a product – for example, the contours and appearance of a particular model of mobile phone or a mineral water bottle. Designs can be registered, providing statutory protection against their unauthorised use by third parties.

The *Industrial Designs Act, 2001* (giving effect to EU *Directive 98/71/EC*) established a design registration system in Ireland and provided for the protection of registered design rights. Design right protection by way of registration lasts for an initial period of five years and is renewable up to a maximum period of 25 years, subject to payment of applicable renewal fees every five years.

There is a more limited form of protection available for unregistered designs that are new and have "individual character". The protection is provided on an EU-wide basis under *Council Regulation (EC) No 6/2002*, under which unregistered designs enjoy protection from copying for a period of three years from the time they are first 'disclosed' (for example, the launch of a new product range of clothing). However, to protect their unregistered design in court, a person must be in a position to prove the date of disclosure of their design, the novelty and individual character of the design and the fact that it subsequently has been copied.

In Ireland, the Controller of Patents maintains the registers of Patents, Trade Marks and Designs in the Patents Office. Registration of a patent, trade mark or design with the Irish Patents Office provides protection on an Ireland-wide basis only.

See also

www.epo.org – European Patent Office.

www.oami.europa.eu – OHIM, the EU Trademark and Design Registration Agency.

www.patentsoffice.ie – Irish Patents Office.

www.wipo.int - World Intellectual Property Organisation.

Q84   What is copyright?

Copyright is a form of intellectual property and automatically comes into existence as a matter of law when an original idea is given written or recorded expression in a copyright 'work'. Under the *Copyright and Related Rights Act, 2000*, a 'work' means a literary, dramatic, musical or artistic work, sound recording, film, broadcast, cable programme, typographical arrangement of a published edition or an original database and includes a computer program (section 2).

Copyright is a property right that entitles the copyright-owner to undertake – or authorise others to undertake – certain acts in relation to a copyright work (section 17(1)) (see **Q86**).

Copyright does not apply to the ideas that inspire the creation of a copyright work (section 17(3)); it subsists in the form in which those ideas are expressed. A literary, dramatic or musical work must be written or recorded in some form before copyright can be deemed to subsist in it (section 18).

The core factor in determining the subsistence of a copyright work is its originality. Copyright does not subsist in a work that infringes another copyright work (section 17(5)). Copyright disputes arise in situations where a new work is so similar to, or appears to be so closely derived from, a pre-existing work that the new work potentially can be regarded as a copy or an adaptation of the original – in which case, a breach of copyright may be found to have occurred.

A US court in 1976 found George Harrison of The Beatles liable for breaching the copyright in a song entitled *He's So Fine*, released by The Chiffons, when he wrote and released the song *My Sweet Lord*. Harrison maintained that he did not deliberately copy any element of the previously-released song but was found by the judge to have 'subconsciously' plagiarised *He's So Fine*.

The *Berne Convention* of 1886, to which over 160 countries are now party, is an important multi-lateral treaty that establishes the international basis for copyright protection. Updated and amended since

1886, the *Convention* provides 'base line' protection (currently copyright duration of life of author plus 50 years), although signatory states may provide for longer terms of copyright protection (for example, copyright duration is for the life of the author plus 70 years for literary, dramatic, musical and artistic works in EU States).

The term 'author', under copyright law, is not confined to the creator of a literary work but refers to a person who creates any form of copyright work.

See also

Q82   What is intellectual property?
Q85   Who owns the copyright in a copyright work?
Q86   What rights does copyright confer on a copyright-owner?
Q87   How can a copyright-owner protect their copyright?
Q88   What is the duration of copyright?

Q85 Who owns the copyright in a copyright work?

The person who first creates a copyright work is known as the 'author' of that work. The term 'author' in copyright law is not confined to its colloquial literary meaning; it also refers to a person who creates a song, a photograph, a film, a computer program (the list is not exhaustive).

Section 23 of the *Copyright and Related Rights Act, 2000* provides that the author of a copyright work shall be the first owner of the copyright in that work, although there are exceptions to this rule (see below).

Where two or more people collaborate in the creation of a copyright work and their respective contributions to the work are not distinct from each other, then the work is regarded under Irish law as a work of joint-authorship (see section 22). It is a matter for the joint authors to agree between themselves how to deal with the copyright in terms of licensing it or assigning it. The principles that apply are the same as those that would apply to joint ownership of any other form of property, such as a house or a piece of equipment. A film is a work of joint authorship by the producer and the principal director, unless they are one and the same person (sections 21(b) and 22(2)).

Where the elements contributed to a copyright work are distinct from each other – for example, where the lyrics of a song are written by one person and the melody by another – two separate copyrights are deemed to exist in the one work.

When clearance is required for the use of a copyright work (for example, the use of a photograph on a website, or of a short story as the basis for a film script), some detective work may be involved in tracing the owner of the copyright or the person authorised to grant a licence to use it. An individual or company may believe mistakenly, or even falsely represent, that they own or control the copyright in a work. Hence the importance of obtaining a written warranty from the person granting a licence to use a copyright work that they have the legal entitlement to grant that licence.

Where, for example, a short story is being adapted into a screenplay for a feature film, the film producer's lawyer will inspect the 'chain of title' documentation evidencing the original ownership of the copyright in the short story and the intervening assignments of and / or licences to use it as the basis of a screenplay.

An important exception to the rule that the author is the first owner of the copyright in a work concerns employees. If a copyright work is made by an employee in the course of their employment, the employer will be the first owner of the copyright – unless the employer and employee have made a specific agreement to the contrary (section 23(1)(a)). The position is different for a freelancer or independent contractor; such individuals are not employees, although they may be supplying services to a company. Accordingly, they hold the copyright in any work they create in the course of supplying services (such as writing a script or composing a piece of music), subject to any contractual arrangements they enter into assigning or licensing the use of that work to the person or business to whom they supply those services.

Staff journalists with periodicals and newspapers thus do not own the copyright in the articles they write for their employers. However, by virtue of section 23(2), a staff journalist may use copyright work they produce in the course of their employment for purposes not related to publication in newspapers or periodicals, without infringing their employer's copyright in that work. There tends to be a lack of clarity in the newspaper industry about the precise copyright status of work created by freelance journalists who often work 'shifts' alongside staff journalists or who contribute regularly to one particular publication.

Misunderstandings frequently arise where a photograph or DVD (such as a promotional film) is commissioned by an individual or organisation that believes that, because they commissioned and paid for the work, they own the copyright in the resulting images or film footage and can use it for whatever purposes they wish. This is not the case; the copyright in a film or photograph is owned by the person who made the film or photograph. If a commissioning client requires the unencumbered ownership of the copyright of the film or image, they must negotiate with the producer or photographer for an assignment of the copyright in that film or image. A more common arrangement in respect of commissioned photographs is for the photographer to grant a licence to the commissioning client to use the image or film for agreed purposes for an agreed fee; any further use beyond that is agreed between the photographer (as licensor) and the commissioning client (as licensee).

In relation to photographs and films commissioned for private and domestic purposes, section 114 of the 2000 Act creates an important right of privacy for the commissioning client in the resulting film or photograph. The copyright-holder is not entitled to publicly display or show the commissioned photograph or film without the consent of the commissioning client.

The copyright in a work made by an officer or employee of the Government or of the State in the course of his / her duties vests in the Government – this is known as 'Government copyright'. Government copyright subsists for 50 years from the end of the year in which the work was first made (section 191). Copyright in legislation vests in the Oireachtas (section 192). This copyright similarly has a duration of 50 years from the end of the year in which the Bill or Act or other form of legislation was published (section 192).

See also

Q84 What is copyright?
Q86 What rights does copyright confer on a copyright-owner?
Q87 How can a copyright-owner protect their copyright?
Q88 What is the duration of copyright?

Q86 What rights does copyright confer on a copyright-owner?

Under section 37 of the *Copyright and Related Rights Act, 2000*, the owner of the copyright in a copyright work has the exclusive right to:

- Copy the work.
- Make the work available to the public.
- Make an adaptation of the work – and copy and / or make that adaptation available to the public.

These three actions are described in section 37(1) as "acts restricted by copyright" and can only be undertaken by, or with, the authorisation of the copyright-owner.

A breach of copyright – also referred to as a copyright infringement – takes place where, without the consent of the copyright-holder, any of these restricted acts are carried out in respect of the whole or a substantial part of a copyright work (section 37(2) and 37(3)). What amounts to a "substantial part" of a work in the context of a claim for copyright infringement is a question of fact, decided on a case-by-case basis by the courts. Broadly speaking, any use of copyright work is potentially in breach of copyright, unless that use is permitted under what are known as the 'fair dealing' provisions of the Act.

Certain aspects of copyright are given explicit recognition and protection by the 2000 Act:

- The reproduction right – the right to make copies of a work (section 39).
- The making available right – the right to make copies of a work available to the public, including by way of broadcast by wired or wireless means (section 40).
- The distribution right – another aspect of the right to make copies of a work available to the public that includes putting copies into circulation in any particular territory (section 41).

- The rental and lending right – the right to rent or lend copies of a work to the public (section 42).

In general, any form of copying, publication or other dissemination to the public or adaptation of a copyright work can take place only with the authorisation of the copyright-holder – subject to certain exceptions set out in the Act, known as the 'fair dealing' exemptions, and (in respect of sound recordings) certain collective licensing scheme arrangements (see **Q97** and **Q98**).

The 2000 Act also is concerned with what are described as 'related rights'. Typically, related rights – sometimes referred to as 'neighbouring rights' – are enjoyed by:

- Performers.
- Phonogram producers – producers of sound recordings, such as record companies.
- Broadcasters – in their broadcasts.

Under Irish law, the copyright enjoyed by sound-recording / phonogram producers in the sound recordings they produce and the rights of broadcasters in their broadcasts are included in the definition of works protected by copyright (section 17 of the 2000 Act). Performers' rights are given explicit recognition and protection by Part III of the 2000 Act.

An extensive body of case law has emerged through the UK courts relating to copyright which, due to the similarity of the common law legal systems and copyright legislation in both Ireland and the UK, carries some weight as precedent law before Irish courts. Much of this UK case law is concerned with disputes over the extent to which a work was so closely derived from a previous work that it can be regarded as a substantive copy of the previous work.

An interesting case involved Random House, publishers of the best-selling novel, *The Da Vinci Code* – see *Baigent and Another v Random House Group Ltd [2007] EWCA Civ 247*. Two non-fiction writers, Baigent and Leigh, had written a book entitled *The Holy Blood and the Holy Grail* (HBHG), which articulated and discussed the evidence for the contention that Mary Magdalene, as referred to in *The Gospels*, had married and conceived a child with Jesus Christ and that a secret society had protected the royal lineage descended from that child over the centuries. Subsequent to the publication of *The Da Vinci Code*, a modern-day thriller, the plot of which was predicated on the same premise, Baigent and Leigh brought an action claiming damages for breach of copyright against Random House, the publishers of the novel. They claimed that the author of the novel, Dan Brown, had copied a substantial part of the 'central theme' of their book when writing several chapters of his novel. They did not claim *verbatim* copying of their book but, rather, claimed that Brown had copied the 'central theme' of their non-fiction work. This contention was rejected both by the trial court and by the Court of Appeal. While ideas expressed in the non-fiction work could also be found in the novel, "what he [Dan Brown] took from HBHG amounted to generalised propositions, at too high a level of abstraction to qualify for copyright protection" (see Lord Justice Lloyd at paragraph 99 of his Court of Appeal judgment agreeing with the findings of the trial judge). The Court of Appeal agreed with the trial judge that whatever elements of HBHG had been copied (if any) by Brown did not amount to a substantial part of the non-fiction work and no breach of copyright had occurred.

See also

www.bailii.org – database of Irish and UK case law.

Q87 How can a copyright-owner protect their copyright?

One of the principles informing the *Berne Convention* is that copyright is deemed to arise automatically in a copyright work and is not dependent on any form of registration.

Some countries, such as the US, have established a voluntary copyright registration scheme, where registration supports copyright-owners in proving their ownership of a particular copyright in the event of a legal dispute over ownership or breach of copyright. Neither Ireland nor the UK maintains such a copyright register.

The core element of a copyright work is its originality and how much time has elapsed since its creation. For this reason, the date of creation of a copyright work is relevant to determining the subsistence of copyright in a work.

The convention of using the symbol '©' to indicate an assertion of copyright on all copies of the work, accompanied by the name of the copyright owner and the date of creation of the work, is a widely-accepted convention for asserting the copyright ownership in a work.

Section 139 of the *Copyright and Related Rights Act, 2000* provides that any "name, statement, label or mark indicating that a person is the author or the exclusive licensee" of the copyright in a work shall be admissible as evidence in a civil or criminal claim for copyright infringement, of the ownership of the copyright in that work. Further, the section provides that this notice of copyright shall be "presumed to be correct" unless the contrary is proved. This places the burden on the defendant to prove that the person whose name appears in the copyright notice is *not* the rightful owner of the copyright in the work. Featuring a copyright notice on all copies of a copyright work therefore puts the copyright owner at a distinct advantage in the event that she / he needs to resort to the courts to vindicate her / his copyright in the work.

To protect their copyright, a copyright owner – who may be the 'author' (the creator) of the work or someone who holds the copyright under an assignment or licence from the author – should clearly mark all copies of the work with:

- The copyright symbol ©.
- Their name.
- The year in which copyright is first asserted in the work.

All copies of the work created or disseminated by the copyright-owner should carry this three-part assertion of copyright.

The author of a copyright work needs to negotiate and agree in clear, unambiguous terms the basis on which her / his copyright work may be used and exploited by another, whether by way of assignment of the copyright or the grant of a licence to use it.

Copyright-owners (who may be the author, their assignee or licensee) need to be vigilant and prepared to take decisive action to vindicate their entitlements if they become aware of a breach of their copyright.

In order to be able to demonstrate, in the event of a dispute, the existence of their copyright in a work on a particular date, authors of copyright works frequently take precautionary measures to create evidence of their copyright-ownership as of a particular date. This can involve posting a copy of the work to themselves by registered post and leaving the registered envelope, on which the date of posting is marked by the post office, unopened unless or until it is opened before a court or on the advice of a lawyer at a later date. It needs to be evident, however, that the seal has not been tampered with or re-sealed since the date of posting. This method of demonstrating the existence of copyright in a work can be of assistance but may not provide conclusive evidence of the date of copyright-ownership arising. An alternative is to deposit a sealed envelope containing a copy of the copyright work with, for example, a lawyer on a date recorded by the lawyer. A lawyer is likely to charge a fee for this service.

In the UK, there exist companies that provide registration facilities, whereby a copyright-owner may make a safe deposit of a copy of the work with the company in a specially sealed envelope and the date of deposit is recorded. Only reputable services should be used, as there can be no guarantee that such a company will be in existence should the deposited work need to be retrieved to resolve a copyright dispute at some distant date in the future. The Irish Copyright Licensing Association contains information in this regard on its website, **www.icla.ie**.

People involved in the origination of content ideas in the film, television and radio industry often are concerned that their ideas will be taken, copied or used without their consent by people to whom they pitch those ideas with a view to further development and production. A precaution commonly taken in such circumstances is to request the person to whom they are pitching to give a written commitment by way of a non-disclosure (NDA) / confidentiality agreement to treat the copyright work (being the written / recorded treatment or pilot for a proposed programme) as confidential and not to disclose it to third parties. Legal advice can be taken on the form of agreement to be used. While this precaution does not prevent unauthorised copying or plagiarism by the person to whom they are pitching, it puts that person on notice that they could be held liable for damages for breach of confidentiality should they show the copyright work to others without authorisation.

Note that a format for a television or radio show is not a separately recognised form of copyright. A format for a television show usually comprises a bundle of copyright works and other intellectual property (such as specific devices or features used in a show; technical and creative know-how on the part of the producer and / or director; specific backing music, lighting or sounds, etc). Usually, the more detailed and specific the various elements of a show and how they hang together in a production, the more likely it is that a format will exist. It is frequently the case that people come up with an idea for a television or radio show that may be original and / or a variation on a generic theme but that does not necessarily mean it comprises a format in the sense that it comprises a package of intellectual property rights that can be licensed to third parties in return for a fee.

Individual production companies or advertising agencies must decide whether to adopt a policy of accepting unsolicited ideas for programmes, advertising copy, jingles or music. Once they have seen or heard a copyright work, and the copyright-owner can show that the company /

agency saw or heard it, it is more difficult for the company / agency to maintain that any similar work produced by them in the future was not based on or influenced by the copyright work submitted to them. Accordingly, many production companies and advertising agencies adopt a policy of not accepting unsolicited copyright work.

Freelance journalists and photographers should be very clear when submitting copy or images to newspaper and other media outlets about the permitted uses of that copy or those images in return for the fee paid. Even where the scope for negotiation of terms by the journalist or photographer is limited, they are within their rights to require a clear statement of the proposed uses of content supplied for publication.

See also

Q84   What is copyright?
Q85   Who owns the copyright in a copyright work?
Q86   What rights does copyright confer on a copyright-owner?
Q89   What is the difference between an assignment and a licence of copyright?
Q90   What remedies are available where a breach of copyright has occurred?
Q91   What steps can a copyright owner take to protect their copyright online?
Q92   What is 'fair dealing'?

Q88   What is the duration of copyright?

Copyright is not a right that endures for ever; it has a limited duration provided for by law.

Different durations of copyright attach to different types of copyright work. The EU has sought to harmonise the duration of copyright across the EU Member States, principally by way of the *Copyright Directive, 1993* (*Directive 93/98/EEC*, as repealed and re-stated in amended form by *Directive 2006/116/EC*). Along with the provisions of certain other EU Copyright Directives, the *Copyright Directive, 1993* was incorporated into Irish law by the *Copyright and Related Rights Act, 2000*.

The duration of copyright in Ireland is set out principally in sections 24 to 36 inclusive of the 2000 Act. Below is a summary of the most commonly-occurring copyright works and the duration of copyright in those works:

- Literary, dramatic, musical or artistic works or an original database: Copyright expires 70 years after death of author (section 24). Note that a computer program is included in the Act's definition of a literary work, as is a photograph in the definition of an artistic work (section 2).

- Films: Copyright expires 70 years after the death of the *last* of the following to die:
  - The principal director.
  - The author of the screenplay.
  - The author of the dialogue.
  - The composer of any music composed specifically for the film (section 25).

- Sound recordings: Copyright continues for 50 years after the recording is made *or* 50 years after the date on which it is first made available to public, so long as it is made available to the public within 50 years of being recorded (section 26). An EU proposal for the extension of the duration of sound recordings from 50 to 70 years was approved by the EU Parliament in April 2009 but, at the time of writing, has not been issued as an EU

Directive. The copyright interest in a sound recording usually is held by the record company that makes the sound recording and is subject to clearance of the underlying rights in the material contained in it – for example, composer's rights in the musical work recorded, or performers' rights of the musicians performing on the recording.

- Broadcasts: Copyright continues for 50 years after first transmission (section 27). Note that a broadcaster holds a distinct copyright in its broadcasts, although that copyright is subject to the underlying copyright interests inherent in its content.

- Typographical arrangement of a published edition: Copyright continues for 50 years after the date on which a published edition is first made available to the public (section 29). Note that a publisher of a book or a newspaper has a copyright in the typographical arrangement, layout and presentation of that book or newspaper that is separate from the copyright in the literary work, comprising the text of the book or newspaper (see section2 for a definition of "published edition").

Note that the duration of copyright protection is calculated from 1 January of the year following the event giving rise to that term (section 35). So, for example, the duration of copyright in a literary work is 70 years from the death of the author; that term of 70 years is calculated from 1 January of the year following the death of the author.

See also

Q84   What is copyright?
Q85   Who owns the copyright in a copyright work?
Q86   What rights does copyright confer on a copyright-owner?

Q89 What is the difference between an assignment and a licence of copyright?

The terms 'assignment' and 'licence' have the same meanings when applied to copyright as they do to any other form of property.

An assignment takes place when a copyright-owner (the assignor) transfers ownership of their copyright to another (the assignee). The assignee then is at liberty to use and exploit that copyright as their property. An assignment contract may contain conditions such as a condition obliging the assignee to pay a share of any earnings from exploitation of the copyright to the assignor (for example, royalties on book sales paid by a publisher to an author), or a condition that the copyright will revert to the assignor if the assignee goes into liquidation or goes bankrupt.

The whole, or part only, of the copyright in a work may be assigned. An author of a book, for instance, may retain certain elements of their copyright, such as the dramatisation rights or overseas publication rights but assign the remaining elements of their copyright in the literary work to a publisher.

In order to be legally binding, an assignment must be made in writing by the assignee or someone authorised to do so on her / his behalf (section 120(3) of the *Copyright and Related Rights Act, 2000*).

A licence is a grant of permission by a copyright-owner to another to use and exploit all or part of the copyright in a copyright work. The copyright work remains the property of the copyright-owner, subject to the licence they have granted as licensor to the licensee. A licence usually will be subject to conditions that specify the extent to which the licensee is, or is not, permitted to use the copyright in the work.

A licence may be 'exclusive' in that it is granted to one person only. A non-exclusive licence is one that allows the copyright-owner to grant similar rights to use the copyright work to a number of different licensees. It is possible for a licence to be granted other than in writing. Reflecting the form of a licence in a written agreement, however, provides evidence of the existence of a licence and the extent of its terms.

It is for the copyright-owner and the assignee or licensee to negotiate such terms and conditions of assignment / licence as they see fit. While there may be certain broad industry norms, such as the rate of commission paid to film distributors in respect of the fees they secure for the distribution of films in various territories, individual contracts can be individually negotiated. The terms and conditions on which assignments and licences of copyright can be made are infinitely varied.

The rapid emergence of new forms of digital media means that potential future digital uses of copyright works need to be contemplated when, for instance, licensing the use of a musical composition or a radio or television programme. Within the book publishing industry, the emergence of ebooks means that provision should be made in copyright assignment or licence contracts for the publication of a literary work by way of an ebook and for the payment of royalties to the author in respect of ebook sales. Where a composer (or her / his publisher, if their copyright has been assigned to a music publisher) is licensing her / his copyright in a musical composition, it is necessary to negotiate for the payment of fees in respect of various forms of digital exploitation of that music (such as use as ringtones or distribution through iPhone apps).

A licence agreement typically includes:

- A warranty by the licensor that she / he is the owner of the copyright being licensed or holds sufficient rights in the copyright to grant the licence.
- A warranty by the licensor that any underlying rights in the copyright work being licensed are cleared (for example, performers' rights, music copyright) – or not, as the case may be.
- A condition agreeing to the media and / or format and / or purpose for which the copyright may be used (for example, online streaming and / or catch-up availability of a television programme as well as broadcast use; use in a commercially-released DVD; use of a photograph in a book).

- A condition specifying the duration of the licence (for example, indefinite or expiring after a period of time or subject to the payment of additional fees after a specified period of time).

- A condition specifying the fees to be paid – when, how and to whom.

Though not exhaustive, these terms illustrate some of the basic issues that need to be considered in negotiating and drafting a licence agreement in respect of a copyright work.

A licence agreement usually contains a term either permitting or prohibiting the licensee from granting further sub-licenses to third parties to use or exploit a copyright work. The chain of licences, sub-licences and / or assignments of a copyright work can become extremely complex. Some licence and sub-licence agreements, particularly in the film and music industries, will involve detailed accounting and reporting procedures to facilitate the collection of revenue share by all those entitled to receive a portion of the revenue earned from the exploitation of that copyright.

See also

Q84   What is copyright?
Q85   Who owns the copyright in a copyright work?
Q86   What rights does copyright confer on a copyright-owner?
Q97   How do music collection societies work?

Q90   What remedies are available where a breach of copyright has occurred?

A person who has unlawfully infringed the copyright of another person can be liable either to criminal prosecution and / or to being sued for damages in the civil courts. The criminal law tends to be invoked in respect of mass-counterfeiting operations, whereas the civil law usually will be the recourse of copyright-holders whose copyright has been breached on a once-off basis.

Criminal penalties
It is a criminal offence under section 140 of the *Copyright and Related Rights Act, 2000* to import (other than for private and domestic use), sell, rent or lend an infringing copy of a work. Bootleg DVDs of films are an example of infringing works. Lending under the section excludes lending to a family member or a friend for private and domestic use. The section also creates similar offences in respect of articles specifically designed or adapted for making infringing copies of copyright work and "protection-defeating devices" (devices used to break or circumvent rights-protection measures, such as illegal decoding cards for satellite signals). The penalties comprise a fine and /or imprisonment.

The court, in a criminal prosecution for copyright infringement, may order the 'delivery up' by the accused person (prior to or after conviction) of an infringing copy of a work, an article specifically designed or adapted for making infringing copies or a protection-defeating device (section 142). Further, a District Court judge may issue a warrant to a Garda, where there are reasonable grounds for suspecting that copyright is being infringed, for the search of a premises and seizure of copies of a work, an article specifically designed or adapted for making infringing copies of a work or a protection-defeating device (section 143).

A court has power under section 145 to order that copies, articles or devices delivered-up or seized be handed over the copyright-owner or destroyed.

It is also an offence, under section 141 of the Act, to falsely claim, for financial gain, to be the owner of the copyright in a work.

Civil remedies

Section 127 of the 2000 Act provides a statutory right to bring a civil claim for copyright infringement and to seek relief by way of "damages, injunction, account of profits or otherwise" (section 127(2)). An award of damages may include aggravated and /or exemplary damages (section 128(3)).

An 'account of profits' involves a defendant who has unlawfully breached the copyright of the plaintiff accounting for the money they have earned as a result of that breach of copyright and paying all or an appropriate share of those earnings to the plaintiff, as ordered by the court.

Where a single incident of copyright infringement has occurred, it is more common for a copyright-holder to take up the matter directly with the person they believe has infringed their copyright under the civil law rather than seek to have the matter dealt with under the criminal law.

Under section 131 of the 2000 Act, a copyright-owner may apply to the court for an order requiring the 'delivery up' to the copyright holder (or such other person as the court may direct) infringing copies of a work, articles specifically designed or adapted for making infringing copies or a protection-defeating device. The Court may also, at the request of the copyright-holder, order the seizure by a Garda of infringing copies, articles specifically designed or adapted for making infringing copies or protection-defeating devices (section 132). If an application is made by a copyright-holder for seizure by a Garda under section 132 and it transpires that there was no breach of copyright and that the application was made maliciously, an aggrieved person may be awarded damages against the copyright-holder who applied for the order (section 132(5)).

There is a limited entitlement conferred on a copyright-owner by section 133 to seize infringing copies, articles for making infringing copies or protection-defeating devices herself / himself. This entitlement is subject to strict statutory conditions, however, and an aggrieved person from whom items have been seized in accordance with section 133 may be awarded damages against the copyright-owner if it transpires no copyright infringement took place and there were no reasonable grounds for the seizure.

References to the Controller of Patents

Although not concerned with breach of copyright as such, certain disputes in relation to the collective licensing of rights by collection societies / licensing bodies may be referred for adjudication to the Controller of Patents under the 2000 Act.

Thus, for example, a television station that requires a licence from a music rights collection society / licensing body in respect of the incorporation of sound recordings into its television programmes may refer the terms of a proposed licence to the Controller of Patents. The Controller may make an order confirming or varying those terms as she / he deems reasonable in the circumstances (sections 157 to 161).

A person or entity that has been refused a licence by a licensing body / collection society to use copyright material under a licensing scheme as described in the Act may to apply to the Controller of Patents for an order granting them that licence on such terms as are applicable under the relevant licensing scheme or as the Controller deems reasonable (section 154).

The equivalent adjudicating body in the UK is known as the Copyright Tribunal.

See also

Q2	What is the difference between civil law and criminal law?
Q9	What are damages and how are they assessed?
Q87	How can a copyright-owner protect their copyright?
Q91	What steps can a copyright-owner take to protect their copyright online?
Q92	What is 'fair dealing'?
Q97	How do music collection societies work?

Q91 What steps can a copyright-owner take to protect their copyright online?

Apart from technical measures implemented to protect copyright material online from unauthorised use, there are other measures by which copyright can be protected online.

No less than in any other form of publication, the owner's copyright in a work made available online should be clearly and visibly asserted by way of a copyright notice.

When a copyright-holder becomes aware of an infringement of their copyright online, prompt action is essential. Where a copyright work appears, without the owner's consent, on an Internet platform, the proprietor of the platform – be it a website, blog or social media page /account – may be contacted and requested to remove it. However, it may be impossible to trace the person or entity that owns or is responsible for that platform. Alternatively, if contactable, they may refuse to take the infringing item off the website or other online platform in question. In such circumstances, copyright-holders may direct their complaint to the Internet service provider or other intermediary service provider through which that site, blog or social media page / account is made available on the Internet.

It should be noted that online service providers are granted protection from liability for online copyright infringement, subject to certain conditions – concerned principally with removal of the offending material on being notified of its presence on a site, blog or social media page / account made available through the services of that service provider.

By virtue of section 40 of the *Copyright and Related Rights Act, 2000,* the provider of 'facilities' for making infringing copies of copyright work available to the public is not liable for copyright infringement unless the facilities-provider, having been notified that the facilities in question are being used to disseminate infringing copies of a work to the public, fails to remove the infringing material "as soon as practicable" after being notified of the presence on its facilities (which term encompasses

Internet facilities) of that infringing material. This section was applicable to an ISP in *EMI Records (Ireland) and Others v UPC Communications Ireland [2010] IEHC 377* (see below).

Section 40 reflects (in part) the provisions of the *Electronic Commerce Directive (Directive 31 /2000 / EU)*, which was incorporated into Irish law by the *Electronic Commerce Regulations* of 2003 (SI 68 of 2003). The Directive and Regulations afford protection from liability for unlawful activity on a 'relevant service' (as defined in the Regulations) in the form of three specific defences:

- The 'mere conduit' defence available to an intermediary service provider that enables the transmission of information *via* the Internet (Regulation 16).

- The 'caching' defence available to an intermediary service provider that temporarily stores information in order to render the process of onward transmission *via* the Internet more efficient (Regulation 17).

- The 'hosting' defence available to an intermediary service provider that stores information for the recipient of an Internet service, where the intermediary service provider is neither aware of the unlawful material nor aware of facts or circumstances whereby the unlawful nature of the material is apparent (Regulation 18).

The caching and hosting defences can be availed of only where the intermediary service provider has acted expeditiously either to remove the unlawful material or to disable access to it on obtaining knowledge of the unlawful nature of the material (both caching and hosting) or on becoming aware of facts or circumstances from which the unlawful nature of the material is apparent (hosting only).

The question remains to be explored under Irish case law as to what services will be regarded as "relevant services" provided by an intermediary service provider for the purposes of the *Electronic Commerce Regulations* defences. Regulation 3 (reflecting the terms of the EU *Electronic Commerce Directive*) defines a "relevant service" as "any service normally provided for remuneration, at a distance, by electronic means and at the individual request of a recipient of the service, other than a service specified in Schedule 1 to these Regulations" (the Schedule 1 exemptions include television and radio services). As is provided for in the Directive, the term "for remuneration" is given a broad interpretation and does not require that a charge be made to the recipient of the online service (see Recital 18 of the Directive).

While the extent of online services that will be regarded as "relevant services" provided by an intermediary service provider under the Regulations is not certain, generally speaking, the provider of a reputable online service is likely to respond promptly to a notification that copyright-infringing material is present on a website, blog or social media page / account provided or facilitated by it, in anticipation that it will be able to rely on the defences available for intermediary service providers in the event of being sued for damages for breach of copyright. Notification of online copyright-infringement by the copyright-holder to the relevant intermediary service provider is therefore a key aspect of copyright protection online.

In the US, copyright-specific procedures may be invoked by a copyright-holder under the *Digital Millennium Copyright Act*, 1998 (DMCA). The DMCA offers protection to online service providers from liability for breach of copyright, subject to compliance with DMCA notification and take-down procedures. Under these procedures, a copyright-holder will notify an online service provider of material online that they allege violates their copyright. To avoid liability for copyright infringement, the service provider must act expeditiously to remove it and notify the service-user who originally posted the material of the complaint. The alleged infringer may counter-claim that they have the right to use the copyright work in question. In such instances, the copyright-holder giving the original notice has 14 days within which to issue civil proceedings for breach of copyright, failing which the online service provider will re-activate access to the material in question and cannot be held liable for breach of copyright.

Social networking sites such as YouTube and Facebook provide procedures for reporting copyright-infringement on their websites which can be relied on as notifications for the purposes of both the Irish / EU 'hosting' defence and for the purposes of the DMCA.

Under the increasingly popular creative commons online licensing system (**www.creativecommons.org**), a copyright-holder can make her / his copyright work available online and indicate to other Internet users its availability for use, subject to certain restrictions imposed by the copyright-holder. To do this, the copyright-holder selects a standardised creative commons licence and then marks the work clearly with a creative commons symbol indicating which form of creative commons licence applies to the use of the work. An example of one form of creative commons licence is the 'Attribution, Non-Commercial licence', whereby other Internet users know that they can take, re-mix and use the copyright-holder's work, subject to crediting the original copyright-holder and not using the work for commercial purposes.

An alternative to a request for take-down of copyright material used online without consent is to request that a fee be paid in respect of the use of the material, either retrospectively and / or in the future. There may be occasions where this would be a practical avenue for the copyright-holder to explore. In effect, the copyright-holder in such circumstances is granting a retrospective licence to use the work and / or a licence to use the work in future.

The international nature of the Internet and the speed of transmission of information online means that the online dissemination of copyright material without the consent of the copyright-owner can often be impossible to track or prevent – unless significant technological and legal resources are deployed, such as those deployed by Getty Images to track down copyright infringement of its images online. There are measures that can be taken, however, to seek to have infringing material removed from online sources and these measures are supported by the law in Ireland.

The key to availing of any of these legal protections is two-fold:

- The clear indication by the copyright-holder of their copyright in any copyright material made available online.
- The prompt notification by the copyright-holder to any online service provider on whose service copyright-infringing material is present requesting the removal of the material or (if practicable,

and desirable) requesting payment in respect of its retrospective and /or prospective use.

Case law

EMI Records (Ireland) and Others v UPC Communications Ireland [2010] IEHC 377

A number of Irish record companies sought an injunction requiring UPC, a major Internet service provider in Ireland, to disable the Internet access of customers found to be repeat offenders in downloading the plaintiffs' sound-recordings by way of peer-to-peer file-sharing sites.

UPC was held to be 'mere conduit' for the purposes of the *Electronic Commerce Directive, 2000*. The judge was trenchant in his condemnation of illegal downloading of musical sound-recordings. However, the injunction sought was refused on the grounds that section 40 of the *Copyright and Related Rights Act, 2000*, on which the plaintiff relied in its application for an injunction, referred to a provider of [Internet] "facilities" not being liable for copyright infringement if it removed the offending material from those facilities as soon as practicable after being notified of its presence. The judge noted that sound-recordings were no longer available for removal from UPC's service once down-loaded. He also noted that, despite reference in the *Electronic Commerce Directive, 2000* to injunctive relief being provided for by way of ordering the disablement of a user's access to infringing material (see Recital 45 of the Directive), section 40 made no reference to the option of disabling user access to copyright-infringing material. He held, therefore, that he could not grant an injunction ordering UPC to disable user-access to copyright-infringing material (by way of cutting off their Internet access) because section 40, as currently worded, did not entitle him to do so. He pointed out that a legislative amendment to section 40 would be necessary to entitle him to grant such an injunction. At the date of writing, such an amendment has not been made.

See also

Q86   What rights does copyright confer on a copyright-owner?

Q87 How can a copyright-owner protect their copyright?

Q89 What is the difference between an assignment and a licence of copyright?

Q90 What remedies are available where a breach of copyright has occurred?

Q93 What does 'public domain' mean?

Q92   What is 'fair dealing'?

The *Copyright and Related Rights Act, 2000* allows for the lawful use of copyright material without the consent of the copyright-owner in certain circumstances, where the use can be classified as 'fair dealing'. Part II, Chapter 6 (sections 49 to 106 inclusive) of the 2000 Act concerns fair dealing. The fair dealing exemptions most-commonly relied on (apart from educational use) are contained in sections 51 to 52 inclusive.

It should be understood that, while the 2000 Act provides for the exemptions, the actual scope and extent of the exemptions cannot be specified with certainty in every situation. Accordingly, there is extensive case law – principally in the UK courts – concerned with the extent and application of the fair dealing exemptions of copyright law. Since Irish and UK copyright law is very similar, UK case law can be cited to support a case made before an Irish court.

Fair dealing with copyright work is subject to two overriding criteria:

- The work already must have been lawfully made available to the public.

- The use must be for a purpose and to an extent that will not "unreasonably prejudice" the copyright-owner's interests (section 50(4)).

There are three principal categories of fair dealing exemption relevant to the media:

- Research or private study (section 50).

- Criticism or review – including reporting current events (section 51).

- Incidental inclusion – including the use of quotes or extracts (section 52).

Research or private study

Section 50 of the 2000 Act allows for the use, including copying, of a copyright work for the purposes of research or private study without the copyright-owner's consent. However, the extent of this copying is restricted, such that multiple copying of material for students by university and other educational establishment libraries is not permitted under this exemption. The 2000 Act provides for a licensing scheme that permits university, school and college libraries to make multiple copies of copyright work available for educational purposes, subject to the terms of a licence granted by the Irish Copyright Licensing Agency. There are further exemptions set out under sections 53 to 58 concerning the use of copyright material for educational purposes, subject to very specific criteria set out in those sections.

Criticism or review – including reporting current events
Section 51 of the 2000 Act provides an exemption for the use of a copyright work for the purposes of criticism or review of that work or another work or a performance of a copyright work.

This exemption is subject to the use being accompanied by "sufficient acknowledgment" (section 51(1)), which means identifying the work by its *title or other description* and identifying *the author* (section 51(3)).

So, for example, publishing a short extract from a recently-published novel in a newspaper literary review will not amount to a breach of copyright, so long as the title of the novel and the name of the author are acknowledged in the review.

An important exemption from the point of view of journalists and news reporters is set out in section 51(2), which permits the use of a copyright work without the copyright-owner's consent for the purpose of reporting current events, subject to the report containing sufficient acknowledgement.

Note that the current affairs reporting exemption does not apply to photographs. This means that press photographs cannot be used by other news outlets on the basis of current events reporting fair dealing exemptions; specific clearance for the re-use of photographs for current affairs reporting must be obtained.

Case law in the UK has held that the defence of fair dealing by way of criticism and review can apply to criticism and review of an idea or matter other than the copyright work used in that critique or review. See *Time Warner Entertainments Co v Channel Four Television Corp plc [1994] EMLR 1*, in which the use in a television documentary of extracts from director Stanley Kubrick's film, *A Clockwork Orange*, was held to be fair dealing. The UK Court of Appeal held that the use of these extracts to critique the decision taken by Time Warner some 20 years previously to withdraw the film – apart from critique of the film itself – was fair dealing. The film contained scenes of graphic violence and had been withdrawn after allegations arose of incidents of copycat violence.

Incidental inclusion

Section 52 allows for a copyright work to feature in some background or ancillary way in another copyright work – for example, in a television documentary. The parameters of what amounts to 'incidental inclusion' have not been explored under Irish case law to date.

The deliberate inclusion of a substantial part of a piece of music or literature in a new copyright work would suggest that its inclusion was not merely incidental.

Section 52(3) states that inclusion of a copyright work in another work will not be regarded as incidental if the manner of inclusion is such that the interests of the copyright-owner in the included work are "unreasonably prejudiced".

Section 52(4) allows for the use of quotations or extracts from published works. This use must be such that it "does not prejudice" the interests of the copyright-owner in that published work and must be accompanied by sufficient acknowledgment (title / description and author). This test of prejudice to the copyright-owner is more stringent than the test of "no unreasonable prejudice" referred to in section 50(4). A precautionary approach is for audio / audio-visual producers and book publishers to obtain clearance from copyright-owners for the use of quotations and extracts from previously-published works – unless, of course, an alternative ground of exemption, such as the criticism or review exemption, is to be relied on to justify the use without consent of those quotes or extracts.

It should be noted that buildings and sculptures are copyright works. However, section 93 of the 2000 Act allows for the photographing, filming and drawing of buildings, as well as sculptures that are located in public places or in premises open to the public, without infringing the copyright in those buildings and sculptures. The same section permits such films or photographs to be made available to the public without infringing the copyright in the building or sculpture featured in the film or photograph. It should be noted that this provision relates to copyright law only; as a matter of privacy law, the proprietor's consent may be required for filming or taking photographs at a private location albeit one to which the public has access.

Two further useful exemptions for media outlets from liability for breach of copyright are:

- Section 89, which permits copies or recordings of speeches ("spoken words") made directly at an event to be used for the purpose of reporting current events or broadcasting the contents of the speech. This provision applies to the extent that the speech itself may comprise a literary or dramatic work. The speech itself (*if* it qualifies as a copyright work) must not infringe a pre-existing copyright and the person giving the speech must not have prohibited the recording of the speech.

- Section 90, which permits the public reading or recitation by one person of "any reasonable extract" from an already-published literary or dramatic work, subject to "sufficient acknowledgment" (title / description and author). It is also permissible to record or broadcast that reading or recitation without infringing the copyright in the work being read / recited (subject to sufficient acknowledgement). However, offering copies of that recording for sale, rental or loan or otherwise making them available to the public is not exempted from liability for copyright infringement. It should also be remembered that a person who gives a recitation or reading of a literary work holds performer's rights. As a performer, their consent will be required to the recording and / or broadcast of their reading / recitation.

It is specifically recognised by section 49 of the Act that it is possible for the use of a copyright work under the fair dealing provisions to be exempted under one or more categories of exemption.

Sections 220, 221 and 222 of the 2000 Act set out fair dealing exemptions by way of criticism and review, current events reporting and incidental inclusion in relation to performers' rights similar to those described above in respect of copyright.

While the laws of some countries (for example, France) provide a specific fair dealing exemption for parodies of copyright works, there is no such statutory exemption under the 2000 Act in Ireland. It should be noted that, under Irish law, composing or releasing to the public a parody of a song without the consent of the copyright-owner can infringe the copyright-owner's copyright – and possibly their moral rights also – in the song.

Case law
Fraser-Woodward Ltd v BBC and Brighter Pictures Ltd [2005] EWHC 472 (Ch)
A UK case where an infringement claim was made by the holder of copyright in certain photographs of the family of David and Victoria Beckham. The photographs had appeared originally in particular tabloid newspapers. The producer of a television documentary programme used on-screen shots of the photographs as they appeared in those newspapers. The BBC (as broadcaster) and Brighter Pictures (as producer) argued that the use of the photographs was defensible by way of criticism and review. They argued that the programme "intended to and did criticise and / or review tabloid journalism and the methods employed by the tabloid press and / or the celebrities featured to build and exploit a story to their advantage".

Apart from one photograph that was on screen for about four seconds, the others were shown for no more than two or three seconds each. The court ultimately held that the use of the photographs amounted to fair dealing within section 30(1) of the *Copyright, Designs and Patents Act, 1988* (equivalent to section 51 of the Irish *Copyright and Related Rights Act, 2000*). The trial judge articulated seven guidelines that he said were relevant in deciding whether the unauthorised use of the claimant's (the UK term for 'plaintiff') copyright in the photographs was fair dealing (see paragraph 55 of judgment), summarised as follows:

(i) It is relevant to have regard to the motives of the user.

(ii) Whether there is a fair dealing is a matter of impression.

(iii) If some degree of use would be fair dealing, excessive use can render the use unfair.

(iv) In assessing whether the dealing is fair, the court can have regard to the actual purpose of the work and will be live to any pretence in the purported purpose of the work.

(v) The amount of the work used can be relevant.

(vi) The guideline at (v) must be carefully applied in relation to photographs where any use is likely to include most of the photograph.

(vii) Reproduction should not unreasonably prejudice the legitimate interests of the author or conflict with the author's normal exploitation of the work.

See also

Q70 How is privacy protected under Irish law?
Q71 What legislation provides for the protection of privacy under Irish law?
Q72 Are image rights protected under Irish law?
Q85 Who owns the copyright in a copyright work?
Q86 What rights does copyright confer on a copyright-owner?
Q87 How can a copyright-owner protect their copyright?
Q90 What remedies are available where a breach of copyright has occurred?
Q93 What does 'public domain' mean?
Q99 What is the role of the Irish Copyright Licensing Agency?

www.bailii.org – database of Irish and UK case law.

Q93 What does 'public domain' mean?

In copyright law, a work is 'in the public domain' when it is no longer subject to any copyright restrictions because the term of copyright in that work has expired or, in some cases, because the work pre-dated international copyright protection laws.

For example, since Mozart and Beethoven both died well over 150 years ago (Mozart in 1791 and Beethoven in 1827), there is no question of their compositions being in copyright and, therefore, their musical works are in the public domain.

However, publications of those composers' musical works in sheet music form that have been published within the last 50 years are copyright works. Such publications comprise copyright works in the form of "typographical arrangements of published editions" (section 17(2)(c) of the *Copyright and Related Rights Act, 2000*).

Sound recordings made of those composer's musical works also are separate copyright works. The underlying musical compositions that are performed on those sound recordings may be in the public domain but each sound recording (such as is contained on a commercially-released CD) is a distinct copyright work (section 17(2)(b)).

Book publishers are at liberty to publish texts of literary works that are out of copyright and therefore in the public domain; they do not need the author's consent to publish those texts. *The Prince*, a political treatise by Niccolo Machiavelli, was written in the early years of the 16th century; Machiavelli died in 1527. The treatise continues to be published by various publishers to this day. Each publisher has a separate copyright in their own typographical arrangement of the published edition of Machiavelli's original literary work although the literary work itself is clearly in the public domain.

It is a widespread practice in Ireland for musicians to make a new arrangement of a traditional air or melody and to assert a copyright in the newly created "trad. arr.".

Some creators of copyright work deliberately choose to make their work freely available without asserting copyright over that work, giving rise to the term "copyleft" often used to describe the practice.

Initiatives such as 'creative commons' increasingly are relied on by creators of copyright work who wish to make their works available to the public on terms that remove to an extent chosen by the author, some of the copyright restrictions that would otherwise apply to the work. Creative commons (see **www.creativecommons.org**) is a not-for-profit organisation based in the US that has established a licensing system using symbols by which a copyright-holder can communicate to the public the extent to which the work may be used. One symbol, for instance, indicates consent to virtually unrestricted use, subject only to the author being acknowledged (Attribution licence), while another indicates consent to use, subject to the author being acknowledged, to no commercial use being made of the work and no adaptation or further works derived from the original being made (Attribution, Non-Commercial, No Derivatives licence). Irish versions of the creative commons licences are being developed in association with the Law Faculty of University College Cork.

In open source software development, the GNU General Public Licence provides a licensing regime for sharing and using copyright computer programs (see **www.gnu.org**).

There is no provision under Irish law for formally 'renouncing' copyright. The world-famous iconic image of Ché Guevara, which has featured on countless posters, tee-shirts and other merchandise is an interesting case-study in this regard. This image was created by Irish artist, Jim Fitzpatrick, in 1968. Fitzpatrick pro-actively and publicly declared his intention to make the image available "copyright free" by reason of his deep personal admiration for Ché Guevara whom he, in his own words, "idolised". Fitzpatrick never sought to assert copyright in his poster-image of Guevara until February 2011, when he announced his intention to claim his copyright in the image, saying that he wished to donate it, for the benefit of the Cuban people, to Guevara's family. The Ché poster-image in turn was based on a photograph of Guevara taken in 1960 by a Cuban photographer, Alberto Korda. Cuba did not become a party to the

Berne Convention, which provides international protection for copyright, until 1996. Korda never sought to assert his copyright until the year 2000, when he took exception to the use of a Ché image, based on his photograph, for the advertising of Smirnoff vodka. He sued the advertising agency that created the campaign images and the photographic agency that supplied the image for breach of copyright. The case was settled and Korda died not long afterwards.

Thus, Internet users need to bear in mind that the fact that an image or other copyright work is publicly available online does not mean that, from a legal perspective, it is in the public domain. Consent to further use may be required from the copyright-owner of that work.

See also

Q84   What is copyright?
Q85   Who owns the copyright in a copyright work?
Q88   What is the duration of copyright?

www.creativecommons.org
www.gnu.org

Q94 What are moral rights?

Moral rights for copyright-holders are set out in Part II, Chapter 7 (sections 107 to 119 inclusive) of the *Copyright and Related Rights Act, 2000*. They are:

- The paternity right.
- The integrity right.
- The false attribution right.
- The privacy right in commissioned films or photographs.

The first two rights are the most frequently encountered moral rights.

The paternity right
The paternity right is the right to be identified as the author of a copyright work. This right also extends to any adaptation of a work (section 107). The term 'author' refers to the creator of the copyright work and is not restricted to the author of a literary work in the colloquial sense.

The most significant of several exceptions set out in the Act to the paternity right is contained in section 108. This section provides that the paternity right does not apply to a copyright work made in the course of employment where, in accordance with section 23 of the Act, copyright in a work vests in the employer. Neither does it apply to work created for reporting current events, for a newspaper or periodical or for an encyclopaedia, dictionary, yearbook or other 'collective work of reference'. This exception means there is no statutory entitlement for a journalist to a by-line on a news story or article written for a newspaper or magazine – unless, of course, that right to a by-line has been negotiated separately as part of a contract (for example, a contract for the supply of a weekly column to a newspaper). The 'incidental inclusion' fair dealing exemption applies, however, to the paternity right (section 108(1)).

The integrity right

The integrity right is the right of the author of a copyright work "to object to any distortion, mutilation or other modification of, or other derogatory action in relation to, the work which would prejudice his or her reputation". This right also applies to an adaptation of a copyright work (section 109). The 'criticism or review' fair dealing exemption applies, however, to the integrity right (section 110(2)(b)).

Whether changes made to a copyright work have this prejudicial effect can be a very subjective – and potentially controversial – judgment. Accordingly, most contracts for television, radio or film contributions (for example, with script writers) will contain a clause requiring a waiver of moral rights by the author. This leaves the producer at liberty to make edits and changes to the underlying copyright work in question without incurring the risk of a claim that the integrity right has been infringed.

Section 110(1) exempts from the integrity right copyright work made for reporting current events, for a newspaper or periodical or for an encyclopaedia, dictionary, yearbook or other 'collective work of reference'. Such works therefore can be edited without risking infringement of the integrity right of the author.

Section 110(2) provides that anything done to a copyright work to avoid contravention of the civil or criminal law, to comply with a statutory duty, or to avoid the inclusion in a broadcast of anything likely to offend public morality or which is likely to encourage or incite to crime or lead to public disorder will not be regarded as an infringement of the integrity right. This leaves editors and producers at liberty to edit, change or alter a copyright work for those specified purposes without risking liability for infringement of the integrity right.

In order for the section 110(2) exemption to apply, however, the Act requires that the author be identified, along with a "sufficient disclaimer" indicating that changes have been made to the copyright work without the consent of the author (section 110(3) and (4)). In most publishing, script-writing and other contracts commissioning copyright work, clauses will appear by which the author / producer of the work permits changes to be made and waives their moral rights in the work. Therefore, the question of giving a sufficient disclaimer for 'unlicensed' changes to the work does not arise.

The false attribution right

This is the right of a person not to have authorship of a copyright work falsely attributed to her / him (section 113). The false attribution right survives for the benefit of an author's estate for 20 years after the author's death (section 115(2)).

The right to privacy in photographs

The 2000 Act grants a right to privacy in a film or photograph to the person who commissioned that film or photograph for private and domestic purposes (section 114). While the copyright in the film or photograph usually will be held by the producer or photographer (subject to any written assignment of the copyright), the right to privacy in relation to the public display of that film or photograph is held by the commissioning client. The 'incidental inclusion' fair dealing exemption applies, however, to the use of a photograph or film to which section 114 applies (section 114(3)).

Moral rights cannot be assigned to a third party (section 118). This means that, while the copyright in a work may be assigned to a third party (such as a literary or music publisher), the original author of the work will retain their moral rights in that work. However, moral rights can be waived – in writing – by the author of a copyright work (section 116).

Moral rights (excluding the false attribution right) have the same duration as the copyright work in respect of which the moral rights subsist (section 115). Moral rights, therefore, can be inherited as part of a deceased author's estate (section 119). This is why the consent of relatives or other beneficiaries of a deceased author's estate who control the copyright in a work is required to make an adaptation of that work (for example, to adapt it as a stage play or a feature film screenplay). Consent is required from those relatives or other beneficiaries not only to the making of the adaptation (copyright) but also may be required in respect of the manner of the adaption (moral rights).

The 2000 Act also grants moral rights similar to those enjoyed by authors of copyright works to performers in respect of their performances (sections 309 to 319 inclusive). Contracts securing creative work from authors and performers usually will contain a clause by which the author or performer waives their moral rights. Such contracts also usually will contain a clause that the author or performer will be given a credit on the finished work incorporating their work or performance. In effect, the author or performer waives their paternity and integrity right under copyright law but then is granted a contractual right to a credit. If the credit is not given on the finished work (for example, a film or television programme) as agreed under the contract, the author or performer can claim damages for breach of contract.

Section 137 provides a statutory right to the holder of moral rights to claim damages for infringement of moral rights. Section 319 provides a similar right to performers in respect of performers' moral rights.

See also

Q95   What is meant by 'underlying rights' in a copyright work?

Whenever an individual or company wishes to create a new copyright work – for example, a television or Internet advertisement – and that new work will incorporate other copyrights held by one or more other people, the law requires that the necessary consents be obtained from those copyright-holders to enable the new copyright work to be made and disseminated to the public. This requirement to clear these 'underlying rights' can apply to the creation of any new work, including literary anthologies, the use of illustrations in books or magazines, the use of archive footage in television or radio programmes and the use of music in computer games.

A copyright work containing underlying rights can be compared in a very practical way with a sponge cake with several layers in it. The 'work' is a single product (the cake) but, within that product, there can be several different layers of copyright being the 'underlying rights'.

An example is a feature film based on a novel. The author is the first owner of the copyright in the literary work that is published as a novel (copyright 1). The novel is adapted as a screenplay by a screen-writer (copyright 2). Additional script-writers may be brought in by the producer to work on the script (copyright 3). Actors perform roles in the film (performers' rights 1). A composer is commissioned to write the score for the sound-track of the film (copyright 4). Musicians perform on the recording of the sound-track (performers' rights 2). The director creates the look / style of the film and decides how the story will be realised on screen and that is filmed (copyright 5) in liaison with the producer, who arranges the financing and production of the film and contracts with all the various rights-holders. The producer usually holds the copyright in the final product, which is the film.[1]

The extent and variation of underlying rights in most feature films are in reality more complex than those given in the example above but it serves to illustrate in broad terms the categories of underlying rights present in a feature film. It is the job of the film producer, through her / his production company, to ensure that contracts are concluded with all underlying rights-holders that assign or license those underlying rights to the production company to an extent and on terms sufficient to enable the producer to exploit the finished film.

A similar analysis can be applied to a commercially-released CD or mp3 of a piece of music. The composer of the song featured on the recording holds the original copyright in the song. The musicians who perform on the recording have performers' rights in their performance. The record company that arranges for the production and marketing of the recording holds the copyright in the sound-recording. If a number of songs are released as an album on CD, the graphic designer who designs the CD cover usually will have copyright in the artwork, as will the author of the sleeve-notes in the text of the sleeve-notes. All of these underlying rights must be cleared contractually by the record company to an extent sufficient to enable it to market and exploit the sound recording.

See also

Q85   Who owns the copyright in a copyright work?

---

1. By virtue of sections 21(b) and 22(2) of the *Copyright and Related Rights Act, 2000*, the producer and principal director of a film are the joint copyright-holders in that film. To enable the producer to arrange for the exploitation of the film, the director is usually required by contract to assign her / his copyright in the film to the producer. Depending on the terms of the contract she / he signed, this can be to the detriment of the director if there is secondary exploitation of the film by the producer. In some countries, there is a well-established system for the collection of fees for directors in respect of secondary exploitation of films they have directed, regardless of the fact that they have assigned their copyright in a film to the producer; in others, there is not. For a comparison of film rights law in EU jurisdictions, see *Film Copyright in the European Union by* Pascal Kamina, published by Cambridge University Press.

Q86   What rights does copyright confer on a copyright-owner?

Q96   What are performers' rights?

Q97   How do music collection societies work?

Q96   What are performers' rights?

The *Copyright and Related Rights Act, 2000* provides for specific rights known as 'performers' rights' in performances and recordings of performances. A 'performance' for the purposes of the Act is a live performance by any actor, singer, musician, dancer or other person of any literary, dramatic musical or artistic work or work of folklore and includes a variety act or similar presentation (section 202). Performers' rights are a form of 'related right' or 'neighbouring right' to copyright; they are not the same as, but are akin to, copyright.

By virtue of section 203 of the 2000 Act, a performer has the exclusive right to authorise or prohibit:

- A recording of their live performance.
- The live broadcast of their live performance.
- The recording of a broadcast of their live performance.

The right relates to the whole or any substantial part of a performance.

Section 203 describes performers' rights generally; four specific performers' rights are also recognised and protected by the 2000 Act. They are:

- The reproduction right: The right to authorise or prohibit the making of copies of a recording of a performance (section 204).

- The making-available right: The right to authorise or prohibit the making-available to the public of copies of a recording of a performance (section 205).

- The distribution right: The right to authorise or prohibit copies of a recording of a performance being put into circulation in different territories (section 206).

- The rental and lending right: The right to authorise or prohibit the rental or lending to the public of copies of a recording of a performance (section 207 – the lending aspect of this right was modified by section 11 of the *Copyright and Related Rights (Amendment) Act, 2007*).

These rights also apply to the whole or any substantial part of a live performance.

Note that making recordings of live performances for private and domestic use (such as by making a recording on a mobile phone at a concert) is not in breach of performers' rights (section 204(4)). However, making that private recording available to the public (for example, on an Internet social networking site) without the performer's consent can be an infringement of performers' rights (section 204(5) and section 205(5)(a)) and renders the recording an illegal recording for the purposes of the Act.

Note also that a person or entity that provides 'facilities' for making a recording of a performance in breach of performers' rights available to the public will not be liable for breach of performers' rights so long as, having been notified by a rights-holder that those facilities (such as, for example, a website) are being used to infringe her / his performers' rights, the facilities provider removes the recording "as soon as is practicable" (section 205(7) and (8)). This defence is helpful to a website owner or ISP where a recording that infringes performers' rights is posted online by a third party.

Clearing performers' rights in a live performance before recording it, broadcasting it or making copies of it available for commercial use is important. Failure to do so potentially can give rise to a claim for damages for infringement of performers' rights (sections 303 and 308). There are also provisions in the 2000 Act, similar to those provided by the Act in relation to copyright infringement, for delivery-up or seizure of illicit recordings of live performances, articles specifically designed or adapted for making illicit recordings or what are known as 'protection-defeating devices' (sections 255 to 257 inclusive). Similarly, the Act provides for criminal prosecutions in respect of, among other acts, the importation (other than for private and domestic use), renting or selling of copies of illicit recordings that breach performers' rights (sections 258 and 259).

The specific rights of performers provided for by sections 204 to 207 inclusive (the reproduction right, making-available right, distribution right and rental and lending right) belong to a category of rights referred to in the 2000 Act as "performers' *property* rights" (section 292). Performers' property rights can be assigned (in writing only), licensed and inherited (section 293). This means that rights, such as the distribution right – for example, the right to distribute in any particular territory copies of DVDs containing a recording of a concert – can be assigned by the performer to her / his recording company The recording company, or its licensed distributor, then would be entitled to enforce that distribution right if it were breached by way of the distribution of bootleg copies of that DVD.

By contrast, the more general performers' rights described at section 203 are known as performers' *non-property* rights; these rights cannot be assigned or licensed so that they are exercisable by another person, but they can be inherited (section 300). This means that the estate of a deceased performer is entitled to enforce those non-property rights.

The rental and lending right carries with it a right to equitable remuneration in respect of any rental of a copy of a recording of a performance (section 297(4)). This right to equitable remuneration for rentals remains in place even where the performer has transferred her / his rental right. The rental right of performers is presumed, under section 297 of the Act, to have been transferred to the film's producer under a film production contract. The term 'film' as defined in the Act applies to a television programme (section 2). The right to equitable remuneration for rentals of copies of recordings of a performance cannot be waived; nor can it be assigned except to a collection society (section 298). Frequently, a contract between a film or television producer and a performer will contain an acknowledgement by the performer of the fee paid as equitable remuneration in respect of future rental of copies of the film or television work featuring their performance. Any attempt to contract out of the right to equitable remuneration, however, will be void by virtue of section 298(6).

Performers on commercially-released sound recordings have a right to equitable remuneration payable by the copyright-owner of that sound recording (usually the record company) in respect of the playing in public or broadcasting of that sound recording (section 208). This represents a potential source of revenue for musicians who perform on commercially-released sound recordings, especially session musicians whose performances in the past would simply have been 'bought out' by the payment of a once-off fee. Musicians who perform on sound recordings should be aware of the importance of registering those performances with the Recorded Artists Actors Performers collection society (**www.raap.ie**). The equitable remuneration right provided by section 208 cannot be assigned, other than to a collection society.

The 2000 Act also confers what are known as 'recording rights' on persons / entities (such as record companies) with which a performer has entered into an exclusive recording contract to make commercial recordings of her / his performances. Recording rights can be infringed when unauthorised recordings are made, played in pubic, broadcast, imported, sold or rented out (see sections 215 to 219 inclusive). A record company or other entity that holds recording rights in a performer's performances is entitled to sue for damages for infringement of recording rights (section 308).

Fair dealing exemptions, as well as educational use and certain other exemptions, are provided in respect of performers' rights (sections 220 to 254 inclusive). These sections include fair dealing exemptions for criticism or review of a performance or recording, for reporting current affairs or by way of incidental inclusion of a performance or a recording of a performance in another recording or work. There is no reference in the relevant sections (as there is in respect of fair dealing exemptions for use of copyright material) to "sufficient acknowledgment" of the performance rights-holder but the use must not "unreasonably prejudice" the interests of the rights-holder (sections 220 to 222). However, an acknowledgment of the performer should be given – if this is practicable – where the 'criticism or review' exemption is being relied on (see sections 221, 309 and 310).

Moral rights, similar to those held by a copyright-holder, are also held by performers (sections 309 to 319 inclusive). Performers' moral rights cannot be assigned (section 317) but they can be waived – in writing (section 316). Performers' paternity and integrity rights pass to the estate of the performer on their death if the performer dies before those rights have expired (section 318).

Performers' rights and performers' moral rights have a duration of 50 years from the end of the calendar year in which the performance takes place or 50 years from the date on which a recording of the performance is first made available to the public, so long as it is made available to the public within 50 years of the date of the performance (section 291 and section 315). There is currently an EU proposal for the extension of the duration of performers' rights from 50 to 70 years, which extension was approved by the EU Parliament in April 2009. However, at the time of writing, this proposal has not been passed as an EU Directive.

See also

Q86 What rights does copyright confer on a copyright-owner?
Q90 What remedies are available where a breach of copyright has occurred?
Q92 What is 'fair dealing'?
Q94 What are moral rights?
Q95 What is meant by 'underlying rights' in a copyright work?
Q97 How do music collection societies work?
Q98 What music collection societies operate in Ireland and what do they do?

Q97   How do music collection societies work?

When a piece of recorded music is played in public (such as airplay on a radio station) or incorporated into another work (such as a television or radio programme or audio-visual advertisement), the rights-holders in that musical recording must consent to that use and may charge a fee for the use of their copyright in that recording.

The composer of the music (or their music publisher, where copyright has been assigned by the composer to a music publisher) is one such rights-holder. Where a piece of music has been recorded on a sound recording, the person who produced that sound recording (usually the record company) will have a separate copyright interest in the sound recording also. These underlying rights in music must be cleared if that music is to be used in another copyright work, or by way of public performance or airplay.

The practicalities of rights-holders consenting to and collecting fees for each use of a melody, song or sound recording are such that it is not feasible for each individual composer or record company to individually licence all use of their copyright work and collect fees for that use. So, a system whereby rights-holders can authorise music collection societies to licence their copyright and collect fees on their behalf has evolved. Music collection societies are 'licensing bodies' for the purposes of the *Copyright and Related Rights Act, 2000* (see Part II, Chapters 16 and 17).

Music returns

In order to distribute fees collected by music collection societies among their rights-holder members, collection societies need information about the pieces of music and / or the sound recordings used, including the media in which they have been used. Where a specific licence is granted in respect of a specific use of an individual song, melody or sound recording, that information is given directly to the collection society granting the licence. Where a 'blanket licence' is granted to an organisation such as a broadcaster, this usage data must be collected by the broadcaster and provided to the various collection societies. The data required is provided by way of music returns (also known as 'music cue sheets' or 'music logs') and includes:

- Title of track.
- Composer's / publisher's name.
- ISRC (International Standard Recording Code) of sound recording.
- Artist's name.
- Record company's name.
- Duration of use.

Where a producer or distributor supplies a programme or film to, for example, a television station, they must supply a music cue sheet in respect of that programme or film to enable the broadcaster to make the necessary music returns as required by its blanket licences with the various music collection societies.

See also

Q84 What is copyright?
Q86 What rights does copyright confer on a copyright-owner?
Q90 What remedies are available where a breach of copyright has occurred?
Q95 What is meant by 'underlying rights' in a copyright work?
Q96 What are performers' rights?
Q98 What music collection societies operate in Ireland and what do they do?
Q99 What is the role of the Irish Copyright Licensing Agency?

Q98   What music collection societies operate in Ireland and what do they do?

The following music collection societies are established in Ireland:

- Irish Music Rights Organisation.
- Mechanical Copyright Protection Society of Ireland.
- Phonographic Performance Ireland.
- Recording Artists Actors Performers.

Each of these societies is linked, by way of reciprocal international agreements, into a network of similar bodies in other jurisdictions. Through this network, rights-holders can license and collect fees in respect of the use of their music internationally.

Irish Music Rights Organisation
The Irish Music Rights Organisation (IMRO) is the collection society that grants licences and collects fees for composers (including songwriters) for the public performance of their music, including airplay, online streaming of music and the playing of music at concert venues. A composer (or their publisher, where they have assigned their copyright to a music publisher) must become a member of IMRO and register their musical work with IMRO so that it forms part of the IMRO repertoire. Each composer / publisher authorises IMRO to licence the use of that work on their behalf and collect fees for that use. The fees collected are passed on, after deduction of a percentage to cover administration costs, to the composers / publishers.

IMRO negotiates and collects fees from a wide range of users of music, including broadcasters, concert promoters and business outlets where music is publicly played (such as pubs, hairdressing salons and waiting rooms).

IMRO negotiates a 'blanket licence' with broadcasters whereby a single annual payment is made by each broadcaster in respect of the public performance of IMRO members' copyright music across their broadcast output. Broadcasters are obliged to compile and return information to

IMRO about the pieces of music given direct airplay on their broadcast stations (by way of music returns / cue sheets / logs). This usage data forms the basis for the allocation among IMRO members of the sums collected under a blanket licence.

Mechanical Copyright Protection Society of Ireland

The Mechanical Copyright Protection Society of Ireland (MCPSI) also represents composers / their publishers and is closely allied to IMRO. Its role is to grant licences and collect fees on behalf of composers / publishers in respect of the reproduction of their music in a new copyright work (such as a commercially-released CD) and / or the synchronisation of a piece of their music with a new audio or audio-visual (for example, a radio or television programme, or an audio-visual advertisement). This right traditionally was referred to as the 'mechanical right', as it involved mechanically copying the original musical work into a new work; in the digital era, this recording / synchronisation takes place digitally.

In respect of MCPSI, it is important to understand the distinction between what is known as 'production music' (also called 'library music') and 'commercial music'. Production music is music specially composed and recorded for use as backing-track or sound-track music in audio and audio-visual productions, including radio and television programmes and audio / audio-visual advertising. By contrast, 'commercial music' is music released on commercial sound recordings and sold to the general public for musical enjoyment, such as albums released by popular singers and bands.

MCPSI grants licences for the synchronisation of production music with new audio or audio-visual works on behalf of both the composers / publishers of that music and the owners of the copyright in the sound recordings on which that music was originally recorded.

In respect of commercial music, in many circumstances, MCPSI can grant licences on behalf of composers / publishers for the re-use of that work in other copyright works, particularly for use in Irish radio and television programmes for broadcast in Ireland. Producers of new works should check with MCPSI to ascertain the clearance position for any particular song / piece of music they wish to use if they are not sure of the position.

A separate consent in respect of the clearance of the rights of record companies – as holders of the sound recording copyright in commercially-released recordings – is required. In most cases, this can be obtained through Phonographic Performance Ireland (see below).

MCPSI collects fees for its members on foot of 'blanket licences' negotiated with Irish broadcasters. Broadcasters are obliged to make returns of usage data for the music incorporated into the programmes they broadcast. The fees collected – after deduction of a percentage to cover administration costs – are then distributed among MCPSI members.

Phonographic Performance Ireland

Phonographic Performance Ireland (PPI) is the collection society that acts on behalf of the record companies that own the copyright in commercially-released sound recordings. PPI licenses and collects fees for the public performance (including airplay, playing of music in pubs, clubs and waiting rooms) of its members' sound recordings. PPI issues licences to broadcasters that permit broadcasters to use sound recordings in their broadcasts, whether by way of direct airplay or by way of incorporation into television programmes. This fee is collected and distributed to its members by PPI.

PPI publishes a tariff card in respect of different categories of use of its members' sound recordings.

In respect of broadcast use of sound recordings, PPI negotiates and collects payment on foot of 'blanket licences' entered into with broadcasters. Broadcasters have an obligation to make returns of usage data for the sound recordings featured in broadcasts across their schedules. On the basis of this data, PPI then distributes the fees it receives from broadcasters – after deduction of a percentage to cover administration costs – among its members.

Music returns

In order to distribute fees collected by music collection societies among their rights-holder members, collection societies need information about the pieces of music and / or the sound recordings used, including the media in which they have been used. Where a 'blanket licence' is granted to an organisation such as a broadcaster, this usage data must be collected by the broadcaster and provided to the various collection societies. The data required is provided by way of music returns (also known as 'music cue sheets' or 'music logs') and includes:

- Title of track.
- Composer's / publisher's name.
- ISRC (International Standard Recording Code) of sound recording.
- Artist's name.
- Record company's name.
- Duration of use.

Where a producer or distributor supplies a programme or film to, for example, a television station, they must supply a music cue sheet in respect of that programme or film to enable the broadcaster to make the necessary music returns as required by its blanket licences.

Performers on sound recordings

RAAP (Recording Artists Actors Performers) was established in 2001 to collect fees on behalf of performers on sound recordings following the implementation of the *Copyright and Related Rights Act, 2000*. Section 208 of the Act grants a right to performers on commercially-released sound recordings to 'equitable remuneration' from the holder of the copyright in a sound recording (usually a record company) where that recording is played in public or included in a broadcast.

RAAP has entered into an agreement with PPI whereby PPI pays an agreed percentage of the fees it collects to RAAP for distribution among the artists who have performed on commercially-released sound recordings. It is important that artists who perform on commercially-released sound recordings, register their performances with RAAP so that they can share in the distributions made to performers on those recordings.

Licensing bodies for copyright-holders in non-musical works

Licensing bodies have been established in Ireland in respect of the copyright of literary authors / their publishers (Irish Copyright Licensing Agency), as well as for the rights of screen directors (Screen Directors Collection Society of Ireland). Several overseas licensing bodies collecting fees on behalf of copyright-holders internationally are also registered with the Irish Patents Office – see the 'Register of Copyright Licensing Bodies' on the copyright section of **www.patentsoffice.ie**.

AGICOA

The attention of film and television producers is drawn to the importance of registering any copyright interest they may hold in a film or television production with the collection body known as AGICOA. This is an international collection society collecting fees in respect of the re-transmission (particularly, by cable) of television programmes across Europe. Significant fees are collected by AGICOA and are available for distribution to copyright-holders in Ireland whose work features in those international re-transmissions.

See also

Q86   What rights does copyright confer on a copyright-holder?
Q97   How do music collection societies work?

   www.agicoa.org
   www.icla.ie
   www.imro.ie – website for both IMRO and MCPSI.
   www.ppiltd.com
   www.sdgi.ie

Q99 What is the role of the Irish Copyright Licensing Agency?

The Irish Copyright Licensing Agency (ICLA) provides a 'one stop shop' for businesses, educational institutions and other persons or entities seeking permission to make multiple photocopies of copyright literary works, such as books, journals and periodicals. It is a not-for-profit organisation that distributes the fees paid for those licences, after deduction of administration costs, to authors and publishers of literary works.

Since 2006, ICLA has collected fees in respect of artistic works (for example, illustrations) included in books, journals and periodicals copied under its educational licence. It pays an agreed percentage of its overall fee income to IVARO (the Irish Visual Artists Rights Organisation – www.ivaro.ie), which IVARO in turn distributes to its visual artist members whose works have featured in those books, journals and periodicals. The educational licence granted by ICLA also extends to the digital copying of published copyright works onto educational institutions' intranet sites (for example, by way of programmes such as Blackboard and Moodle).

The *Copyright and Related Rights Act, 2000* provides for the administration of licensing schemes and for the registration of licensing bodies that collectively license rights in copyright material on behalf of categories of copyright-owner (Part II, Chapters 16 and 17 of the Act). ICLA is registered as such a body and its objectives and licensing schemes can be accessed through the Copyright Licensing Bodies section of the Irish Patents Office website (www.patentsoffice.ie), as well as through the ICLA website (www.icla.ie).

See also

Q84   What is copyright?
Q86   What rights does copyright confer on a copyright-owner?
Q100   What is the Public Lending Remuneration scheme?

Q100   What is the Public Lending Remuneration scheme?

The Public Lending Remuneration (PLR) Scheme is a statutory scheme under which authors can collect payments based on the number of times their books are lent out by public libraries.

The Scheme was established on foot of section 42A of the *Copyright and Related Rights Act, 2000*, as inserted by section 7 of the *Copyright and Related Rights (Amendment) Act, 2007*. It was brought into effect by the Minister for Environment, Heritage and Local Government on 31 December 2008 (see SI 597 of 2008).

Authors must register the books they have written with the PLR scheme, which is administered by the Library Council of Ireland. Information about the scheme and how to register copyright books with the scheme is provided on the PLR website, **www.plr.ie**. To be eligible to register as an author with the scheme, an author must be a citizen, domiciled or ordinarily resident in a country within the European Economic Area (comprising the countries of the EU plus Iceland, Liechtenstein and Norway).

The scheme was introduced as a modification of the rental and lending right (section 42 of the 2000 Act), whereby a copyright-owner has the right to authorise (and a correlating right to decline to authorise) the public lending of a copyright work. However, EU *Directive 92/100/EEC* (repealed and re-enacted with amendments in consolidated form by *Directive 2006/115/EC*) permits a derogation from the lending right if authors receive remuneration for public lending. This derogation and the required scheme for remunerating authors was established in the PLR scheme, which is funded by public funds allocated for that purpose by a vote of the Oireachtas.

Irish authors also can register their books for payments under the UK PLR Scheme (**www.plr.uk.com**). The website **www.plrinternational.com** provides information about international PLR Schemes. Irish writers whose work is lent by Dutch libraries can collect fees due to them through collection facilities offered by ICLA. This arrangement between the Dutch PLR scheme and ICLA may extend to other jurisdictions in due course. What is important is that authors themselves must take the initiative to have their work registered for PLR payments whether in Ireland or overseas.

See also

Q84 What is copyright?
Q86 What rights does copyright confer on a copyright-owner?
Q99 What is the role of the Irish Copyright Licensing Agency?

Appendix: Glossary of Legal Terms

Accused: The person charged with a criminal offence (see also 'Defendant'). By convention, the term 'Accused' usually is used where the charge is to be heard by a jury.

Act of the Oireachtas: A piece of primary legislation, passed in accordance with the procedures set out in the Constitution by both the Dáil and Seanad and signed into law by the President (spelt with a capital 'A').

Affidavit: A statement by which a person sets out in written form certain facts within their own knowledge and / or which they believe to be true and swears on oath that the contents of the statement are true; may relate to a court case or a non-judicial process.

Common law: The traditional system of judge-made, precedent-based law that developed originally in Britain and, later, in countries colonised by Britain. Under common law, judges in the higher courts can further develop and refine legal principles, drawing on the principles and precedents established by higher court judges in previous cases.

Damages: Financial compensation ordered by a court to be paid by the defendant to the plaintiff in a civil claim to compensate for the wrong found by the court to have been done to the plaintiff by the defendant.

Defendant: In civil law, the person (both a natural person and a legal entity, such as a limited company) against whom a claim is brought in the civil courts; in criminal law, the person against whom a criminal charge is laid (see also Accused). By convention, this term usually is used where the charge is tried summarily in the District Court.

Directive: A form of EU legislation used to harmonise and standardise certain areas of law across all EU States. Member States usually have a specified period of time within which to incorporate the provisions of a Directive into their domestic law. In Ireland, implementation of a

Directive is effected by the making of a SI or the passing of an Act of the Oireachtas.

Discovery: A legal process whereby documentation relevant to an ongoing court case is disclosed to one or more of the parties involved in that litigation. Discovery may be made voluntarily or on foot of a court order. Discovery may be made by any of the parties to the litigation or by a third-party who holds relevant documentation.

Director of Public Prosecutions (DPP): The State legal officer responsible for reviewing Garda crime investigation files, deciding whether to prosecute, preparing the prosecution case and prosecuting criminal charges.

Estate: Where used in reference to a deceased person, means the totality of the property – assets and liabilities – of a deceased person as administered by the person(s) with legal authority to do so.

Interlocutory order: A court order made prior to the final determination of a civil action that provides a form of temporary relief to one of the parties, or decides an issue that has arisen in the case but does not make a final decision on the entire case.

Plaintiff: The person (to include both a natural person and a legal person, such as a limited company) by whom a claim is brought in the civil courts; in UK court procedure, the plaintiff is referred to as "the claimant".

Pleadings: Formal court documents issued by the parties to a civil claim in accordance with court rules, in which the case made by each party to the claim is set out; pleadings are lodged with the relevant court office and made available to both parties to the claim.

Regulation: This term (spelt with a capital 'R') can have one of two meanings: (i) A form of EU law that has direct application in Member States without needing to be incorporated specifically into domestic law by each Member State; (ii) A statutory instrument may provide that its contents are to be referred to as 'Regulations'.

Statutory: Indicates a legal principle, rule or procedure set out in legislation.

Statutory Instrument (SI): A form of secondary legislation passed by a Government Minister or State body authorised to do so by an Act of the Oireachtas, by which the provisions of an Act are implemented; can also be used by a Government Minister to give effect to an EU Directive or an Act. Sometimes referred to as 'enabling legislation'.

Summary trial: A trial that is heard by a judge sitting without a jury.

Tort: The legal term used to describe a wrong done by one person to another for which the person who has been wronged has the right to seek redress from the courts, usually by way of an award of damages.

Waiver: A form of declaration, usually made in writing, by which a person forgoes their entitlement to exercise a particular right or privilege. The waiver may be limited in duration or extent or may be indefinite and unqualified.

Warranty: A contractual statement given by one party to a contract to the other that a particular state of affairs or circumstances exists / is true and / or will at a future date exist / be true. The person in whose favour the warranty is given may sue for damages should that warranty be false or dishonoured by the person making it. A warranty, in certain circumstances, may be implied even if it is not explicitly stated in a contract.

ABOUT THE AUTHOR

ANDREA MARTIN is a lawyer with over 23 years' experience and has practiced exclusively in media law since 1998. She worked for a number of years as part of the in-house legal team for Ireland's State broadcaster, RTÉ, before returning to private practice in 2003. She is now a Consultant with the Media Law Group of Eugene F. Collins, Solicitors in Dublin, advising clients from individuals and independent production companies to large corporations in traditional and digital media-related matters.

Andrea is in demand as a trainer throughout the media sector in Ireland and is the legal trainer for the Learning Waves training project for the commercial radio sector. Andrea guest-lectures extensively in media law at universities and colleges throughout Ireland and is a frequent contributor to radio and television discussions about media law topics

ABOUT THE QUICK WIN SERIES

The **Quick Win** series of books, apps and websites is designed for the modern, busy reader, who wants to learn enough to complete the immediate task at hand, but needs to see the information in context.

Topics published to date include:

- QUICK WIN B2B SALES.
- QUICK WIN DIGITAL MARKETING.
- QUICK WIN LEADERSHIP.
- QUICK WIN MARKETING.
- QUICK WIN SAFETY MANAGEMENT.

Topics planned for 2011 include:

- QUICK WIN ECONOMICS.
- QUICK WIN FRANCHISING.
- QUICK WIN LEAN BUSINESS.
- QUICK WIN SMALL BUSINESS.

For more information, see **www.oaktreepress.com**.